Modern Jewish History

Robert A. Mandel, series editor

Contesting Histories

Contesting Histories
German and Jewish Americans and the Legacy of the Holocaust

Michael Schuldiner

Texas Tech University Press

This book is typeset in Sabon. The paper used in this book meets the minimum requirements of ANSI/NISO Z39.48-1992 (R1997). ∞

Designed by Kasey McBeath

Library of Congress Cataloging-in-Publication Data
Schuldiner, Michael Joseph.
    Contesting histories : German and Jewish Americans and the legacy of the Holocaust / Michael Schuldiner.
        p. cm. — (Modern Jewish history)
    Includes bibliographical references and index.
    Summary: "A history of Holocaust understanding (and misunderstanding) in German- and Jewish-American communities. Focusing on both past and recent debates in academia, Schuldiner provides expansive historical context for understanding the Holocaust's reception and place in American historiography"—Provided by publisher.
    ISBN 978-0-89672-698-7 (hardcover : alk. paper) 1. Holocaust, Jewish (1939–1945)—Historiography. 2. Holocaust, Jewish (1939–1945)—Influence. 3. Public opinion—Germany. 4. Public opinion—United States. 5. Holocaust, Jewish (1939–1945)—Public opinion, German. 6. Holocaust, Jewish (1939–1945)—Public opinion, American. 7. Jews—United States—Attitudes. I. Title.
    D804.348.S38 2011
    940.53'1814—dc22   2011015289

Printed in the United States of America
11 12 13 14 15 16 17 18 19 / 9 8 7 6 5 4 3 2 1

Texas Tech University Press
Box 41037 | Lubbock, Texas 79409-1037 USA
800.832.4042 | ttup@ttu.edu | www.ttupress.org

For the victims, among them my grandparents Manashe and Fayge Bier, and my uncles Shaye, Yankel, and Israel Bier.

And for the survivors, among them my parents Aaron "Max" Schuldiner (of blessed memory) and Toby Schuldiner.

And my wife's parents, Michael and Mirriam Schultz, may they rest in peace.

The idea of making the century's great crime look dull is not banal. Politically, psychologically, the Germans had an idea of genius. The banality was only camouflage. What better way to get the curse out of murder than to make it look ordinary, boring, or trite? With horrible political insight they found a way to disguise the thing. Intellectuals do not understand. They get their notions about matters like this from literature. They expect a wicked hero like Richard III. But do you think the Nazis did not know what murder was? Everybody (except certain blue stockings) knows what murder is. The best and purest human beings, from the beginning of time, have understood that life is sacred. To defy that old understanding is not banality. There was a conspiracy against the sacredness of life. Banality is the adopted disguise of a very powerful will to abolish conscience. Is such a project trivial? Only if human life is trivial.

Saul Bellow, Mr. Sammler's Planet

Contents

Contents

Illustrations

Introduction

Holocaust Debates: From Main Street to Academia

Shortly after I moved to Fairbanks, Alaska, in 1979 to take up my post as a new assistant professor at the University of Alaska, I discovered that a Holocaust denier was running for mayor of the city. I remember the black, red, and white campaign poster advertising his candidacy. It hung on the wooden double-doors to the university pub. I think it was the colors of his poster, reminiscent of the colors found on placards and flags in which the swastika was embedded during the Hitler Reich, that impressed itself on my memory and keeps the poster of the mayoral candidate vivid in my mind. That individual did not win the mayoral race, but he still lives in Fairbanks, and his letters to the editor arguing that the Holocaust never took place still occasionally appear in the daily newspaper. So when I first decided to teach a Holocaust literature course in 1993, I wasn't certain what to expect. University of Alaska students are an outspoken group—"independent" is the way they like to think of themselves. I had in fact thought I might hear some students deny that the Holocaust had taken place. But in all the years that I've taught the Holocaust course—in Alaska and elsewhere—no student has ever suggested any such thing. I also thought that I might hear some students argue that no one knew that a Holocaust was taking place. But no one has ever suggested that either. On the contrary, what I heard during that first term from a small but vocal minority of students is that, indeed, people knew that Jews were being murdered by the Nazis; and, what's more, they—the Jews—deserved it.[1]

According to these few students, the Jews had brought the Holocaust on themselves and what the Nazis did was not really that bad anyway.[2] The opinion that Jews were to blame for their fate took various shapes. One student, for example, indicated that Jews were thieves and cheated Germans, which is how they managed to acquire such wealth; another suggested that during World War I, Jews had been a fifth column and had worked to defeat Germany, so they had to be gotten rid of when World War II broke out; still another student stated that Jews had killed Christ, suggesting that the Holocaust was their punishment; and, to take just one more example of the many such arguments I met with, another student expressed the view that Jews were natural victims, that there was something in their psychological makeup that made them prone to abuse and victimization.

Equally dumbfounding—and I was literally struck dumb the first time I heard these arguments from my students—were the arguments that the Holocaust wasn't that bad. These students were not suggesting that the Holocaust never happened; nor were they suggesting that the Jews deserved it. They were arguing that what the Nazis did was not so unusual under the circumstances, that these murderers of six million Jews and millions of other people succumbed in human ways to ordinary human failings. I heard arguments such as Stalin was as bad as Hitler, and the Russian gulag was as bad as the German death camp; that those who participated in the murder of Jews behaved no worse than anyone else would under similar circumstances—the Milgram study had suggested as much[3]; that the medical experiments of the Nazis produced results that are still of scientific value today; and, to take just one more example, the Nazis were vilified only because they lost the war—had they won, they would be treated as heroes. While one can find an example to support any one of these types of statements—one can always find at least one example to support just about any statement—these were not arguments being made for their own sake, the kind that some students will make simply to lay down an intellectual challenge. These were arguments that, for the most part, were made to justify what the Nazis had done; they were efforts to whitewash the evil committed.

What is more, these were not all arguments that one would hear at local bars from lonely men or women looking for someone, anyone to talk to about anything. These were not the kinds of statements made by people just looking to make conversation. The suggestion that Stalin was worse than Hitler was popularized by Ernst Nolte during the German Historians' Debate of the 1980s; and the German Historians' Debate was introduced to American academics by very distinguished historians of German culture, such as Richard Evans and Charles Maier.[4] Also, as already pointed out, some students were producing arguments based on psychologist Stanley Milgram's study of the manner in which students could be induced to inflict what they thought were painful shocks on ordinary individuals.[5] As I soon discovered, these vocal students who had produced these arguments had been tutored by my colleagues in the History and German Departments at the University. As one of these colleagues pointed out to me after I naively complained to him about what I had met with in my class, "We protect our students." "Protecting students?" I wondered to myself. From whom? And why?

As I subsequently realized, these students were being tutored by my colleagues, ostensibly to protect them from me. I soon discovered that what I had encountered here for the first time in my dozen or so years in Fairbanks was the local German American community. What I had met with was a reaction that was at one and the same time both defensive and aggressive. I had pointed out at the outset of the class, and it was certainly known by my colleagues, that I was Jewish, that my mother's parents had been killed by Nazis in Poland, that my wife's mother was an Auschwitz survivor complete with a tattooed number on her arm, and that I had been born in a displaced persons camp in Germany after the war. It was the view of that vocal minority of students that, by offering a class on the Holocaust—by asking such admittedly naive questions as "How could such a thing like the Holocaust happen?"—I was trying to psychologically revenge myself on them for what their relatives had done to mine. And they were determined not to be victims. It was not the Germans that were responsible for the Holocaust. The Jews were responsible; and, what's more, what the Nazis did to them was not so unusual, as atrocities go.

My first response was to attempt to determine the origins of these arguments, and it seemed to me at the time that the source for these arguments was the German Historians' Debate that took place between 1986 and 1989. As explained, this debate had been brought to the United States by distinguished scholars; and it was the writings of these scholars, I reasoned, that those who had been mentoring my students were reading.

In 1999, my university decided that, having taught Holocaust literature for six years, it was time that I learned something about it. I was given a two-thirds sabbatical to attend Cambridge University, where I duly received a M.Phil. in Historical Studies on July 22, 2000. When I first arrived in Cambridge, it was with the intention of writing a thesis about the German Historians' Debate. In the course of my research, however, I discovered that these arguments could also be found in some of the newspapers published by major German American organizations. I realized then that here was the opportunity to explore, instead of the arguments alone, the state of mind of those German Americans who had produced the arguments and continued to deliver them. I could explore these newspapers that presented the views of German Americans toward Holocaust-related events, which it turned out had never been examined; and in particular, I could try to determine what experiences or circumstances might be responsible for the kinds of statements my students—and others—were making. Many books had of course been written about German Americans. There were books about researching German Americans, such as *Research Possibilities in the German-American Field* by Heinz Kloss and La Vern J. Rippley and *German-American History and Life: A Guide to Information Sources* by Michael Keresztesi and Gary R. Cocozzoli, both published in 1980.[6] There were also books about the experiences of German Americans during World War II when the Holocaust was occurring. Timothy Holian's *The German-Americans and World War II* (1996) and Don Heinrich Tolzmann's multivolume compilation of materials related to the experiences of German Americans during the two world wars, *German-Americans in the World Wars*, published in the 1990s, are perhaps the most significant.[7] There were even books about the German American press, although these were written in the 1960s and therefore were not really relevant to my investigation.[8] Strong reactions from the German American community and from the American community in general toward the Holocaust began when the NBC miniseries, "Holocaust," aired in 1978. It seemed that an exploration of the reactions of German Americans toward the Holocaust in German American newspapers might produce some understanding of what my students were arguing and the experience that lay beneath their arguments.

I discovered in my research that the views expressed by my students, of course, represented only a small segment of the German American community. Reactions to the Holocaust among

German Americans, as one might suspect, range widely. First, there are a great many individuals of German descent who do not think of themselves as an ethnic group, but identify themselves as simply American. The reaction of these individuals probably does not differ from that of other individuals in the United States who view the event as tragic and moving but do not feel any personal involvement in the tragedy. Most Americans, whether of German descent or of any other ancestry, do not really give the Holocaust much thought. Most, of course, are too busy with their studies or diversions, their hobbies or their jobs, doing the best for their family or looking for someone to fall in love with. The people who keep track of the Holocaust are a tiny fraction of the American population. They are primarily the "professional ethnics," primarily Jewish Americans and German Americans, members of the Anti-Defamation League of the B'nai Brith or members of the German American National Congress, but also rabbis and pastors and scholars, as well as, of course, antisemites and Holocaust deniers. More intermittently, thoughts of the Holocaust will come to other portions of the population, as in 1978 when the NBC miniseries "Holocaust" was aired; but more often most people are too busy with other matters to think about it much. It is when the Holocaust falls into the hands of neo-Nazi groups who claim the Jews are using "myths" about a holocaust to stir hatred against "Aryans"—thereby attracting descendants of "Aryans" to neo-Nazism and fomenting acts of violence by neo-Nazis toward Jews and other minorities—that one begins to realize how distortions of the Holocaust can have serious consequences despite the relatively small number of individuals who participate in Holocaust-related events. This small number is representative of a far larger audience.

The reactions of the German American portion of the population who do respond to Holocaust-related events vary from feelings of shame and guilt—although the individuals who experience these emotions probably had nothing whatever to do with the Holocaust—to perhaps the most extreme form of defensiveness short of the physical aggression associated with neo-Nazis: total denial that the Holocaust ever happened. Between these two positions are many different German American responses to the Holocaust. Close to the view that espouses outright denial of the Holocaust, is the view that the Holocaust wasn't that bad and that Jews were responsible for their own fate.

However, it should be pointed out that when individuals present arguments such as "there were worse horrors than the Holocaust," such arguments are not always intended to lessen the experience of the victims or relativize it into something other than the horror it was. Such arguments—when presented by Germans or German Americans—might be intended to defuse the Holocaust of the guilt or embarrassment (or the horror) that thoughts of the Holocaust impose on them. The intention might be only to "normalize" the Holocaust. There is no thought given to how such normalization of the Holocaust might impact Jews or other victims of the Holocaust, that such efforts at normalization might, to the victims of the Holocaust, appear as relativization and minimization of their experiences, or worse. Those whose intentions are to normalize their own response to the Holocaust—by suggesting, for example, that worse fates had occurred to other peoples—without any thought for how such statements might impact the victims can be accused of insensitivity toward the feelings of surviving victims, but they are not antisemites. Their intentions are only to feel more comfortable with themselves, not disparage the experience of others. On the other hand, one should not lose sight of the fact that there are those individuals whose intention it is, by drawing comparisons or by other means, not only to normalize their own feelings toward the Holocaust, but also to relativize the experience of the victims. To compare Jews to victims of other tragedies whose sufferings might be less well-known with the intention of suggesting that Jews are exaggerating their sufferings is indeed antisemitism. In such cases, the comparison is probably motivated by hatred and can be used to stir hatred and violence. It is not surprising to discover that Holocaust deniers (and relativizers) such as David Irving are popular speakers at rallies conducted by neo-Nazi organizations.

But there is also the question of how even such efforts at only normalization, when presented publicly, impact indifferent third parties. Is it possible, for example, to compare the Holocaust to another event with the intention only to normalize it without, in the mind of the third party, relativizing it or the event being compared to it? Is it possible to state that Stalin was just as bad as Hitler without minimizing the evil of Hitler or the evil of Stalin in the minds of an audience that has no particular relationship with either perpetrators or victims? Probably not.

The defensiveness on the part of German Americans toward Holocaust events, of course, is due in large measure to the simple fact that one tends to get embarrassed by not only one's own shortcomings but the shortcomings of those who are close to us. If our relatives even appear to be criminals, it does not reflect well on us; and so we tend to become defensive about it. But the condition of those German Americans who dwell on the Holocaust is aggravated by their own experience during the war, which is only recently being discussed. In fact, discussion of this persecution and particularly the internment of German Americans by the U.S. government during the two world wars has been repressed. Too ashamed to speak of their own persecution in America, some German Americans will dwell either on the persecution of Germans that took place toward the end of World War II or on the liability for the Holocaust that many in Germany still feel very profoundly today. In effect, many who identify themselves as German Americans repress their own feelings of persecution and become defensive about the persecution of Germans in Germany. It is this defensiveness that sometimes manifests itself in "normalizing" or "relativizing" of the Holocaust, and in such reactions as "There were worse horrors than the Holocaust," and "The Jews deserved what they got." This defensiveness, in its extreme form, also manifests itself in denial that the Holocaust ever occurred. It also manifests itself, at times, in acts of physical violence toward Jews and others.

Examination of efforts to relativize the Holocaust also reveals some of the heretofore less well-known types of activities of deniers and denial groups. As shown in the pages that follow, a pattern of behavior emerges: When a well-publicized Holocaust-related event occurs, and criticism of Jews appears most strident among members of the German American community, advocates of Holocaust denial use the opportunity to announce their existence in the newspapers of legitimate German American organizations and they thereby attempt to recruit adherents. These denial groups, through letters to the editor and even editorials, in effect advertise that the "truth" about the Holocaust can be found out by writing to these antisemitic "revisionist" organizations. It is while reactions to Holocaust-related events are most rabidly antisemitic that the positions and objectives of the legitimate German American newspaper and the antisemitic denial organizations are most compatible, if not entirely synchronous in the views that they present.

The point here, however, is that there is an intense defensiveness, as well as an antisemitism and denial that appear in the newspapers of German American organizations and elsewhere that is attributable to two circumstances. First is the experience of German Americans in World War II. This was never spoken of. Instead the experience of Germans in Germany was discussed, thus allowing for "venting" without the shame or embarrassment to German Americans that would come of admitting to their own persecution. The other circumstance is the Holocaust-related event that periodically appears. This type of event conjures up shame but, again, is dealt with by defending the interests of Germany's Germans, as opposed to German Americans. This overt defensiveness about the Holocaust—based as it is in a hidden shame—takes various forms, including Holocaust denial, accusations that vengeance is being taken against all of German descent, and threats toward those who seem to be insisting that German shame never end.

This study, however, is larger in scope. The often silent or hidden conflict between German Americans and Jewish Americans permeates the discussion here, but this book is primarily about the way in which these early arguments between German Americans and Jewish Americans have made their way into the academic arena and have provided the foundation for opposing historical interpretations of the Holocaust.

This book begins with an examination of the way in which German Americans were persecuted during the world wars: the internment of thousands of German Americans and German nationals residing in the United States during both World War I and World War II, as well as some of the other indignities suffered. These persecutions account in some measure for the skittishness even today among German Americans toward any public activity that might portray Nazis—identified, in the view of these German Americans, with all Germans and those of German descent—as evil. It is the experience of Germans during the world wars that has made some German Americans defensive, and this defensiveness would later appear prominently throughout the remainder of the twentieth century and beyond whenever the Holocaust was publicized. The defensiveness would express itself in the form of accusations of anti-Germanism on the part of Jews whenever the Holocaust was memorialized, efforts to relativize the horrors experienced by the victims (other peoples have suffered equally horrible or worse atrocities), and determination to relativize the deeds of those who perpetrated the Holocaust (other nations have done worse; anyone would have done the same under the same circumstances).

During World War II, as shown in Chapter 2, Jewish Americans became aware of the persecutions that Jews were experiencing in Germany and Eastern Europe. They therefore naturally gravitated toward interventionism in the late 1930s as the United States contemplated entering the war, which of course it eventually did in 1941. German Americans were, by and large, isolationists who understood full well that if Americans went to war, German Americans would be forced to fight and kill their relatives in Germany. World War II was perhaps the first instance in which Jewish Americans and German Americans found themselves on opposite sides politically; at stake for both groups was the very blood of their relatives. The argument between German and Jewish Americans became public in September 1941, when hearings were called for by U.S. senators from heavily German American Midwestern states to examine the hawkish productions of the Hollywood film industry, in which Jews were prominent. At these hearings the senators, speaking for their German American constituency, accused Jewish Hollywood producers of making films that portrayed Nazis as evil and that would therefore lead not only to anti-Germanism in America (which occurred during World War I) but also to U.S. intervention in the war in Europe. These Hollywood films, maintained the senators, were motivated by Jewish desire for revenge. The Jewish Hollywood producers, they said, had been listening to false stories of persecution of their kinsmen in Germany. Jews had a persecution complex, the senators maintained. Jews were not really suffering terribly. In fact, Germans were suffering too. As for Hitler, he had learned how to persecute people from Stalin, who was just as bad. The practice of relativizing Nazi persecution of the Jews had already started, even before the Holocaust had reached its most horrifying proportions.

One of the major Holocaust debates to take place after World War II, the debate over the construction of the United States Holocaust Memorial Museum, was one that the newspapers and major German and Jewish ethnic organizations took part in. Chapter 3 explains that, as was the case during World War II, the chief concern of the German American community was that a national Holocaust memorial museum would provoke anti-Germanism in the United States, and this anti-Germanism would be directed against Americans of German descent. It should be remembered, claimed the opponents of the museum—again relativizing the tragedy of the Jews—that Germans were also victims of Nazi institutions such as the Gestapo. And this was not the only effort to relativize the Holocaust that took place. There appeared in the national press as well as in the press of German American organizations the argument that not only were there other atrocities that were just as bad as the Holocaust, but there were also other atrocities that were closer to home and that warranted memorialization in the nation's capital to a greater extent than did the Holocaust. The reply of Jewish Americans was, yes, it is true that other tragedies of history should be memorialized—events such as slavery and the decimation of the Native peoples of America. Today, of course, there is a museum dedicated to Native America on the Washington, D.C., mall, and a museum of American slavery is being built. These would never have been possible had there not been a United States Holocaust Memorial Museum.

By the time of the Bitburg controversy in 1985, created by President Reagan's decision to lay a wreath for German soldiers at the cemetery in Bitburg, Germany, German historians had taken up the matter of Holocaust relativization. Some such as Ernst Nolte insisted that German history should be cleansed of the Holocaust. The way to cleanse German history was to explain that there were other horrors equal to the Holocaust, and the perpetrators of those other atrocities did not continue to carry the guilt for their actions. Nolte probably had no idea that very similar efforts at relativizing the persecution of the Jews had been offered by the Midwestern senators during Senate hearings in 1941, although there were no doubt other sources for Nolte's arguments as well. Other German historians, some of the most prominent such as Hans Mommsen, disagreed with Nolte and seemed to have marginalized Nolte and those who supported his view. However, as Chapter 4 explains, conservative Chancellor Helmut Kohl, whose brother had died a soldier in World War II, no doubt agreed with Nolte. President Reagan, of course, knew nothing of this "battle of the German historians" (*Historikerstreit*) that had taken place when he was invited to Bitburg. Given the staunch alliance that had formed between Germany and the United States since World War II, it seemed to Reagan too that it was time to forgive and forget what had taken place in the past. His explanation for visiting the Bitburg cemetery, however, indulged a comparison quite similar to that which Nolte proposed and which, as already explained, appeared initially back when Jews first started being persecuted in Germany. Reagan did not suggest that others had committed atrocities equal to the Holocaust. Instead, somehow he had managed to discern that those soldiers buried in the Bitburg cemetery were as much victims as those who had died in the Nazi death camps. In his own words, "they were victims," said Reagan, "just as surely as the victims in the concentration camps." President Reagan did not know that there was already something of an ignoble history to this type of relativization of the sufferings of the Jews by suggesting there was some comparison between their hideous deaths and the deaths of German soldiers. He also did not know that many of the German soldiers were Waffen SS, among the most brutal killers in Hitler's army.

The last major debate to be discussed here took place in the early nineties between two American scholars, although German academics and the reading audiences of America and Germany also made their views known very powerfully. The two academicians were Daniel Goldhagen, at that time a young Harvard assistant professor of political science, and historian Christopher Browning, who was already well-known and highly regarded for his work in Holocaust studies. Browning presented what had historically been the German American view, a sympathy that had apparently developed while teaching at Pacific Lutheran University, if not before; Daniel Goldhagen is Jewish American and clearly presented what had historically been the Jewish American perspective, although many Jewish American academicians publicly took issue with Goldhagen and sided with Browning. It was in this debate that for the first time an American academician whose sympathies were primarily with the plight of German Americans and an American academician who espoused a historically Jewish American position argued the responsibility for the Holocaust in the most direct manner possible, given the bounds of academic civility.

As explained in Chapter 5, Browning had examined documents concerning German Reserve Police Battalion 101, a police battalion that was composed of what appeared to be ordinary individuals who participated in the gruesome murder of innocent Jewish men, women, and children. As Browning explains, these policemen had the option of not killing Jews. Browning argues that there might have been a variety of circumstances of time and place that persuaded these policemen to kill, peer pressure, for example, or the desire for advancement within the Nazi organization; and, said Browning, anyone faced with that same situation might have committed the same murders. Browning, here, had again relativized the murder of the Jews. Nolte's argument was refocused. Nolte's relativized the Holocaust by arguing that there were other nations who committed atrocities as horrifying as the Holocaust. Browning relativized the Holocaust by insisting that all people, regardless of the nation they belonged to, are capable of committing the same atrocities under the same circumstances. Browning changed a philosophical argument into a sociological one based on data such as the Milgram studies, which have been disputed. But the relativizing effect is the same: to suggest that what the Germans did to the Jews was not out of the ordinary and was nothing that others might not do and be forgiven for. Goldhagen challenged Browning, arguing that the perpetrators were not primarily motivated by their external circumstances. Instead, they were motivated internally by a virulent antisemitism of the most profound sort. But Goldhagen also recognized that the German perpetrators of the Holocaust were not the Germans of today. Today's Germans had transformed themselves into a liberal people and their country into a model democracy. The Gordian knot—the question of how to condemn the perpetrator and thereby avoid humiliating the victim, while at the same time relieving modern Germans of the sense of guilt they might feel about the Holocaust—had been rent asunder. And all of Germany knew it, even eventually, German academicians such as Jürgen Habermas who awarded Goldhagen the Democracy Prize from the *Journal for German and International Politics*. American academicians, on the other hand, simply could not abide the arrogance of the youthful Goldhagen who had challenged them. Goldhagen is no longer employed by Harvard.

Although the war period gave rise to serious arguments between German Americans and Jewish Americans, after World War II and the Holocaust had run their course, the terms of the argument changed only slightly. The issue was no longer who was persecuting whom; instead it was defining where responsibility for the horrors of the Holocaust lay. While it might have seemed obvious to an objective observer that Jews and others had suffered extraordinarily at the hands of the Germans who had been responsible for World War II as well as the Holocaust, twentieth-century America was a place where, for some, objectivity was no longer necessary.

Literary theorists were arguing for subjectivity, for the view that each observer of the facts was entitled to his or her own interpretation. And by the end of the century literary theory of this type was influencing law and the writing of history. It was not difficult to explain how the Holocaust might not have been so great a tragedy, as tragedies go. It depended on how you looked at it. And Germans were not doing anything out of the ordinary by murdering millions. Such slaughter had been going on for millennia. The Holocaust was just another one of these periodic mass murders. Moreover, the twentieth century had produced philosophers who claimed not that God was dead, but that he didn't much care. It was an age in which man was alienated from other men, and so he was alienated from himself. Man had become an automaton in a mechanized age. The Germans were not to blame. It was the age in which they lived that had turned flesh and blood into cold blocks of stone who could perpetrate the worst of horrors without so much as the blink of an eye. The age was to blame. History had become subject to the same perversions that titillate readers of literary criticism. Goldhagen's theory that antisemitism and profound hatred of Jews were responsible for the Holocaust was "old hat," and simply did not work with observed historical forces found to be at play in the twentieth century. Browning's theory that the circumstances of the place and time were responsible for the murder of millions, and not the Germans, fit in perfectly.

Contesting Histories

One

Holocaust Uniqueness and American Retribution

The feelings of German Americans about the Jewish Holocaust are in part the product of their experience, or their parents' experience, during the two world wars when German Americans endured anti-German discrimination. Anti-Germanism was rampant during World War I. German Americans who were sympathetic to their ancestral homeland favored Germany over England prior to America's entry into the war, and argued that America should not involve itself. When the United States did enter the war, German Americans suffered verbal and physical abuse for the views they expressed earlier. In a few cases, German Americans were murdered. It was that legacy that German Americans brought to World War II. As the war neared and it appeared that a second conflagration might appear, pitting Germany on one side and England and America on the other, German Americans attempted to keep a low profile. The violent anti-Germanism that took place during World War I did not appear during World War II. But acts of discrimination toward German Americans did take place. German Americans were invariably associated by some with German Nazis. The fact that there was a small but highly visible Nazi party in the United States did not help matters for German Americans. The relationships that existed between the American Nazi party and the Nazi government in Germany confirmed for many the opinion that American Nazis, comprised primarily of German nationals in America (legal enemy aliens), were a fifth column, awaiting the opportunity to take power. Many of the pronouncements of the American Nazis did little to dispel that notion. German Americans created anti-Nazi organizations in efforts to avoid guilt by association. As there developed a growing awareness in American society generally of the unexpected barbarities being committed by the Nazis in Germany, Jewish groups and German American groups protested the acts of the Nazis both in Germany and America; but as they did so, the American public became more and more conscious of the German presence in America. Eyewitness accounts of the unique or unprecedented horrors committed by the Nazis were reported in the papers, and almost invariably they were reported along with threats of retribution against German Nazis for the crimes that were being committed. The U.S. government established internment camps for German nationals residing in the country, and some German Americans had their citizenship taken away so that they could be incarcerated as well. Retribution against German nationals residing in the United States and against German Americans was already taking place. Even at present, when the Holocaust is advertised to the American public, it is these events that are brought to the minds of some German Americans.

The negative impact of Holocaust media events on German Americans is a product of their experience during the two world wars, and in particular their experience at the time it became known that the Holocaust had taken place. For while the incarceration of German Americans during World Wars I and II is the single most pernicious event ever to befall a large group of Germans who were either citizens, or as was more commonly the case, would become American citizens, German Americans also experienced other abuses, both verbal and physical, as a result of events that took place during both world wars. It is the cumulative effect of that abuse that is brought to mind when the Holocaust is discussed as unusual in the annals of history and the German people presented as an unusually brutal population.

German Americans and World War I

In 1930, before Hitler's rise to power in 1933 interrupted immigration, there were about seven million Americans with at least one parent born in Germany, and about 1.6 million native-born Germans in the United States, people living in the United States.[1] There are no census figures for individuals with one German grandparent; some estimates suggest that the number of individuals of German descent in 1930 was about 32 million—roughly one-fourth the U.S. population.[2]

German American identity was fostered in America from virtually the outset by a variety of different sources. Certainly, German churches and their associated schools played a major role in maintaining a sense of Germanness among immigrants, even as these immigrants adapted themselves to American customs and surroundings. In 1936, after a considerable decline following the population influx of Germans in the nineteenth century, the German Lutheran Missouri Synod still maintained 281 German-speaking schools with 17,800 pupils.[3] And of course, pietistic communities such as the Hutterites of South Dakota, who opposed relinquishment of the German past in which their religion is steeped, in the 1970s still maintained their own German language instruction for children of public-school age.[4] German-language publications were another factor contributing to the maintenance of a German American identity. Statistics dating from 1930 show that at the time there were 172 German-language publications in the United States, which, while substantial, again represented a decline. These publications served, among other purposes, to maintain the relationship between Germans in America and Germany. The newspaper explained America to the new German immigrant and kept the Americanized German in touch with developments in Germany. German publications, predictably, further declined during World War II to a total of only sixty German newspapers, including only seven dailies, by 1950. The publications that appeared during the war issued from New York, which had the largest number of German publications, followed by Illinois, Ohio, Minnesota, Pennsylvania, and Texas.[5]

German clubs were a regular feature wherever there happened to be German Americans in any significant number. In Manchester, New Hampshire, where the population of the predominantly German Ward 11 numbered 4,825, eleven different German clubs, or sections of national clubs, were holding meetings in 1942. These clubs included the Turn-Verein, the Workingman's Relief Association, the Harugari, and the Sons of Hermann. In Lawrence, Massachusetts, similar clubs existed at which German Americans were known to meet for dancing and lobster feasts.[6] That German clubs were still meeting in the United States in 1942 is noteworthy in light of the distrust of German associations that had developed as a result of the appearance of pro-Hitler groups in the United States.

The period of the two world wars was difficult for German Americans, as one might guess. German Americans' experience during World War I was worse than during World War II, in terms of both verbal and physical abuse, and murders by vigilantes. Anti-Germanism was so strong that all things German were attacked. It was during World War I that many of the German cultural institutions created by German Americans were outlawed by federal and state governments. German Americans blamed Wilson, whose bias for England, they maintained, had brought America into the war on the side of the English and created the anti-German atmosphere in the United States. Discussion of the experience of German Americans during World War I is important here because, even though the experience of that war led most German Americans to keep a low profile when a second world war appeared imminent, the psychological abuse experienced by German Americans during the two world wars was cumulative. When German Americans react defensively to publicity about the Holocaust, they carry with them the psychological baggage of abuse experienced during two world wars.

In the United States almost everyone has ancestors who can be traced to another country, and even if one is not a devout advocate of the nation of one's heritage, one is likely to feel some pride in the accomplishments of one's ancestors and embarrassment or irritation if one's ancestry is disparaged, regardless of whether that ancestry is German or English, Italian, or Irish, Jewish or Catholic or Muslim or Protestant. German Americans by the late nineteenth century had already developed for themselves a sense of ethnic identity;[7] they viewed themselves as a distinctive German community capable of contributing in a significant way to the cultural life of America. It is not surprising that when World War I broke out, and before the United States formally declared its allegiance to England, German Americans and the German American press in the United States supported Germany, even as the English-language press increasingly supported England. Hostility developed between the two camps—German American and Anglo-American—as each side presented its own view of where responsibility for the war lay, and began publishing negative propaganda about their opponents. Supporting the German American press was the German-American National Alliance and the German Literary Defense League.[8]

German Americans cheered German war victories in the streets, public parades and rallies were organized, and German bonds were sold by German Americans in support of the German war effort.[9]

When Woodrow Wilson declared war against Germany in April 1917, German Americans were angered, but not surprised. Even though Wilson had run for president on a platform of neutrality and nonintervention in the war, and on August 10, 1914, had issued a proclamation to that effect,[10] Wilson's preference for England in the conflagration taking place in Europe was made clear long before the U.S. declaration of war. In 1915, he protested Germany's creation of a war zone around England, but had said nothing about England's blockade of Germany. To German Americans this seemed to be an example of callous bias against Germany.[11] While the German American characterization does not appear to be entirely objective—Britain seized ships, whereas Germany sank them and their passengers in a spectacular way; for instance, 128 American lives were lost when the *Lusitania* was sunk by the submarine *Untershoot 20* on May 7, 1915—it is nonetheless clear that Wilson did favor the British.[12] Robert Lansing had succeeded "near-pacifist" William Jennings Bryan as secretary of state in July 1915, and, together with Wilson's close friend and privy counselor Edward M. House of Texas, advocated a pro-English policy and course of action to Wilson, whose emotional sympathy for England, it is generally understood, needed little encouragement.[13] In addition, Lansing and a number of U.S. naval experts believed that Germany represented a military threat to the United States—from its settlements in Latin America, Germany had been eyeing the Philippine Islands since the Spanish-American War. With the Panama Canal nearing completion, the economic stakes were high. By 1910, the U.S. War Department had already drafted plans for repelling a German attack on North America.[14] What is more, for Lansing, Germany represented the rule of autocratic power hostile to democratic principles and bent on world domination.[15] By 1915, there was another matter: Great Britain and the Allies had clearly established themselves as the major market for the sale of American goods and war supplies.[16] In brief, there were territorial and political concerns from the outset, and later there were clearly economic concerns as well that were addressed in Wilson's pro-English policy, although these would not have been apparent to the uninitiated, whether Anglo American or German American.[17] To many German Americans, Wilson seemed to be doing nothing more than indulging his cultural bias.

Subsequently, during the 1916 presidential elections German Americans bolted from Wilson's Democratic Party and flocked to the Republicans because they felt that Charles Evans Hughes would be an acceptable president. Wilson, in the view of German Americans, was running on an anti-German and anti–German-American platform. He repeatedly spoke in disparaging terms of "hyphenated-Americans," which German Americans believed was a thinly veiled slur against the German American community. German Americans responded with the argument that to be American did not mean that one had to identify with the English. Wilson, of course, won the election.[18]

By 1917, it was clear to Germany that the United States was not in its corner; and despite earlier insistence by the United States that Germany's submarines desist from attacking without warning passenger vessels that might carry Americans, Germany began a campaign of unrestricted submarine warfare.[19] On March 12, 1917, a German submarine sank the *Algonquin*, an unarmed American vessel. Three more were destroyed on March 18.[20] Also in 1917, the British-intercepted Zimmerman telegram was published. It had been discovered that German Foreign Secretary Arthur Zimmerman had offered Mexico its "lost provinces" of Texas, New Mexico, and Arizona, in return for a declaration of war by Mexico against the United States.[21] Still there was resistance to

American entry into the war. On April 2, 1917, Woodrow Wilson delivered what is said to be the most impassioned speech of his career, exhorting Congress to declare war. Aware of the concerns of ethnic Germans in the United States, Wilson distinguished in his speech between the autocratic German government and the German people who lived under that government and for whom one felt sympathy and friendship.[22] On April 6, 1917, war was officially declared by Congress. A tidal wave of nationalist hysteria swept the United States, and German Americans in particular suffered, in many instances for simply being of German descent.

On June 15, 1917, Congress passed its first Espionage Act of the war, which started the reign of terror against anyone who seemed in any way to act or speak against what government officials and government committees composed of industrialists regarded as the war interests of America. At lower levels, organizations to keep watch over potential subversive elements in the American population were organized. For example, Attorney General Gregory Thomas organized the American Protective League, a force of 200,000 volunteer detectives who were to inform the Justice Department of any acts of suspected disloyalty by American citizens.[23] Among other targets were leftists. Labor unions, in particular, whose agitation for better wages and hours could be viewed as opposing the war effort, were crushed. It was the beginning of the Great Red Scare. Socialist leader Eugene V. Debs was tried in Canton, Ohio, for having made a speech in which he stated, "The master class has always declared the war, and the subject class has always fought the battles. The master class has had all to gain and nothing to lose, while the subject class has had nothing to gain and all to lose—especially their lives." Debs was sentenced to ten years in prison. Under the new laws, 10 people were arrested for sabotage, 65 for threatening the president, and 1,532 for disloyal statements.[24]

The worst of the Great Red Scare of course was to come. In 1919, Wesley Everest shielded an organizer for the International

Workers of the World, who had been trying to get Washington State lumberjacks payment in federal money instead of company script. Everest was mutilated and hanged from a bridge.[25] This was also the period of the Sacco and Vanzetti trials and appeals. Anarchists Nicola Sacco and Bartolomeo Vanzetti were sentenced to death on July 14, 1921, for robbing the Slater and Morrill shoe factory in South Braintree, Massachusetts, and murdering the paymaster and guard. During the ensuing six-year period of appeals, Celestino Medeiros confessed to the murders; requests for a new trial following the confession were denied. Sacco and Vanzetti were electrocuted in August 1927.[26]

German Americans were the other major targets of government officials. In fact, in order to keep watch on German Americans, independent organizations were formed, such as the National Security League with a membership of 100,000. The National Security League produced such publications as *The Tentacles of the German Octopus in America*, which accused German Americans of belonging to a worldwide German conspiracy. Actions against German Americans can be thought of as having eight targets. First, and among the most important for the discussion to follow, residents of German descent who had not yet acquired U.S. citizenship were treated as "enemy aliens." Six thousand of them were removed from their home and livelihood, and placed in an internment camp at Fort Oglethorpe, Georgia. Among these individuals were musicians such as Ernst Kunwald, concertmaster of the Cincinnati Symphony Orchestra, and the actors of the German Theater of Cincinnati. Second, use of the German language was outlawed in twenty-six states. Fines ranged from $25 to $100, with terms of imprisonment ranging from ten to ninety days. By 1921, the number of individuals who had been found guilty of using German in public was 17,903. Of these, 5,720 were sentenced to terms in prison. Third, the language laws facilitated a movement to eliminate German instruction in the schools. In South Dakota, public schools were ordered to eliminate German instruction at all levels; in Nebraska both public and private schools were ordered to remove German from the curriculum. At the University of Michigan at Ann Arbor, the German Department was eliminated, resulting in the dismissal of five faculty members. Fourth, lists of banned books prepared by the U.S. War Department and state councils on defense began to appear in 1918, and many German-language publications were ordered removed from local libraries. The Cincinnati public library placed its German collection in storage, but other libraries disposed of their collections leaving permanent gaps in their collections. Fifth, anti-German sentiment forced the decline of German American publications. Newsstands refused to sell German American publications, and advertising boycotts of the German American press were organized. These circumstances and a new law that permitted the local postmaster to determine the loyalty of a publication resulted in the number of German American publications falling from 537 in 1914 to 278 in 1920.[27]

Sixth, German American organizations such as the German-American National Alliance were attacked. The Alliance, established in 1901, was the foremost German American organization with forty-seven state chapters, two journals (*Mitteilungen* and *German-American Annals*), and three million members.[28] Its mission was to work politically and socially for the interests of the German American community, which ranged from opposing U.S. immigrations restrictions to fostering German language and literature.[29] In January 1918, Senator William Henry King of Utah introduced a bill in Congress to repeal the Alliance's charter. Hearings were held at which German Americans were slandered and witnesses humiliated. Although the Alliance disbanded on its own in April, Congress decided to repeal the Alliance's charter on July 2, 1918, and attacked it as fostering German culture and sowing the seeds of disloyalty.[30]

Lastly, individuals of German descent became targets of verbal abuse and violence. Terms like "Hun," although first applied to Germans by the Kaiser himself,[31] became commonplace terms of derision for Germans and German Americans, and could be found almost daily on the front pages of newspapers. Groups of citizenry came to German American homes, churches, and businesses, and demanded that they buy war bonds to prove their loyalty. Anti-German mob actions occurred. A popular activity was to humiliate German Americans by marching them through town and then forcing them to pledge allegiance and sing the national anthem. Pacifists, both German and non-German, who refused, might be brutally punished or worse. At Bishop, Texas, a German Lutheran minister was publicly flogged. In 1915, the Reverend Edmund Kayser was shot and killed near Chicago. Charges of disloyalty in the case of Robert P. Prager, a German American coal miner in Collinsville, Illinois, led to his seizure by local vigilantes. Although he was rescued by the police, they offered no resistance when the jail was later stormed by a mob and Prager was lynched. These appear to have been the worst of the acts of violence perpetrated against German Americans, but there were many others.[32]

German Americans and World War II

World War I did significant damage to the German American psyche. They had done nothing wrong and were abused. The German sense of self among Americans of German descent was severely wounded. Indeed, as World War II approached, some German Americans hid the fact that they were of German descent because they feared another outbreak of anti-Germanism.[33] During World War I, the barbarities were all on the side of German Americans' persecutors. The persecutors had taken away their language and their books, and beaten and even murdered some of those who protested. German Americans were the victims. World War II was another matter. Nazi barbarities were genuine; and insofar as these barbarities were German and some German Americans continued to identify with Germans, and felt embarrassment, shame, and guilt.

Among the results of World War I is that German Americans, at least at the national level, decided that the Democratic Party, to say the least, was not the party for them; and their experience of World War II would confirm them in that decision. When the 1936 elections came around, Roosevelt, like the Democratic candidate Wilson who had brought America into World War I, was viewed by German Americans as pro-British and anti-German. German Americans supported a German American candidate, William Lemke, who ran on the Union Party ticket and who was supported by the radio personality Father E. Coughlin. In 1940, they supported another German American, Wendell Willkie, the Republican candidate, who ran against Roosevelt and promised not to get involved in the European war. German Americans, as in the case of World War I, felt an attachment to their ancestral homeland. But this time there was also the fear that anti-German hysteria similar to that which appeared during World War I would reappear. Roosevelt, like Wilson before him, promised that if elected for a second term, he would not bring America into the war.[34] War, of course, did come to America after the Japanese attack on Pearl Harbor, but as it turned out, little of the thug violence against German Americans that seemed to have characterized the anti-Germanism of World War I appeared during World War II.[35] However, many of the sanctions against German American institutions that had been put in place during World War I were still in effect. For example, while language laws had been revoked, there was no effort to reinstate German-language programs, so schools went without.[36] Moreover, the Second World War was a period in which new calumny would be heaped upon German Americans as American Nazism reared its head.

After the experience of World War I, the German Americans

were generally far more circumspect about advocating for Germany when it appeared that Germany might again fight England, and perhaps the United States, in a second world war. Fearing another outbreak of anti-Germanism, German Americans advocated isolationism prior to U.S. entry in the war, but once war was declared, German Americans immediately and enthusiastically pledged their loyalty to the American effort. In 1919, the Steuben Society of America was formed, an organization composed of Americans of German ancestry who emphasized their loyalties as Americans.[37] The Steuben Society of America is today the oldest existing organization of Americans of German descent. But pro-German nationalism again appeared among Germans in America during World War II, this time clearly from outside the country, as Nazi organizations in America recruited members primarily from recently arrived German immigrants.

The first Nazi groups in the United States were supported by recently Nazified agencies or new Nazi agencies created in Germany in 1933. It was known that about one-fourth of the U.S. population was of German extraction, and it was estimated that German was the primary language of about five to six million Americans.[38] America appeared to be well prepared to contribute to the German world order that Hitler envisioned; Germans living in America could be useful, politically effective allies for the new Germany. By 1935, however, American Nazis proved themselves a burden to Germany, and Germany severed most of its connections with the American groups. However, these organizations created by German agencies did not die out in 1935. They survived until December 1941. Their target was the American Jew, who, in their view, held great power in the United States and was corrupting the German American, producing in America an unfavorable image of the new Germany. Among other serious flaws in their policy, neither the German agencies that sponsored the Nazi groups in America nor the Nazi groups themselves—composed, as explained, primarily of recent German emigrants—realized how profoundly the governmental actions and public violence directed against German Americans during World War I had impacted the German American community. Most German Americans at this time and for some time to come would adhere to the melting-pot philosophy and present themselves as simply—and emphatically—American.[39]

Among the pro-Nazi groups to appear in America was the Bund der Freunde des neuen Deutschland (Society of the Friends of the New Germany), formed by Heinz Spanknoebel, a nominal member of the German Nazi party, who had been empowered by Berlin in March 1933 to establish the organization.[40] Spanknoebel's short career as leader of the Friends is worth brief discussion here since it includes an early instance of confrontation between American Nazis, and German and Jewish Americans—a confrontation in which German Americans and Jewish Americans united against a bid for the takeover by American Nazis of one of the chief German American organizations of the day. The Spanknoebel affair, in addition, led to the creation of what would become the most notorious committee in the history of the American Congress, the House Unamerican Activities Committee (HUAC). Spanknoebel, having used an endorsement from Rudolph Hess himself to unite various small, pro-Nazi German groups in the United States, in 1933 attempted to bring under his control one of the larger German American groups, the United German Society of Greater New York (UGS), an umbrella organization that claimed a membership of 10,000.

It is important to note here that, as in Germany itself, Jews were many times prominent members of the German community in America. Fritz Schlesinger, the Jewish treasurer of the UGS, and Robert Rosenbaum, leader of the German Israelite National Guard, along with several important Roman Catholic families, were urging the group to take an anti-Nazi position. Nazi antisemitism was already well-known. The Nazi-organized boycott of Jewish businesses in Germany when Hitler came to power had already been met by a counterboycott of German products by Jewish Americans, although the counterboycott did not deter Hitler in the least.

Spanknoebel began by approaching the leading German American newspaper of the day, the *New Yorker Staats-Zeitung und Herold*. He was met by Victor Ridder, one of the two brothers who published the paper, whom he ordered to publish material favorable to Hitler and Nazi Germany. Ridder was not impressed and threw Spanknoebel out of his office. Spanknoebel subsequently turned his attention to the UGS itself. Spanknoebel managed with the help of Edwin Emerson, prominent in the German American community and one of the leaders in the Friends, to get his name on the agenda of a UGS meeting. Reminiscent of Hitler's rise to power, Spanknoebel packed the meeting hall with his brown-shirted Ordnungs-Dienst, a division of the Friends that wore the uniform of Hitler's Sturm Abteilung (known as Storm Troopers or Brown Shirts). They chanted, "Out with the Jews, out with the Jews," and Spanknoebel threatened to club anyone who disagreed. Representatives of four Jewish groups left the hall and the remaining sixty-six representatives, when asked to vote Spanknoebel a seat on the UGS board of directors, did so. After additional business, Spanknoebel asked for a vote on a resolution to raise the German flag, which included a swastika, at the upcoming German Day celebrations. On this matter, Spanknoebel failed to get a majority of the votes. The entire board of directors of the UGS resigned. Spanknoebel, at the next meeting of the UGS, asked again for a vote to fly the German flag at the German Day celebrations, which would be held at the Manhattan Armory, a U.S. military installation, and the measure passed.

Spanknoebel, at this point significantly emboldened by his victories, allegedly had his Brown Shirts paint swastikas on the doors

17

of several Jewish synagogues in Manhattan.[41] Mayor John Patrick O'Brien convinced Reverend William Popcke of the Zion Lutheran Church, who led the exiled UGS board of directors, to cancel German Day activities. In the meantime, Congressman Samuel Dickstein, chairman of the House Committee on Immigration and Naturalization asked the Labor Department to deport Spanknoebel on the grounds that he had not registered with the State Department as an agent of a foreign nation. Spanknoebel, apparently recalled by Hess, fled the country on October 29, 1933. On November 20, the House Committee on Immigration and Naturalization began preliminary hearings on Nazi activities in the United States. On the first day of the new session of Congress, January 3, 1934, Dickstein proposed the formation of the House Unamerican Activities Committee (HUAC) to investigate Nazi activities in the United States. In March, funding was provided by Congress. Spanknoebel had inadvertently given Dickstein and others support for the belief that Hitler was infiltrating German American organizations with his agents. As the "Spanknoebel affair" was reported and gained currency with the American public, the story was magnified and in the public imagination virtually every German American became a potential spy.

Friends of the New Germany, or "the Bund" as it was sometimes called, was now led by Ignatz Griebl, handpicked by Spanknoebel before he was recalled.[42] Under Griebl, the Friends of the New Germany focused its recruitment efforts on not only German nationals in America, but also German Americans. Through the offices of the German consulate, the Bund cultivated friendship with the German-American Business League (Deutschamerikanischer Wirtschaftsausschuss, or DAWA), a group of German American businessmen who created the organization in order to counteract the Jewish counterboycott of German goods sold by German Americans, by advocating boycott of Jewish stores in the United States. In 1935, DAWA became a division of the Bund, which offered the service of walking up and down streets with advertising boards hung from shoulders, or handing out leaflets that read "Buy German" or "Boycott the Boycotters!" Some Bundists went so far as to try to shake down German-Jewish shop owners, many of whom had their shops in the same streets as other German Americans. In general, the relationship between the Bund and the German American businessmen who composed DAWA lent the Bund an air of respectability: the Bund was defending the small German American businessman against the discriminatory practices of the Jewish community.[43]

It should be pointed out, however, that as early as the middle of 1934, as newspaper reports and firsthand reports of Nazi terror reached German Americans, many flocked to join the Jewish instigated boycott of all goods coming out of Germany. The Carl Schurz Memorial Foundation, established to foster relations between Germany and United States, in 1934 divorced itself from Nazism, and changed the name and sponsorship of its journal. During the war, a number of German American organizations worked with labor unions and other sectors of U.S. society specifically to promote loyalty to the American war effort and to counter the perception that German Americans were sympathetic to Nazism. Among these were the Loyal Americans of German Descent, the German-American Congress for Democracy, and the German-American Anti-Nazi League.[44]

The propaganda message that German Americans started receiving from the Bund was very much different from any that they had received before from anyone. It was not the melting pot theory, certainly, that was being promulgated by the Bund (German Americans were not asked to become first and foremost Americans, which had been asked of them by the Steuben Society), nor were they told by the Bund to recognize that, while owing allegiance to America, they should remember their German heritage. The message of the Bund was that they were Germans, and Germans only, who happened to be living in America. Walter Kappe, national editor of Bund publications, would write, "[T]o give

America our souls, as many of our fellow countrymen have done, nobody can ask of us; to become German-American *mongrels*, who do not know where they belong, nobody can ask of us; WE ARE AND REMAIN GERMANS. GERMANS IN AMERICA." The purpose of the Bund was to make all German Americans aware of their essentially German character. Of its members, primarily German nationals or recently naturalized citizens, the Bund demanded loyalty to the internal and foreign goals of national socialism. These demands, in the view of Samuel Dickstein and his colleagues, required of Bund members that they compromise their loyalty to the United States.[45]

New York Congressman Samuel Dickstein—especially after the HUAC investigations of the Bundists got underway—became in the eyes of the Bund America's number-one German hater. Dickstein was characterized by the Bund as a Satanic Bolshevik, evil incarnate, and a loud-mouthed Jew. All of Roosevelt's Jewish friends were maligned by the Bundists, including Justice Louis Brandeis and Henry Morgenthau (long before he wrote his ill-conceived and never-implemented plan for the postwar fate of Germany). In Bundist publications, Jews in general were stereotyped and smeared as loud and greedy communists with an inborn hatred of Germans. Jews, according to Bund publications, were trying to revive the anti-German feelings of World War I, and brand all Germans in America as foreign agents bent on destroying America. The intent of the Jews was that the U.S. government deport German Americans. The immediate goal of the Bund's propaganda effort was to change the unfavorable impression that the New Germany had in the United States; its long-term goal was in fact to create a united Germandom that would eventually take the place of the Jews who they thought were running the United States. As Walter Kappe would make plain, Anglo-Saxons sooner or later would understand the benefits of race politics and join Germans to create a new America based on Adolph Hitler's teachings.

Dickstein's House Unamerican Activities Committee, co-chaired by John McCormack of Massachusetts, eventually forced Berlin to withdraw its support for the Friends of the New Germany, a decision it had already been contemplating because of the embarrassment of the Spanknoebel affair. But HUAC did not put an end to Nazism in the United States. Dickstein tactics toward Bund members who appeared before him were intimidating. He accused witnesses of treasonous activities in a manner that would later become characteristic of Senator Joseph McCarthy when he chaired the Committee and brought before him individuals thought to be communists. Dickstein was accused even by former supporters of violating the constitutional rights of witnesses. However, Dickstein did accumulate evidence that Germany was sponsoring the Bund. Among other testimonies, Sergeant Gottlieb Hass of the New York National Guard testified that Berlin had encouraged Bundists to join the Guard in order to use its Peekskill, New York, training camp. About 20 percent of his company were Bundists, said Hass. Germany claimed it knew nothing of the activities of its nationals in the United States. The Committee threatened Berlin with exposure of its subversive activities. At that point Germany finally decided, having contemplated dissolving the Friends for the previous two years, to pull the plug.[46]

The Friends, or the Bund, consisted of about five to six thousand members.[47] Roughly four to five thousand were either German nationals who arrived after World War I looking for better economic opportunities than existed in Germany, or recently naturalized American citizens born in Germany.[48] No more than 10 percent were naturalized Americans who had arrived before 1900 or Americans of German extraction.[49] In November 1935, German nationals, including those who had officially declared their intentions of becoming American citizens, were forbidden by Germany from belonging to the Friends of the New Germany.[50] They were warned that their passports would be confiscated and might lose their German citizenship, if they remained within the Bund.[51] Rudolf Hess himself supported the Foreign Ministry edict.[52] Most of the leadership and rank and file were not American citizens, and Berlin hoped that the organization would quickly dissolve itself.

Instead, the reins of the Friends of the New Germany were turned over to a new leader, Fritz Kuhn, who on March 29, 1936, renamed the movement the Amerikadeutscher Volksbund (known as the German-American Bund, or, again, simply the "Bund"). Kuhn created an auxiliary to the Bund, a Prospective Citizens' League, that German nationals seeking American citizenship could belong to after Germany's deadline without fear of having their passports revoked. Kuhn had appeal. He was dynamic and flashy; he wore his Nazi uniform and jackboots regularly, and aped the mannerisms of Hitler when he spoke to crowds. Although he lacked Hitler's oratorical abilities, his efforts to provide Americans with the experience of National Socialism did not go unappreciated or unrewarded. Kuhn continued the policies of the Friends, but turned the organization into a money-making venture by reorganizing or incorporating six of the Bund's potentially lucrative divisions, such as its press. He also instituted membership dues, and sold Nazi paraphernalia and summer cottages at the Bund youth camps in Wisconsin, Pennsylvania, New Jersey, California, New York, and Michigan. The membership of the Bund under Kuhn's leadership rose to almost twenty-five thousand and each member was required to pay dues of nine dollars per year, which would have grossed the organization in membership dues alone roughly a quarter of a million 1936 dollars. The Bund's propaganda-laden, antisemitic newspapers in Los Angeles, Chicago, Philadelphia, and New York had generally turned a profit, and continued to do so; but Kuhn also published antisemitic books such as Hitler's *Mein Kampf*, and required Bundists to buy and read it; he published antisemitic pamphlets such as *The Protocols of the Elders of Zion*, as well as a magazine for German youth, *Junges Volk*. In fact, Kuhn created a small corporate empire.[53]

The highlight of Kuhn's career was his meeting with Hitler during the Berlin Olympics in 1936. For several years thereafter, Kuhn would rally his supporters around him with the claim that his leadership was endorsed directly by Hitler. Hitler had provided no such endorsement, and in fact later realized he had committed a political blunder by meeting with Kuhn. Two years later, Martin Dies, who took over the chairmanship of the HUAC, would take Hitler's meeting with Kuhn and Kuhn's own words at face value, and point out that "we have always believed that the German-American Bund was the spearhead of Hitler's attempted penetration into this country."[54] The Bund was Germany's fifth column in the United States. But Kuhn had never broken any federal law.

By December 1938, public opinion against Hitler in the United States had spread dramatically, and as his stock fell, so did Kuhn's. The *Kristallnacht* (Night of the Broken Glass) on November 10, 1938, had produced an outcry the world over, including statements of outrage from the German American community. A young Jew, Herschel Grynszpan, had murdered Ernst vom Rath of the German Embassy in Paris because his mother had been in a convoy that was deported from Germany and dumped in no-man's land on the Polish border. In retaliation, synagogues were looted and burned, Jewish shop windows were smashed (hence the name "Night of the Broken Glass") and the premises ransacked; and Jews were beaten and shipped to concentration camps. It was a well-orchestrated and well-publicized pogrom that had taken place in the New Germany. A storm of protest appeared in most American newspapers as the American public displayed what was characterized by the German Foreign Ministry as a "violent and bitter" attitude toward the Nazi Reich.[55] The United States recalled its ambassador to Germany; and Germany retaliated by recalling the German ambassador in America. After years of silence, the Steuben Society of America officially condemned the Nazi dictatorship; and the Ritter brothers, publishers of German-language newspapers in the United States, did likewise. The outburst of public sentiment after Kristallnacht, combined with the HUAC's renewed investigations, particularly its request that the Federal

Bureau of Investigation (FBI) look into the activities of Bundists working in shipyards and plane factories, encouraged an exodus of German nationals—always the backbone of the Bund—back to Germany that had already been underway for two years.

Kuhn's downfall, however, came when he was accused and tried on November 9, 1939, for embezzling $14,548 of proceeds from a Bund rally. The federal government had been trying to jail and deport Kuhn on the basis of his pro-Nazi activities, but no relevant laws existed at the time. Laws did, however, exist that had brought to justice such gangsters as Al Capone, and it was these laws that, it was eventually discovered, Kuhn had broken. Thomas Dewey, who had experience "racket busting" in New York City, acquired the Bund's accounts. The defense made the argument that under the "leadership principle" adopted by the Bund, Kuhn had total control over the organization's finances; and apparently the argument was very convincing. Eventually, the government's case rested on the allegation that a legal fee of $500 that was supposed to have been paid to a lawyer who had defended several Bundists the previous year had never been paid, but had been pocketed by Kuhn. The court found Kuhn guilty and he was sentenced to a term of two and one-half to five years in Sing Sing prison. For all practical purposes, the Bund was dead. On May 27, 1943, Kuhn was convicted of violating the Nationality Act of 1940, which made it illegal to retain allegiance to a foreign nation at the time of naturalization. He was stripped of his American citizenship and transferred to a government internment camp in New Mexico. After the war, Kuhn was deported to Germany where he died in 1951.

The American Nazi party had been an embarrassment to German Americans. Certainly most German Americans made considerable effort at the time to distance themselves from the American Nazis, most of whom were emigrants or recently naturalized. The exceptions were the members of the German American business community, who became members of the Bund to combat the Jewish counterboycott of goods produced in Germany. To be sure, the German American community at large deserves praise for its early creation of anti-Nazi organizations, if only to distance themselves from the Bund, as does the Steuben Society of America and the Ritter brothers' newspapers for their open denunciation of Hitler after Kristallnacht in 1938. Certainly, it must have been embarrassing, to say the least, knowing that the HUAC, and later, the FBI was looking into the activities of German Americans, as well as Germans residing in America. But the problems of the German American community certainly did not end with the dissolution of the Bund. The horrors being committed by the Nazis in Europe against the Jews and other peoples in Europe were only beginning in the early 1940s, and as they became known, German Americans were apprised of the threats of retribution for Nazi crimes that were being leveled. The call for retribution seems to have been linked in many instances to the astonishment of the observer upon witnessing the horror that had occurred during the Holocaust, or the astonishment of the reporter listening to the account of such horror from a reliable witness. It seems also that the call for retribution and sense of horror were very frequently accompanied by remarks concerning the unprecedented or almost unprecedented nature, in the observer's view, of the murders that had occurred.

German Americans Experience the Threat of Retribution

Knowledge that a Holocaust was occurring seems first to have made its way to the English-speaking world, not surprisingly, through Britain. From the time that the Holocaust began, Polish statesmen residing in exile in Britain and British statesmen themselves were apprised of the heinous murder of civilians being perpetrated by the Nazis and spoke of the unprecedented nature of Nazi evils—as well as the punishment for those crimes that awaited the perpetrators.[56] The American public, including the German American community, was apprised of the unprecedented nature of Nazi crimes by British authors writing for the American press, and German Americans who visited concentration camps also would speak, albeit less graphically, of Nazi horrors.[57] The U.S. government recognized the barbarity of Nazi crimes;[58] and retribution was not merely threatened by the American government,[59] it was being executed as early as 1941 with the establishment of camps in the United States for the internment of German nationals.[60] Such retribution was not limited to German nationals. A considerable number of German Americans were also interned in these camps.[61] These of course included American Nazis such as Fritz Kuhn, but they also included many more far less notorious Americans of German descent.

In 1942, the Polish Ministry of Information, operating out of London, published an English-language pamphlet compiling various allied statements of an official nature discussing the horrors perpetrated by Nazis in Eastern Europe. These are important because they provide a precedent for associating the idea of the uniqueness of the Holocaust with the need for retribution for German horrors during the Holocaust. It was because German horrors during the war were so startling and without precedent—unique—that the Allies argued some form of retribution was necessary.

The title given the pamphlet is a phrase from a brief document, also included in the pamphlet, by Brendan Bracken, British Minister of Information. The full title (ellipses, parentheses, and all) reads:

> Bestiality . . . unknown in any previous record of
> history. . . . (Mr. Brendan Bracken on July 9th, 1942).

And it is the perceived unprecedented nature of the "bestiality" of the Nazis that is emphasized throughout the fifty-six–page pamphlet. Detailed accounts are provided of the mass murders and tortures meted out to inmates of Nazi concentration camps,[62] and an early account is provided of the medical experiments and gassings at Auschwitz.[63] Also included is a map identifying twenty-two other concentration camps in Germany and Poland.[64]

Polish leaders of the government in exile were, of course, most concerned about reports that filtered out of Poland about the mass murders taking place, but they were also distressed by the confiscation of Polish property and the destruction of Polish culture that by 1942 had become apparent. In that year, General Wladislaw Sikorski, head of the Polish government in exile, himself broadcast to Poland and other nations within listening range the unprecedented nature of the crimes committed by the Germans, warning of the reprisals that Germans could anticipate with the Allied victory. Sikorski's broadcast, in his words, was warranted because the Nazi "wave of terror"

> assumed such vast dimensions in Poland in the spring of this year, that is to say, after Himmler's visit to this country, the Polish government again decided to call the attention of the Allied Nations to these crimes unheard of in history.[65]

The crimes "unheard of in history" include not only the destruction of the Jews, but also the nature of German reprisals upon the Polish population for partisan actions. According to Sikorski, Germans were seizing hostages "in mass from amongst well-known social and political workers, and every class of the nation."

> A month ago, in Warsaw, a hundred of them were shot as a reprisal for the shooting of one German, and in the Lublin district 400 were executed for the killing of one German henchman.[66]

These German crimes, said Sikorski, can only be stopped if the Allies announce retribution for these crimes in the future and begin reprisals immediately:

> The perpetrators of these crimes must be brought to account, and this principle ought to become the guiding policy of the Allies. Only the announcement of retribution and the application of reprisals, wherever possible, can stop the rising madness of the German assassins, and save hundreds of thousands of innocent victims from certain death.[67]

The particular aspect of Nazism that the authors in this pamphlet identify as "unheard of" is the brutal punishments inflicted by the Nazis on their victims—the word "bestiality" recurs repeatedly in this context—and invariably these authors threaten retribution.

Brendan Bracken's own essay on behalf of the British Ministry of Information was one that spoke of the unprecedented nature of the horror inflicted by the Nazis. Further, Bracken also warned of the retribution that awaited the Nazis for these unprecedented acts.

> We are about to hear a tale as ghastly as any ever known to history. 700,000 Jews alone have been murdered in Poland. The treatment of every other religion, including the Catholic religion, has been marked by a bestiality unknown in any previous record of history. The Germans have excelled themselves as the most brutal nation which has ever defaced the annals of the human race. WHAT GIVES ME SOME SMALL SATISFACTION IS THAT I, AS A MEMBER OF THE GOVERNMENT, CAN REASSURE OUR POLISH FRIENDS THAT THE PEOPLE RESPONSIBLE FOR THESE MURDERS AND OUTRAGES IN POLAND WILL BE BROUGHT TO JUSTICE. . . . I can assure you that the Government of Great Britain and all the Governments of

the United Nations are in complete agreement on this question, that every care should be taken to secure the names of
the persons responsible for these crimes; that they should be
brought speedily to justice at the conclusion of the war, and
that their punishment will fit their crimes; and believe me, in
view of the crimes committed by the Germans, the punishment will be in many cases the most severe known to any
law, and I hope that that fact will be rubbed steadily into the
minds of the beasts responsible for the terrible happenings in
Poland.[68]

The murder of the Jews here is only "as ghastly as any ever known
to history." It is the treatment of other religions that is unprecedented, that "has been marked by a bestiality unknown in any
previous record of history." The context in which the nature of
Nazi crimes can be thought of as unique is more narrow. The perpetrators, in any case, "have excelled themselves as the most brutal nation which has ever defaced the annals of the human race."
And it is justice that awaits them. Bracken's intentions, like those
of General Sikorski, were, on the one hand, to provide some con-
solation to the Poles under Nazi domination, and at the same time
to try prevent more horrors from occurring by warning those who
might be contemplating such crimes of the justice that awaits
them.

American officials were less likely to think of the Holocaust as
unprecedented, or to use such hyperbolic phrases as "unheard of
in history" when speaking of Nazi crimes, perhaps because they
were not as close to the horror as the British were. The British
people, of course, experienced the ferocities of world war in a way
that American civilians did not. But also significant here is the fact
that the Polish government in exile was situated in London. Firsthand reports of entire Polish villages being murdered and individuals being brutally tortured could be made known to British

officials in face-to-face encounters with the Polish members of the underground who had witnessed these horrors and had come to London to report them. That simply was not the case across the ocean in America. It also seems that there was some skepticism in America as to whether reports of Nazi atrocities were true. Reports of German barbarity had also appeared during the First World War and had turned out to be false.[69] This is not to say that there were not a good many reports in America of war crimes being committed by the Nazis. One such report in 1942 by *Life* magazine of the German slaughter of Russian POWs went so far as to suggest a thoroughness to the executions "rarely seen before in history."[70] There were also discussions of the murder of Jews, but more often than not they seem to have been virtually buried in pages of reports of military movements and wartime politics.

An exception was the story by Arthur Koestler that appeared in the *New York Times Magazine* for January 9, 1944, and which spoke of Nazi crimes against the Jews as unprecedented. Koestler, a native of Hungary, had been imprisoned by the Nazis in France, and had managed to escape to London where he wrote his essay. The story, titled "The Nightmare That Is a Reality," is an angry appeal to the world to take action against the Nazis, and focuses, in particular, on the murder of the Jews. According to Koestler, Jews were being slaughtered by the most brutal methods. He states,

> So far three million have died. It is the greatest mass killing in recorded history; and it goes on daily, hourly, as regularly as the ticking of your watch.

Koestler's point that the unprecedented Nazi murders, "the greatest mass killing in recorded history," were still going on was reinforced by what has come to be a well-known cartoon by David Low of five bodies hanging from a wire between two poles. The bodies are faceless and unidentifiable, as if to suggest that the crime committed is against all humanity and not just the Jewish people. Hitler and Himmler are in the foreground, standing amidst dead bodies. Hitler seems satisfied; Himmler wears an evil-looking grimace. The caption to the cartoon repeats the key language in Koestler's story, the language he used to refer to the murder of three million Jews: "The greatest mass killing in history goes on daily, hourly, as regularly as the ticking of your watch."[71] It is the unprecedented nature of the Jewish murders that was being emphasized with the hopes that the consciences of Americans might be moved to take action against the murders taking place. On May 2, 1944, the same year that Koestler's article appeared in the *New York Times*, the deportation of Jews from Hungary—where Koestler's mother and her family still resided[72]—began. By the end of that summer, 400,000 Hungarian Jews had been murdered at Auschwitz.

German American writers were as appalled by Nazi horrors as anyone. Edgar Snow, in his article for the *Saturday Evening Post* for October 28, 1944, reported on his visit to the death camp at Lublin-Majdanek, and his report indicates that he was clearly shaken by what he saw. But Snow's use of detail when referring to the Holocaust was limited, perhaps reflecting a desire not to further provoke anti–German-American sentiment in the United States. The Nazi methods employed at Majdanek, as Snow explains, represent a perverse use of those German virtues of order and efficiency that he had heard of when a youngster from the German side of his family.

> It happens that two of my own great-grandparents were Germans, and from that side of my family I heard in my youth a great deal about those German virtues. Indeed no one can say that American society hasn't benefited by them either. But here at Lublin you got a complete distortion of the historic genius of a race.[73]

31

Snow remained devoted to the "historic genius" of Germans, from which American society has significantly benefited. Nazi methods comprised a "distortion" of that genius, according to Snow, having produced an unprecedented system of extermination:

> [H]ere at Majdanek is a point of new and clinical interest. It is the diabolical system and efficiency, the comprehensive, centrally directed planning, that for the first time made a totalitarian modern industry out of the reductions of the human being from an upright ambulatory animal to a kilogram of gray ashes.[74]

It was the perverse use of German methods and efficiency by the Nazis that, "for the first time," made an "industry" out of death, says Snow.

But Snow could not bring himself to wish retribution on the German people. It was clear to Snow that such horrors as he witnessed at Majdanek did not bode well for the future of the defeated Germany. As he states, "Majdanek and the ghosts that throng around it will be a living presence at the peace tables to harden man's heart to the inevitable dismemberment of Germany."[75] But Snow does not state that such horrors as he witnessed are deserving of retribution. Instead, the editors of the *Saturday Evening Post* place within Snow's story a boxed insert titled, "This Is Why There Must Be No Soft Peace," in which the editors explain that Americans were too magnanimous toward Germany after World War I, and that was what "permitted Germany to prepare for the next holocaust."[76] The editors go on to insist that

> [t]here are times when sanely administered punishment, of a nation, as of a man, is the only effective quarantine to save a world in danger from a nation bent upon befouling itself and all that it can reach.

The editors of the *Saturday Evening Post* are insistent upon making the point that Snow did not. Nazi crimes, evidenced by what took place at Majdanek, warrant no less than "punishment" of the criminals.

Like the British, American officials did make their views known concerning the punishment that awaited criminal acts performed by the Nazis. Warnings from President Franklin Roosevelt appeared in the course of the war as more became known about the ways in which the Nazis terrorized civilian populations in the territories they captured.[77] In 1943, Roosevelt issued a joint statement along with Prime Minister Winston Churchill and Premier Joseph Stalin, deploring the atrocities being committed by the Nazis as they retreated from territories being taken back by the Soviets, and warning that those who take part in the executions of Allied prisoners or civilian populations in Poland or the Soviet Union "will be brought back to the scene of their crimes and judged on the spot by the peoples whom they have outraged. Let those who have hitherto not imbrued their hands with innocent blood beware lest they join the ranks of the guilty. . . ."[78] But the statement did not mention the murder of Jews, although the United Nations—of which, of course, the United States formed an integral part—had issued in December 1942, a statement condemning the massacre of Jews.

In March 1944, on the eve of the murder of the 400,000 Hungarian Jews at Auschwitz, Roosevelt publicly acknowledged the wholesale slaughter of Jews taking place and spoke of retribution for that crime. In language echoing that of Koestler in his January article for the *New York Times*, the president expressed his sense of how time was not on the side of the survival of Europe's Jewish population:

> In one of the blackest crimes of all history—begun by the
> Nazis in the day of peace and multiplied by them a hundred
> times in time of war—the wholesale systematic murder of

the Jews of Europe goes on unabated every hour. As a result of the events of the last few days hundreds of thousands of Jews, who while living under persecution have at least found a haven from death in Hungary and the Balkans, are now threatened with annihilation as Hitler's forces descend more heavily upon these lands. That these innocent people, who have already survived a decade of Hitler's fury, should perish on the very eve of triumph over the barbarism which their persecution symbolizes, would be a major tragedy.

It is therefore fitting we should again proclaim our determination that none who participate in these acts of savagery shall go unpunished.[79]

Roosevelt's description of the murder of the Jews as "one of the blackest crimes of all history" is the closest he would come to suggesting that the Jewish Holocaust was unprecedented or unique. All of these statements by Roosevelt, of course, amounted to far too little too late. The murder of Europe's Jews went on. But it was clear that Roosevelt was determined to demand retribution from culpable Germans for the crimes being committed against Jews and others.

It is of course true that German Americans were perceived during the war as something of a threat, a fifth column, operating in the United States; and that the internment of German Americans by the U.S. government was intended, in part, as a precautionary measure. It is also true, however, that when the Polish government in exile called upon the American government to intern Germans in the United States, they were asking that the United States do so not as a precautionary measure, but as a form of retribution. The Polish government wanted a warning issued to the Germans that abuse of allied civilians in German-occupied territories would have dire consequences for German civilians in Allied countries. Stanislaw Mikolajczyk, who, at the time, was Polish minister for home affairs, called for the incarceration of Germans in the United States:

> The people in Poland think that the reaction to the unexampled torture inflicted upon them is too weak, as much on the part of their own Government as on the part of the Pope and the Allies. They demand that an equivalent code should be applied to the Germans in the United States; at least some tens of thousands of them should be imprisoned in concentration camps and regarded as hostages. The mere threat of a tribunal in the future and the inexorable application of reprisals does not help at all.[80]

It is not clear what Mikolajczyk means when he speaks of the "unexampled torture" inflicted upon Poles by Germans and asks that "an equivalent code be applied to Germans in the United States." What is clear is that his call for the internment of Germans in the United States has nothing whatsoever to do with any concern about espionage activity that might be taking place.

Internment of German Americans—Seagoville, Texas

Retribution by the United States for crimes committed by the Nazis had in a sense already started. The internment of German nationals and some German Americans in camps in the United States during World War II began in 1941 and extended in some cases for several years beyond the end of the war. A total of 25,655 Germans or individuals of German descent from the United States, Hawaiian Islands, and Latin America were interned in various U.S. facilities from Washington State to New Jersey. Most were resident aliens, or Germans who had not yet been naturalized. It was thought that these people might be traded for American hostages held in Germany. Among the interned were 10,905 Germans residing in America and German American citizens. As pointed out, individuals such as Fritz Kuhn, leader of the German-American Bund, were among them. German Americans were "denaturalized," their American citizenship taken away from them, so that they could legally be interned.[81] Also included in the figure of 10,905 are the wives and families who "voluntarily" interned themselves to be with the forced internee.[82]

It should be noted at the outset, however, that the United States was not the only country to intern German aliens living on foreign soil or denaturalize citizens of German descent who were thought to be a security threat. Nor was the United States the first to intern German enemy aliens. England began interning them in 1940. As one European nation after another fell to Hitler's army, the English, of course, felt the threat of occupation by Germany more acutely than did the United States. As refugees poured in from beleaguered European nations, including anti-Nazis and Jews from Germany, suspicion mounted and procedures were put in place for screening the 75,000 Germans and Austrians living in Britain. The hearings proceeded rapidly and were conducted in brief. In January 1940, 528 enemy aliens were interned and 8,356 had been placed under restrictions. By June 13 of the same year, almost eleven thousand enemy aliens had been interned. England interned more German enemy aliens than any other country during World War II, including the Unites States. Some 22,000 were arrested by the British government, 11,000 of whom were shipped to internment camps in Canada and Australia for safekeeping.[83] Canada became subject to about the same level of apprehension concerning enemy aliens that existed in the United States. Like the United States, Canada first interned German enemy aliens during World War I. Canada at the time had a total population of about eight million. About a half million were of German or Austro-Hungarian descent; of these, 8,500 were interned. Germans living in Canada and Canadian Germans fared better during World War

II because, among other reasons, Canadian Prime Minister Mackenzie King was favorably disposed to the German Canadian population, a substantial number of whom had supported him in his early first efforts to win political office. Nonetheless, in September 1939, an initial 303 Germans and German Canadians were interned; and in May 1940, an additional 1,200 were placed in custody. These numbers, however, dropped considerably by the end of the war as hearings and rehearings found no basis for holding many of these individuals. By the end of 1942, 411 individuals remained, 40 of whom had their Canadian citizenship taken away. Ninety-eight German enemy aliens were repatriated to Germany by the Canadian government.[84]

Contrary to what one might have anticipated, documents edited by Don Heinrich Tolzmann and compiled by Arthur D. Jacobs and Joseph E. Fallon—all highly regarded within the German American community—present a rather pleasant picture of life in U.S. internment camps. The three camps for which substantial information exists—inspection reports of facilities and camp life— are Seagoville, Texas; Crystal City, Texas; and Ellis Island, New York. Although not the largest of these facilities, the Seagoville camp is the one for which the most extensive documentation exists. The Seagoville facility was first established on October 10, 1940, as the nation's second Federal Reformatory for Women. It was a minimum-security, open institution based on the progressive model of the Aldersville, West Virginia, women's reformatory, the first of its kind in the United States. The Aldersville reformatory consisted of cottages, each of which had its own kitchen. Among the more impressive and innovative features of the Aldersville facility is that the women governed themselves. Eleanor Roosevelt visited the facility several times. One congressman called it a "women's seminary." The Seagoville Reformatory was similarly designed as a "cottage" community for women offenders and similarly permitted the inmates to govern themselves. The Seagoville reformatory was built to house 400 women and was situated on farmland on which the women could grow their own produce. In March 1942, the prisoners vacated the facility and it was made a federal detention station for Japanese, Germans, and Italians.[85] When the Swiss legation, representing German interests, visited the Seagoville detention facility two years later on August 22, 1944, they found 337 German nationals, including 49 women who had voluntarily interned themselves to be with their husbands. There were no children of German nationals at Seagoville. Camp residents also included thirty-six German Americans (thirty-five women and one child) who had also voluntarily interned themselves to be with their husbands and father. Of the total 373 people housed in Seagoville, 288 individuals, or 80 percent, had been arrested by the U.S. government. Twenty percent had come of their own volition.[86]

The U.S. government, of course, did not stop to think that Germans residing in the United States or naturalized German Americans might consider internment a form of revenge. Internment served more practical purposes. For one thing, German internees were needed to trade for Americans being held by the Nazis in Europe. Second, while there was never really the possibility of a fifth column, the United States was clearly vulnerable to espionage. Military and war-related plans and designs were stolen by Nazi agents in the United States from the U.S. companies who produced them. Interning individuals, even American citizens, who had openly declared their loyalty to Germany seemed an obvious means of curtailing Nazi recruitment in the United States and espionage activities that might directly cost the lives of American soldiers fighting overseas.

By the standards of the day, living accommodations in Seagoville were quite good, by some measures better than that of the average American citizen. The main portion of the camp consisted of twelve colonial-style, red-brick buildings with cream limestone

Seagoville, Texas, Camp, circa 1942. Internment camp primarily for German nationals, 1942–1945. Institute of Texan Cultures, University of Texas at San Antonio, photo #085-0910. *Courtesy of Seagoville Federal Correctional Institution.*

Two of the red-brick colonials as viewed from the Industry Building, circa 1942, Seagoville, Texas, Camp. *Record Group 85, PHO-G1, National Archives, Washington, D.C.*

trim, the whole of which was surrounded by spacious lawns. According to one report, "visitors remarked that the camp resembled a college campus."[87]

The living quarters at Seagoville consisted of six red-brick colonials and sixty cottages. Each adult individual had either a private eight-by-ten–foot room in one of the buildings or shared a sixteen-foot-square cottage with a spouse. Cottages were also sometimes given to single women. In all probability, a single room would have been a step up for some internees compared to their own homes. The U.S. Census for 1940 indicates that one in five American homes had more than one person per room, a condition the Census defined as overcrowded.[88] Furnishings in the dormitories were of maple and included a bed, chest of drawers, clothes closet, desk, and chair. All had electric lights and were heated with gas or steam heat. The average room does seem to have been similar to the average dormitory room on a college campus today. The dormitories also had dining areas with tables for four and recreational lounges that were furnished with lounge chairs, tables, lamps, a combination radio and record player, and a piano. Perhaps more importantly, the dormitories were equipped with complete indoor plumbing, while bathhouses provided similar facilities to the cottages. According to the Census Bureau, in 1940 nearly half the houses in the United States lacked "complete plumbing facilities"; in some states, this rate was as high as 80 percent. Complete plumbing facilities were defined by the Census as hot and cold piped water, a bathtub or shower, and a flush toilet. These facilities, according to the Census, had to have been for the exclusive use of a housing unit's inhabitants in order to qualify as "complete plumbing facilities." The Seagoville camp had "complete plumbing facilities."[89]

Other structures in the camp included an educational building, which housed classrooms, a beauty shop (used for courses in cosmetology), an auditorium, and a library. It appears that a number of the internees were able to make use of their free time to develop their talents. In 1943, the camp school enrolled 158 people who took courses in subjects such as English, German, French, Italian, Spanish, portrait painting, oil painting, wood-burning craft, technical drawing, mathematics, bookkeeping, and beauty shop technique. In addition, lectures were provided weekly by the internees themselves on subjects such as "china and porcelain," and "Simon Bolivar" (a number of the internees were German nationals brought to the United States from Latin America). The American Friends Service Committee also arranged occasional lectures. Three were scheduled for fall 1944, two of which are identified in the documents as having been delivered by Mrs. Jean T. Joughin of the University of Texas at Austin. The titles of her lectures were "What Americans thought of their frontier 100 years ago!" and "How economic causes contributed to the break between the North & South!" The equipment available for lectures was quite good for the time and included a 16-mm "sound movie projector," slide projector, film strip projector, opaque projector, a standard-size motion projector screen installed in the auditorium, as well as a portable screen for use in a classroom that had dark shades for daylight operation.[90]

Each internee received an allowance from the government and the opportunity to perform work for pay. The daily allowance was ten cents, about the equivalent of $1.50 in 2007, according to the Employment Policies Institute.[91] A dollar fifty was not a great deal, but it was enough for a beer or a coke at the canteen, and maybe a few cigarettes. Even when one considers that room and board were free, the allowance was hardly adequate. Complaints were registered by the internees and recorded by the Swiss legation, but no one complained of the wage or living conditions at Seagoville. Apart from the daily allowance, internees also received $5.25 (about $77 in 2007 currency) per month in scrip to purchase clothes from the canteen.

Seagoville scrip, used in internment camp.
Photos courtesy of Jerry Adams.

When a special need arose, the canteen clerk would purchase items for internees in Dallas. In 1943, the Camp Committee (elected by the internees) and its chairman, Franz Wurz, drew up a set of house rules that required all internees to spend time working in the kitchen and share the responsibility of keeping their houses and rooms clean. By 1944, internees were no longer being forced to work, even at feeding themselves or cleaning their homes. During the month of June 1944, 329 internees were on the payroll. A total of 310 internees were being paid to work part-time in the kitchen, 41 were working in "house management," and 10 were "cleaning." There were also, however, a number of other forms of employment. Some were working as carpenters, electricians, clerks, or in shoe repair. Several worked at more than one job. All earned 10 cents an hour.[92] The minimum wage at the time was 30 cents an hour. However, internees, as has been pointed out, also received room and board gratis, as well as a monthly clothes allowance and a small amount of pocket money each day. It is difficult to say how much was lost in pay by these workers due to their internment. Some were skilled laborers and no doubt could have netted more in savings had they lived outside the camps. However, it should be noted that almost all the males were German nationals and recent immigrants at a time when the United States was at war with Germany. They were not likely to be offered the best-paying jobs.

For diversion, there was a library that consisted of about forty-five hundred books, approximately three thousand in English and fifteen hundred in German. The internees were well-informed on events taking place in the world through the over 250 English-language periodicals that were regularly received. On a lighter note, the internees staged musical and theatrical productions in the auditorium, which seated four hundred. A seven-piece internee musical group had been formed that played at musicals and variety shows that were staged; and all internees had use of the camp's eight upright pianos, one grand piano, one Hammond electric organ, and nine combination radio-phonographs. For the more academically inclined among the patrons, weekly lectures were provided by the internees on musical topics, and these were accompanied by recordings. Further, the American Friends Service Committee arranged on October 31, 1944, for a piano recital by Harlow Mills, whose program consisted of German, American, and Latin-American music.[93]

Services for both Catholic and Protestant internees were held each Sunday. The Catholic mass was held in the morning and the Protestant service in the evening. Priests and ministers were hired for the purpose on a contract basis and paid for by the U.S. government. Services were held at the discretion of the minister or priest in either German or English.[94]

Sufficient attention seems to have been given to the physical health of the internees. There was a health-care facility in the camp that was operated under the direction of the U.S. Public Health Service, as well as a sports and physical fitness program at Seagoville. The health facility was staffed by two full-time physicians and a full-time dentist who made themselves available to internees five days a week. Internees who had need of specialist care were taken to the Dallas Hospital twenty miles away. There, on the regular payroll of the Seagoville facility, were four consultants, including an eye, ear, nose, and throat specialist, surgeon, radiologist, and urologist. An obstetrician, second radiologist, pediatrician, and neurosurgeon from the Dallas Hospital consulted on a fee basis. Although relatively few participated in the sports program (there were only eight children in the camp, seven of whom were under the age of four; all other internees were aged thirty and older), some did play tennis (for which two courts had been built), soccer, fistball, volleyball, softball, track, high and broad jump, discus, shot-put, and quoits (horseshoes). Equipment existed for baseball, but there was no real interest in learning to play the game among the internees. The same was true of basketball. For indoor recreation, there were four ping-pong tables.[95]

The Seagoville station was run by Superintendent Dr. Amy N. Stannard. Stannard had been assistant warden to Helen Hironimus when the facility was a women's reformatory, and became warden of the reformatory when Hironimus moved to Alderson. When Seagoville became a federal detention station, Stannard stayed on as the administrator, although all the women staff and, of course, the inmates, were transferred to Alderson.[96] The new name given to the facility was the Seagoville Detention Station. Internees at the facility were represented by a Family Camp Committee, which consisted of seven elected spokesmen, one from each the seven housing units. These seven then elected a speaker to represent them. The Family Camp Committee on various occasions would meet directly with the superintendent. The concerns of the internees were numerous and ranged widely. Among the issues raised by the Camp Committee at its meetings with Stannard were the essentials of daily living, such as accommodations, foodstuffs, and clothing. The following two paragraphs present a sampling from committee minutes.

The German internees complained that the meat was inferior, and that it wasn't fresh. They wanted better meat, more milk, and more fresh vegetables. The delivery of beer was neither regular nor adequate. In addition, the local dealers in Dallas needed to be informed that the 3.2 percent alcohol content restriction that applied to U.S. Army bases did not apply to Seagoville. They asked, could the cottages on the premises be used for private meetings with visitors? Such was the case at other facilities, the internees pointed out. Bulbs of higher wattage were needed for their rooms; and the ventilators in buildings 10 and 11 needed repair. Dr. Stannard had reported that some new cots had arrived for which there appeared to be no immediate need since no new internees were expected. Requests from current internees for these cots, however, outnumbered the cots that had been received, and a way of fairly distributing them would have to be implemented. The issuance of warmer underwear and clothes needed to be discussed, but this subject would be better broached at a future meeting with the Clothing Committee present. The Administration was asked to "ease up" on the regulation requiring official roll call, which was performed at noon when the internee Fire and Safety men, who worked at night, slept. Could the monthly payroll be paid out earlier in the month than it has been in the past?[97]

Internees were encouraged to be creative and find solutions of their own whenever they could. Dr. Stannard asked the members of the Camp Committee to report to their constituency that there was a growing demand for the finished products that they were producing in the camp facilities, by which she presumably meant the crafts objects being produced in the crafts huts. The internees' request that they be permitted to raise rabbits near the garden project was welcome, but the spokesmen were advised to get the reaction of the garden owners first and report back before permission would be granted. The chicken farm project would have to be put on hold. The Central Office did not want to invest so much money in the project at this time. They would reconsider the matter in late winter or early spring if, in the meantime, suggestions were submitted explaining how the project could be executed at considerably less cost. The main item is the chicken wire for the fencing. Efforts will be made to purchase materials secondhand through government surplus.[98]

But there were also of course other issues related more directly to the fact of internship. The Family Committee did not understand why their letters could not be returned to the sender when they contained material thought objectionable by the authorities, instead of being sent forward with the censor's embarrassing deletions. Dr. Stannard agreed, and thought that returning the letters would educate the sender concerning "censorship requirements." (Regulations prohibited, for example, any discussion of the numbers of individuals interned in the camp.) She suggested that letter writers enclose a slip of paper asking that edited letters be returned instead of sent to the addressee.[99]

On November 22, 1943, Dr. Stannard reported to the Family Camp Committee that she had recently received a communication from Mr. Kelly of the Central Office that no nationalistic symbols, emblems, or pictures were to be displayed. Dr. Stannard reminded the Committee that the American flag had been withdrawn from the school building because of protests from some of the internees, and an agreement had been reached at that time between the camp administration and the Family Committee not to display any national symbols or pictures. Stannard also pointed to a second agreement between herself and the Family Committee that had permitted a Memorial Day celebration on November 9. At this celebration, a "special program" was provided using a "special method." (Neither the special program nor the special method is specified.) November 9 was the anniversary of Hitler's 1923 beer hall putsch, and celebrations were held on that day throughout Nazi Germany. Apparently a commemoration of some type was allowed to go forward at the Seagoville facility. However, the new communication that Stannard had recently received from the central office meant that no such commemoration could take place in the future. Mr. Kelly, Stannard explained, felt that exhibiting national symbols might create "disharmony and unrest" among the "divergent groups in this camp." However, individuals were permitted to display such symbols or pictures in their private rooms.[100] It is quite remarkable that Stannard would have permitted a celebration of early Nazi exploits (and failed exploits at that) while Americans were being killed fighting those same Nazis. However, the minutes of this meeting between Stannard and the Family Committee suggest that such commemorations were permitted in POW camps.

Most of the internees were German nationals who were ardently in favor of the Nazi party and admired Hitler enormously. When it was proposed by the Camp Council in April 1944 that they be permitted to hold a celebration in honor of Hitler's birthday, the chairman of the Council explained that he expected 80 percent of the camp population would want to attend. The program, which was to begin at 8:30 pm, called for Hans Ackerman, the speaker of the Family Camp Committee, to start with "words of welcome"; these were to be followed by the chorus singing a "salute to the Fuehrer" and the orchestra playing Hitler's favorite marches, the "Badenweiller marches." At that point the curtain would rise on the stage, and Mrs. Jackie Weik would recite the "flower greeting to the Fuehrer." At the same time, the chorus would sing several pieces: "Der Gott der Eisen Wachsen liess" (God lets the sword advance) and "Volk ans Gewehr" (People to your weapons/to arms). Frau Schram would recite a poem, "Prolog," written by Miss Zanglein, and also recite something called "Treuspruch" (Declamation). The orchestra would play an old German march called "Preussens Gloria" (The Glory of Prussia), an address would be given with quotations from some of Hitler's speeches, and the program would end with the community, accompanied by the orchestra, singing the German national anthem.[101] Apparently, the program was not approved by camp officials and the public celebration never took place. An angry letter exists from the camp speaker to camp authorities complaining of the fact that the wishes of by far the majority of the internees were not accommodated as they should have been.

What is remarkable here is that the internees should have even thought that such a program would have been acceptable. Songs titled, "God Let the Sword Advance" and "People to Arms," obviously call upon Germans to do battle with their adversaries, among whom of course were Americans who were dying by those same swords and arms the internees would sing of. More heinous was the fact that at about the same time Germany was rounding up the 400,000 Hungarian Jews that would be sent to their death at Auschwitz. The Western world, including the United States, knew of the action and warned Germany not to massacre these people. The internees at Seagoville were certainly well aware of what was taking place in Europe. They had a library of regular subscriptions to magazines such as *Time* and *Life* to keep them apprised of developments.[102]

Then too there was the matter of rehearings by the Alien Enemy Control Unit that had incarcerated German Americans. Stannard reported to the Family Camp Committee that the Alien Enemy Control Unit was in the process of sending around to all the internment camps in the United States a traveling hearing board that would listen to the arguments of those who felt that they had been wrongly interned. Supplementing these would be additional field officers assigned to one station at a time to perform personal interviews. Those who wished for rehearings were advised to file their applications. The traveling board was expected at Seagoville in January or February 1944, but not everyone who requested a rehearing would be granted one. The names of those who were selected for rehearings would be known beforehand so that they could prepare their cases. Apparently the rehearings produced the desired outcome, at least in a good number of cases. According to the Swiss delegate for war prisoners, who visited Seagoville on August 22, 1944, as of January 1, 1944, thirty-five individuals (including twenty-two family units) had been provided "interim parole," and twenty-one people had been placed in "internment at large." Also, an additional twenty-five had had their request granted for transfer to the Crystal City internment camp.[103]

There were significant numbers of Seagoville internees who wanted to go back to Germany, at least during the early years of the war. Toward the end of the war, when everyone realized that Germany was in ruins, that Nazis were being imprisoned in Germany, and that in all likelihood the former Seagoville internees would take their place inside the same German prisons that now held loyal German Nazis, many of those who had formerly desired "repatriation" in Germany recanted and expressed their desire to remain in the United States. The desire for repatriation among some of the inmates at Seagoville is evident in the minutes of a meeting of the Camp Council on February 19, 1944, at which W. F. Kelley, assistant commissioner for alien control, was present. The minutes were taken by Franz Wirz, the chairman of the Family Camp Committee, and present Kelley's views on repatriation in very clear detail. According to Kelley, diplomatic exchanges were underway and the U.S. government was awaiting a reply to an offer it had recently made. Kelley was quick to add, however, that the Immigration Department was not directly involved in exchange negotiations. However, the Immigration Department worked closely with the International Red Cross to help repatriate individuals who were suffering particular hardships. Kelley went on to point out that, for example, 634 people had been released from the internment camp at Crystal City, but only 357 individuals had actually been exchanged for Americans being held abroad, and all of those 357 individuals had been arrested in South America. The others, all of whom were from the United States, were not exchanged, but, rather, "repatriated" to Germany, some because they were deemed unfit to be of use in Germany's war effort. Kelley further stated that he understood that Seagoville inmates were anxiously looking forward to leaving for Germany on the next sailing of the Scandinavian ship *Gripsholm*, but that the next sailing would carry only the sick and badly wounded German prisoners of war. There would be no room for civilians. Kelley also stated that he was committed to doing his best to provide a means of repatriation at some later date. Kelley and those who desired repatriation to Germany apparently met with some success. In August 1944, the Swiss delegate reported that Seagoville at that point in time housed 268 individuals of German descent from the continental United States and sixty-eight such individuals from elsewhere. The delegate went on to point out that as of January 1, 1944, fifty-nine individuals had been repatriated to Germany and two to Panama.[104]

Copies of some of the letters sent by inmates of Seagoville to their friends and family elsewhere still exist in a file collected by Stannard. As one might expect, many of these letters glow with descriptions of how wonderful life at Seagoville is. Particularly disparaging remarks about Seagoville would have fallen under the scrutiny of the censor, who was known to delete portions of letters and who would have been charged with reporting subversive or suspicious statements had she not made the deletions. Mrs. Irma Spohr, a voluntary internee, wrote to her friend Herta Mueller in Chicago that Seagoville is a "paradise": "I enjoy everything thoroughly, the flowers of blue and gold in the meadows, the shrubs with their white and yellow blooms, the wonderful sky or the magnificent cloud formations, the sunset, the starry skies at night, the still air or the roaring wind, everything in God's nature contains a beauty for me and is an adventure for me." Internee Hans Lein was impressed with the leisure activities available in the camp. He wrote that "entertainment is provided generously." Both movies and orchestral music were provided twice weekly. On his one free evening, he accompanied a pianist on his violin for the entertainment of the Spanish-speaking residents. Seagoville had four ping-pong tables, and he was apparently one the best ping-pong players in the camp. Elli Donath was impressed with the way they were provided for their well-being. He explained in a letter to Otto Donath of Chicago that they received very good underwear at Seagoville. "Many of the internees have perhaps never in their lives been able to afford such clothes." Other letters, however, were more evenly balanced in their judgment of Seagoville. However fine the facilities, their movements and activities were still confined to a well-defined perimeter. Karl Wecker wrote to his wife, Tessie, in New York City expressing his regret that he could not be with her on Christmas. He wrote, "[B]ut let not undue sadness burden our hearts. I'll have a lighted candle in front of your picture and all my thoughts will be with you. We are not the most ill-treated and suffering people in the world. . . . You have been here and know that I am rather pampered than persecuted. And while I profoundly detest being deprived of my freedom, I am treated in a correct and humane fashion by the detaining authorities." Of greater interest here, however, are the letters to Dr. Stannard from individuals who had been interned in Seagoville and released, and who wrote to Dr. Stannard expressing their gratitude for the treatment they received at Seagoville. These expressions would probably not have been feigned. Hilda Zaenglein Braunlich, who made her home in Jacksonville Beach, Florida, after release from Seagoville, wrote to Dr. Stannard that "many who [have] been there will think back like I do, gratefully to you and all the officers who always were very good and understanding to us. I surely will not forget."[105]

Today, however, there are individuals who recall their internment experience and that of their parents and siblings with bitterness and a sense of having been unfairly mistreated. One such individual is Gunther Graber, who was about two years old when he and his family found themselves in the Seagoville detention facility. Graber recalls the day that two neatly dressed men moved in down the street from where he, his brother Werner, and parents lived in Elizabeth, New Jersey. It was then that the freakish visitations began. The first time these new neighbors visited the Graber home they flashed their FBI badges and took Gunther's father, Theo, to the local FBI bureau for interrogation. That was on September 25, 1942. In November they were back to make arrests. Gunther's mother, Emmy, stepped out of the bedroom door as the FBI agents announced the purpose of their visit. Emmy fainted and fell down the stairs. She had been pregnant. Gunther's brother Teddy was born December 2, 1942, two months premature with a deformed right leg and suffering from spina bifida, a birth defect that interferes with the development of the central nervous system, including the brain, spinal cord, and nerve tissues. When FBI Inspector Stern and two Elizabeth policemen came to arrest the Graber family on January 16, 1943, they had to swing by the Elizabeth General Hospital to pick up Teddy. After more than a year, Teddy was still unable to leave the hospital. Because the boys were citizens by virtue of birth on American soil, they could not be forcibly interned, but their father decided they should stay together. Gunther's account does not indicate whether or not there might have been any alternatives for the boys. No mention is made, for example, of near relatives in the vicinity with whom the boys might stay. Their immediate destination was Ellis Island. On January 19, they were again moved, this time by train. Graber recalls that as they waited on the platform they were separated from the crowd and guarded by plainclothes agents. People stared at them like criminals. Their new destination—their new home—was the Seagoville detention facility. The family of five, three of whom were under the age of five, was assigned two rooms. Contrary to the portrait drawn by the official Seagoville records, "life in general," said Teddy, "was miserable." Both his mother and Teddy were constantly sick and spent a good deal of time in the hospital. He calls Seagoville "a desolate, miserable place. . . . I cannot imagine how my mother and father managed all this misery." No doubt young Gunther associated all the tragedy of the sickness experienced by his mother and brother with the physical environment they were forced into. Gunther Graber does not really describe Seagoville in much detail, but there is no reason to believe that the facilities at the Seagoville he experienced differed from those described in the official documents.

A year and a half later, the Graber family was moved to the detention facility at Crystal City, Texas, which Gunther liked a lot better. It was hot in Crystal City, and Teddy still spent most of his time in the hospital, but they lived together in a bungalow, and so could function again as a family. One day his father was approached and asked whether he would like to repatriate to Germany. His father decided to go. Gunther explains that his father's choice to return to war-torn Germany was evidence of how "miserable" and "embittered" his father was. However, it is unlikely that his father knew that bombs were being dropped on the town he would return to in Germany. It is unlikely that anyone would choose subjecting himself and his family to bombardment instead of remaining incarcerated in a facility that offered much-needed medical attention for a disabled son. On January 6, 1945, the family sailed on the *SS Gripsholm* for Germany.

They were part of a group that was being exchanged for Americans who had been in Germany when the Nazis declared war on the United States. These Americans were arrested and interned in Germany in camps where the conditions were far worse than those in internment camps in the United States. Gunther described how in Friedrichschafen in Germany, a one-by-one exchange took place. One internee from the American side walked to the German side; then one internee from the German side walked to the American side. Those who chose the German side clearly got the worst of the bargain. Allied aircraft were still strafing German targets and German anti-aircraft artillery was still operative, attempting to shoot down Allied craft. Germany was in near ruins and the ruin would get worse. There was little to eat, and work for hire was hard to come by. Apparently, the family was refused help from local social service offices because they were not regarded as refugees. There were no such people as refugees from the West, they were told, especially not from America. Refugees were from the East. The Grabers managed to find a two-room living area in a wooden barracks building with running water and toilets outside. An embittered Gunther states, "[I]t was a long way from Elizabeth, NJ, but in many ways like being back in internment camp." The "internment camp" that Gunther alludes to here is, of course, Seagoville, where the family also had two rooms. Gunther neglects to mention, however, that there were considerable differences between the facilities at Seagoville and postwar Germany.

And of course there was considerable difference between Seagoville and the German concentration camps. In fact, the very same ship, the *SS Gripsholm*, which carried the Graber family back to Germany on January 6, 1945, carried Americans interned in the German concentration camp Bergen-Belsen back to the United States just six weeks later on February 22, 1945. Needless to say, the experiences of these Americans at Bergen-Belsen were gruesome. For example, Emil Weiss and his family, who were awaiting repatriation to the United States, were regularly beaten by the guards with a stick for no reason at all. It is possible that the guards knew that the Weiss family was Jewish. Emil Weiss, at the time of his internment, was seventy years old.[106] These and far more horrible stories about Jewish and gentile American inmates in German concentration camps do not absolve Americans of their responsibility to behave humanely. However, one cannot ignore the obvious fact that brutality, by contrast, was almost entirely on the side of the Nazis.

Despite the quality of life that existed in at least some of the facilities, the experience of internship was nonetheless wrenching and caused severe hardships for many. Arrest of German nationals began after the bombing of Pearl Harbor as America entered the war in 1941. Then, too, it seems clear that not all camps at all stages of development were comparable to Seagoville. The major internment center, for example, was in Crystal City, Texas. This camp housed 3,500 to 4,000 people at any one given time, including the families of thirty-five German nationals, roughly 130 Germans. In most cases, internees were rushed from their homes without being able to make any plans or provisions for their homes or families. In many instances, they were not told what their crime was, where they were going, or for how long. Wives and children of internees usually had no choice but to join their interned husbands, largely because of financial reasons. The wives and children were almost all American citizens born in the United States. Inside the internment camp, movement was restricted, but officials tried to make the camp as comfortable as possible. Families had private cottages, although only a few cottages had private bathrooms. Large mosquitoes were a constant nuisance, but of greater concern was the large scorpion population in the area that forced residents to walk warily and shake out their shoes. Otherwise internees were fairly well taken care of, and even opportunities for various sorts of recreation existed.[107] Despite the relatively good conditions, however, internees and their American families felt ashamed, stigmatized by what had happened to them. Inmates would later recall the shame felt when relatives would come to visit them, the humiliation of being in a facility that was guarded with men with guns, and not being able to move freely beyond the perimeter of the camp.[108] No doubt many German Americans alive today who lived in the internment camps, or who were born in them, view their experience of incarceration as unjust retribution for crimes they did not commit. The sense of injustice that German Americans felt during the war years persisted among some, especially when they sensed that Germans or German Americans were still being blamed for what happened during the Holocaust. That sense of injustice manifested itself as anger and defensiveness whenever the Holocaust would later be commemorated or memorialized, and the defensiveness would be especially pronounced when the Holocaust would be identified as somehow unique among the horrors that have occurred throughout history.[109]

Two

Interventionism versus Isolationism or Jewish Americans versus German Americans?

The Holocaust "Debates" of the 1930s and 1940s

The internment of German Americans after America entered the Second World War was only one of several setbacks suffered by the German American community because of the Nazis. The earlier embarrassment of German Americans occurred when Germany declared war on the United States shortly after the United States declared war on Japan for bombing Pearl Harbor. German Americans had been doing their best to keep America from declaring war on Germany. In fact, for some time prior to America's entry into World War II in 1941, a political battle had been raging between "isolationists" and "interventionists." The isolationists were comprised conspicuously—although certainly not exclusively—of German Americans who did not want America to go to war. It was obvious that if America were to enter the war it would do so on the side of the British against their German brethren. German Americans might be called upon to kill their German relatives as had already once been the case. The interventionists, on the other hand, included, among others, some very conspicuous

Jewish Americans who had relatives in Germany being persecuted and murdered by German Nazis. These Jewish Americans wanted America to intervene in some manner—to go to war, if necessary, and defeat the Nazis—in order to stop the persecution of their co-religionists in Germany.

The isolationists were of course comprised not only of German Americans but others, among whom were many well-intentioned individuals who genuinely believed that America was not the world's policeman, that American intervention would only mean Americans being killed, as well as Germans, Englishmen, and others. Among those who espoused the isolationist philosophy, however, were also German Americans who were genuinely pro-German, including those German Americans within the many Nazi or pro-Nazi groups operating in America when World War II began. Yet it is important to emphasize the fact that not all German Americans were isolationists, nor were all Jewish Americans interventionists.

According to the isolationists, the film industry—allegedly controlled by Jews—was the key means by which Jewish goals of intervention might be realized. The key event in the debate between German American isolationists and Jewish American interventionists was the U.S. Senate's Interstate Commerce Subcommittee hearings of September 9 to 26, 1941. At those hearings, testimony was taken regarding proposed Senate Resolution 152: "A Resolution Authorizing an Investigation of War Propaganda Disseminated by the Motion Picture Industry and of Any Monopoly in the Production, Distribution, or Exhibition of Motion Pictures." The hearings were important because they brought together for the first time, in an official forum, unofficial representatives of the German American and Jewish American communities to do intellectual battle over Germany's persecution of the Jews. Representatives of the German American community initiated the hearings in order to begin an investigation into the motion picture industry, which, the German American representatives charged, was owned by Jewish Americans who were producing anti-German propaganda designed to drag the United States into the war on the side of the British. The position of those representatives of the film industry called before the Committee, the position of those such as Harry Warner, was that the film industry was not anti-German but pro-American, and that Nazism was in fact a genuine threat not only to Jews but to the entire free world, including the United States. But in the course of argument, other more foundational tensions were revealed: the German American position was based on the view that the German persecution of Jews, if publicized in the United States, would bring persecution down on individuals of German descent in America.

However, even before 1941 when war between Germany and America became a reality, friction began to develop between German Americans and Jewish Americans over Nazi policy toward Jews. These early conflicts were harbingers of the greater debate between isolationist German Americans and interventionist Jewish Americans concerning U.S. entrance into World War II. From virtually the time Hitler took control of Germany in 1933 and began the persecution of Jews through local boycotts of Jewish businesses and other means, American Jews realized that action was needed. Jewish American organizations, although initially restrained by warnings of German reprisal upon the Jews of Germany, called for the boycott of German goods entering the United States as a response to German persecution of Jews. And in fact, Nazi Germany then responded with state-sponsored boycotts of Jewish shops in Germany, thereby perpetuating and escalating the terror experienced by Germany's Jews. To many Germans in America, and to German American Nazis in particular, German action was justified in a number of respects. According to some, the boycott of German goods by Jewish American organizations could be thought of as intervention into the economic life of Germany and promulgation of a state of opposition between Germany and the United States. While there were considerable differences between actions of the Jewish American organizations toward Germany and actions that the U.S. government might take toward Germany—there is really some question here as to whether Jewish American actions could be thought of as remotely interventionist—the relations between German Americans on the one hand and Jewish Americans on the other became strained, and that strain would persist and grow not only throughout the war period but in one respect or another to the present day.

The Jewish American boycott of German products led to countermeasures not only by Nazi Germany but also by German American businessmen who relied on the sale of German products in America. Many German Americans became, in effect, pro-German (at least from a commercial standpoint), just as many Jewish Americans had become pro-British. Measure followed countermeasure in the United States until many Jewish Americans and German Americans were, in effect, conducting an economic battle of sorts, although individual parties on each side would insist that was not the case; and indeed many Jewish Americans and German Americans made common cause in the effort to stop the Nazis. As war began to loom on the horizon, however, many Jewish Americans, if they had not already committed themselves, became anti-Nazi and interventionist, while German Americans became pro-German and isolationist.

Early Excesses of the Nazi Reich: Individual Actions and Local Boycotts

Hitler's induction as chancellor of Germany in January 1933 gave Brown Shirts everywhere in Germany license to persecute other Germans and vent their rage against Communists, Socialists, and Jews. Initially, the press in English-speaking countries focused on the treatment that political opponents, such as the Social Democrats, were receiving at the hands of the Nazis; but as early as the beginning of March the papers were identifying brutal beatings and other forms of humiliation experienced by Jews. England's

Manchester Guardian on March 27, 1933 reported the following:

> The worst excesses here in Berlin occurred on March 9th, most of the victims living in the Grenadierstrasse. Many Jews were beaten by Brown Shirts until the blood streamed down their heads and faces and their back and shoulders were bruised. Many fainted and were left lying on the streets, and were picked up by friends or passers-by and taken to hospital. A man and his wife walking together were both beaten and robbed.
>
> The Brown Shirts worked in gangs of five to thirty, the whole gang often assaulting one person. Many had the brassards worn by Nazis enrolled in the auxiliary police. Mr. ＿＿＿＿ was beaten bloody and unconscious and several hundred marks (his name and the precise sum are known to your correspondent) were taken from him.
>
> Twelve uniformed men broke into the house of Mr. ＿＿＿, stole several thousand marks and beat him, his wife, and his son until all three were bruised and bleeding (name, address, and precise sum also known).
>
> On the evening of the 15th three Jews were arrested by Brown Shirts in the Café New York and taken in a car (the number of which is in the possession of your correspondent) to the S.A. Lokal in the Wallnertheaterstrasse, where they were robbed of several hundred marks (precise sum also known), beaten bloody with rubber truncheons, and then turned out on the streets in a semi-conscious state.
>
> On the same day four Jews were taken to a Nazi S.A. Lokal in the Schilligstrasse, robbed of 400 marks and beaten bloody until they fainted.
>
> Hundreds of Jews have been beaten, but [no one] . . . dare[s] say so publicly or dare[s] complain without the risk of another beating.[1]

The scenes painted by the *Chicago Tribune* and the *New York Times*, like the scene depicted above, might have reminded the American public more of gangland Chicago than the land of Schiller, Goethe, and Beethoven, so fraught with violence did Germany appear in some of these news stories. Reports in American newspapers told of Jews, men and women, being "insulted, slapped [and] punched in the face, hit over the heads with blackjacks." Already, some were being dragged off to concentration camps where they were held without being charged. Complaints had been lodged against the German Foreign Office by U.S. Consul General George Messersmith concerning specific cases of "molestation" that Americans had experienced. Rumors flew that the Nazis planned to massacre the Jews. The *New York Times* concluded that Germany had suddenly gone "mad."[2]

Local boycotts of Jewish businesses in Germany, which by 1933 had already become a regular feature of the landscape, were occasions for such violence. Even smaller boycotts—outbursts by local party members—concretized what would otherwise have been simply antisemitism in the abstract, the type of antisemitism that existed elsewhere, including the United States. The boycott of the local butcher across the street, however, gave the antisemite a target, a face to look at, to get angry at, and ultimately to violently vent his frustrations on. Boycotts, as used by the Nazis, were a form of incitement to riot, but riots that might be contained. And riots served the very real and practical purpose of giving the Nazis the opportunity to let off steam. If they could be controlled— and boycotts assumed a degree of organization—such controlled violence was certainly better (would be reported more favorably in the international press) than the uncontrolled variety.

Prior to April 1933, Nazi attacks on Jewish businesses in Germany took the form of *Einzelaktionen*, or "individual actions," against specific Jewish retailers, usually Ostjuden or eastern Jews from Poland and points farther east who had settled in Germany.

These Jews, unlike their long-established and well-integrated German cousins were primarily orthodox, religious Jews, conspicuous by their appearance, their black coats and hats, their beards and forelocks, their clannishness, and their poverty. The eastern Jewish German was very easily identifiable; and, in his efforts to make his way in the German world, he might undersell a Christian competitor and bring down upon his head the ire of the other local shop owners as well as a beating from the local Nazis. The following report from Duisburg is not unusual:

> On March 24, a civilian accompanied by an armed member of the SS gained forced entry into the furniture store of the Polish Jew AAC, who apparently had antagonized his competitors by underselling them. The SS man accosted the Jew with his fists and left him covered with blood. AAC proceeded in this condition to the precinct station, where he was told that the police were powerless to act in such cases. On April 1, he was taken into protective custody, since there were fears of further acts of violence.

Comparable, but more severe, was the treatment received by a butcher in Dortmund:

> Members of the SA and SS dragged the butcher Julius Rosenfeld and son from the Dortmund stockyards through the streets of the city to a brickyard at the Voss pit. Rosenfeld and his son were lined up against the wall several times and threatened with pistols. They were forced to sing the "Horst Wessel Song," and were greeted by a rain of blows when they arrived at the brickyard. The young Rosenfeld was forced to set fire to his father's beard with a burning newspaper. After this, father and son were compelled to jump into a clay-pit. After five hours, the elder Rosenfeld was released and sent

home under the condition that within two hours he bring a slaughtered ox to his tormentors as a ransom for the release of his son.[3]

Prior to January 1933, when the Nazis took office, local police made efforts to curtail such incidents by rogue Nazis. After January 1933, those same rogue Nazis *were* the local police.

The primary motivation for these actions against Jews seems to have been economic, rather than race based, although the targets were always Jews. Further, not all *Einzelaktionen* were directed at, specifically, the small Jewish, Polish-German businessmen. Established Jewish-German retail businesses in Western Germany, including larger department stores, were also the targets of violent demonstrations during the month of March 1933. In Cassell, Storm Troopers took over the Tietz department stores on March 10, and threatened the department store's customers. On the same day, Nazi troops in Bottrop and Mullheim-on-Ruhr prevented people from entering Jewish shops, which consequently had to be closed. Official Nazi reports explained that the German population of those towns "would not stand for further existence of Jewish department stores and shops."[4] Nor were such *Einzelaktionen* restricted to attacks on tradesmen. The professions were also targeted, particularly doctors and lawyers. Demands that Jews be disbarred and prevented from practicing law were made by the League of National Socialist lawyers at its convention on March 14, 1933.[5] However, accounts of incidents involving Jewish members of the legal profession had already appeared in the German press. The *Frankfurter Zeitung* for March 10, 1933, reported

In Breslau at noon to-day [a group of] . . . S.A. men forced their way into the Law Courts. Amid shouts of "Out with the Jews!" all offices and conference rooms were opened and all the Jewish lawyers, judges, and public prosecutors were forced to leave the building forthwith. There were exciting scenes in the corridors and court rooms. The barristers' room was cleared within a few minutes and some of the Jewish lawyers had to leave the building before they had time to get their hats and coats. Many cases that were proceeding in the Courts had to be interrupted.[6]

Similar developments had taken place in the medical profession. Jewish doctors, in particular those who belonged to the Association of Socialist Physicians, were targeted for humiliation and boycott by the League of National Socialist Physicians. Jewish doctors were arrested; some were killed.[7]

Not all Americans or all newspapers took these reports seriously. Similar reports of German terror had appeared during World War I, and had proven to be false. The official Nazi position was that all of these reports were lies.[8] When an explanation was offered, one way the Nazi party tried to explain away what was happening in Germany was by comparing the Nazi "revolution" to the Communist revolution in Russia. The view propounded in official Nazi bulletins was that Germany was undergoing a revolution similar to the communist revolution in Russia. Just as the communist government could not be held responsible for the overzealous actions of isolated communist groups acting under their own volition, so too the Nazi government could not be held responsible for pent up anger now being released against Jews by isolated cells of the Nazi party. According to the Nazi bulletin releasing the information, "the government will not be involved any more than the Soviet Government is responsible for actions of the Communist party."[9]

That the Nazis themselves are drawing comparisons between the Nazi party and the Communist party, even at this very early stage in the development of the Third Reich, is important to this study because one of the major rationalizations of the Holocaust that would later be presented by German historians such as Ernst Nolte, as well as others, is that Hitler learned from Stalin how to persecute people. It is revealing that the Nazis themselves first used this "rationalization by comparison" for justifying the horrors that they were committing. From the very outset of the Hitler regime, Communist activities were being used to justify Nazi persecution, just as even today some critics will point to Stalin's reign of terror to justify Nazi horrors, even though they say that is not really what they are trying to do.

American Action and Inaction toward Early Nazi Persecutions of Jews

As reports of these acts of Nazi terrorism reached the United States, Jews in America were outraged, but initially no consensus could be reached by the several Jewish American organizations concerning the action to be taken against Germany, or even whether any action should be taken. As soon as the Nazis discovered that atrocity stories were circulating in the American press and that American Jews were contemplating taking action against Germany by boycott or other means, Nazis in Germany began to threaten that greater harm than any German Jews had yet experienced would come to them if American Jews continued to disparage the new Germany. The American Jewish Committee, founded in 1906 for the purposes of protecting Jews in the United States and abroad, took the Nazis at their word and refused to go through with a boycott for fear that such action would only bring a greater reign of terror down on German Jews. Although it is difficult to say whether, or to what extent, it should have been taken seriously, the Centralverein, the chief organization of Jews in Germany, also asked that no adverse action toward Germany be taken, that such action would only lead to further repression of German Jews. On the other hand, the American Jewish Congress, the second of the three major Jewish organizations (the third was the B'nai B'rith), was insistent that some action should be taken. The American Jewish Committee was comprised primarily of Jews of German descent, who like the Jews still in Germany believed that Hitler could not last very long in the land of Goethe and Beethoven, Meyerbeer and Heine. The membership of the American Jewish Congress, on the other hand, consisted for the most part of Jews from Eastern Europe and Russia who had witnessed the death throes of countless Jewish communities as pogrom after pogrom seared through their provinces. Empowered to take action, they knew it would do no good not to.[10]

Despite significant pressure from its membership, the American-Jewish Congress under the guidance of Rabbi Stephen S. Wise was able to delay for a year or so any action against Germany, and comply with the wishes of the American-Jewish Committee and the B'nai Brith, as well as the Centralverein in Germany. As early as January 1932, delegates from the American-Jewish Congress had met members of the American-Jewish Committee to discuss means of combating Nazi antisemitism. The decision reached was to comply with the wishes of Jews in Germany and trust to Germany's more enlightened citizenry to see to it that the civil rights of Jews were protected and the persecutions ended. It was hoped that Hitler the empowered ruler would be considerably less zealous in his persecution of Jews than Hitler the aspiring demagogue. When by March 1933 the power of Hitler was solidified and still no relief for Jews was in sight, the American-Jewish Congress decided that it was time to act. On March 19, 1933, the American Jewish Congress convened an emergency conference of Jewish organizations, including representatives from the American Jewish Committee. Dr. Samuel Margoshes, one of the vice presidents of the American Jewish Congress, called for a national protest against the treatment of Jews in Germany. J. George Fredman, commander-in-chief of the Jewish War Veterans organization, proposed a boycott of all German goods. Joseph M. Proskauer, judge and prominent member of the American Jewish Committee warned that such actions—whether they take the shape of demonstrations or boycotts—"will kill Jews in Germany." It was voted that a protest rally would be held on March 27 at Madison Square Garden. In Dr. Wise's view,

> the time for caution and prudence is past. We must speak up like men. . . . What is happening in Germany today may happen tomorrow in any other land on earth unless it is challenged and rebuked. It is not the German Jews who are being attacked. It is the Jews. We must speak out. If that is unavailing, at least we shall have spoken.[11]

On March 23, four days before the Madison Square Garden rally was to be held, 2,000 Jewish war veterans along with an additional 2,000 non-Jewish veterans paraded in protest of the treatment of Jews by the Nazis. John Patrick O'Brien, mayor of New York City, reviewed the troops and was given a resolution calling for boycott of German products. Local boards of veterans were instructed to create placards and publicly demonstrate against purchase of German goods. Flyers were circulated that read "Don't Buy German Goods. Don't Sell German Goods, Don't Ship American Merchandize in German Ships, Don't Patronize German Moving Pictures, Do It Yourself, Tell Your Family and Friends to Do It, But by All Means, Boycott, Boycott, Boycott!" The Jewish War Veterans claimed almost immediate success. Two million dollars worth of orders placed in Germany had been canceled, they said, as a result of boycott efforts within the first few days. However, it would be several months before they were joined by other groups in America.[12]

The lead story on the front page of the *New York Times* for Tuesday, March 28, 1933, was the previous day's rally at Madison Square Garden in protest of Germany's treatment of its Jews. Twenty thousand Jewish Americans packed the stadium to capacity, while another estimated 35,000 people packed the streets, some able to listen to the proceedings over loudspeakers that had been set up for the purpose of broadcasting to the overflow crowds. Nor was the protest limited to New York City. The plans were for rallies to be held in eighty other cities apart from New York, including Chicago, Philadelphia, Boston, Baltimore, and Cleveland. The Madison Square Garden rally, moreover, would be broadcast to the metropolitan centers of Europe. It was to be an international day of protest against the treatment of Jews and a day of mourning for the German nation that had fallen so tragically "from a high state of enlightenment to a position of barbaric medievalism." The *Times* reported protest rallies in Tennessee, Chicago, and Poland. An estimated one million Jews had assembled throughout the world to protest the persecution of Jews in Germany. In the United States, resolutions were being introduced in Congress to condemn German treatment of Jews and efforts were being made to convince the president that he should come forward and lend his voice to others who were protesting violence in Germany. At Madison Square Garden, the speakers that Monday included such distinguished non-Jews as William Green, president of the American Federation of Labor, as well as Robert F. Wagner, senator from the state of New York; Alfred E. Smith; and Mayor O'Brien. Telegrams from governors and congressmen throughout the nation were received condemning the German persecution of Jews, including letters of sympathy from Henry T. Rainey, speaker of the House; Joseph T. Robinson, majority leader of the Senate; senators from California and Utah, and the governors of Illinois, Pennsylvania, Iowa, Oklahoma, Oregon, Indiana, Virginia, and Wisconsin.[13]

German Boycott versus the Jewish American Boycott

Germany, of course, used the Madison Square Garden protest and the threat of boycott by Jews as an excuse for still greater persecution of Jews. On the front page of the *New York Times* for March

28 appeared, along with the story reporting the Madison Square Garden rally, a story announcing a Nazi boycott of Jews in retaliation for Jewish "atrocity tales" abroad, *and* the boycott that American Jews were *planning* against German-made products. A recent bulletin of the Nazi party promised that instructions would be forthcoming "for the organization of a gigantic popular movement for the forming of committees to boycott the Jewish stores of Germany in response to the boycott threats of international Jewry."[14] It is revealing, here, of course, that the call for German boycott of Jewish goods is in anticipation of a boycott by Jews of German products. The Nazis were unaware that a Jewish boycott of German goods had already been instituted by the Jewish War Veterans, nor did it matter. No good reason for boycotting Jewish goods was known or really needed by the Nazi authorities, who clearly had every intention, even at this early point, of harassing Jews until there were no Jews left to harass. Nor were the Nazi authorities planning to limit themselves to a boycott. They also called for "nation-wide agitation for a decree immediately restricting the admission of Jews to certain academic professions and public institutions." Already, the governing board of the German Bar Association has resigned in order to make possible new elections and the installation of a new board that would be free of Jews and socialists. The German League of Physicians Associations had similarly requested their local units to dismiss Jews and others unsympathetic to the Nazi regime from their local governing boards.[15]

When the April 1 boycott by Germans of Jewish stores did take place, it turned out to be short-lived but important because it was a first official act of persecution. The boycott had been planned only a few days earlier, on March 28. It was started by the Nazi party on April 1 and, three days later, officially proclaimed a "one-day" boycott by the German government. The German government had legitimized anti-Jewish actions. Unlike the *Einzelaktion-*

en that preceded the boycott, many of the events that comprised or accompanied the boycott were contained, at least in the large cities. Hitler Youth were stationed in the entrance of Jewish concerns with placards that identified the establishment as Jewish and warned customers to stay away. Those who nonetheless attempted to enter the Jewish businesses were photographed and their pictures appeared the next day in the local newspaper. In smaller towns, various degrees of violence accompanied the boycott. Obscenities were written on shop windows, and in some instances windows were smashed and businesses robbed by the local population. In locales such as Dortmund, Duisburg, Saxony, or the Scheunenviertel area of Berlin, where conspicuous groups of Eastern European Jews dwelled, these more egregious types of actions were widespread. Some Germans rebelled against the Nazis by intentionally patronizing Jewish concerns on April 1, by going to Jewish doctors or seeing a Jewish lawyer, but most pretended that nothing unusual was going on and some were even joyous to see such anti-Jewish actions taking place.[16]

What would now amount to a concerted, Jewish "counterboycott" of German goods in America was not so easily organized as the German boycott of Jewish businesses in Germany. As noted, there were three major Jewish organizations in the United States when Hitler came to power in 1933 (American Jewish Committee, B'nai Brith, and American Jewish Congress), as well as the smaller but apparently effective Jewish War Veterans. The views of these organizations on the matter of boycotting differed. Only the Jewish War Veterans were in favor of boycott from virtually the very outset of the Hitler period. The other Jewish organizations dragged their feet, some well into 1934, before putting into place the machinery necessary for an even minimally effective boycott. In the meantime, a new organization materialized which was more clearly disposed to penalizing Germany for its treachery toward Jews. Toward the end of April 1933, the American League for Defense of Jewish Rights (ALDJR) was formed by Dr. Abraham Coralnik with financial backing promised by movie producer Louis Mayer.[17] On May 14, the League held its first conference and among the speakers was Samuel Untermeyer, a former vice president of the American Jewish Congress and the individual who would become president of the League and the major spokesperson for American boycott of German goods.[18] The conference unanimously endorsed implementation of a boycott,[19] but it was not until the National Boycott Conference of September 10, at which the League was the key player, that plans were laid for administration of a boycott on a large scale.

The boycott organization was to consist of an executive department and a fund-raising department. The executive department was divided into three sections. One would be responsible for developing the instruments and avenues for advertising the boycott, the placards, circulars, radio appearances, newspaper publicity, and speaking tours for the leaders of the movement. A second section would be responsible for organizing different sectors of the community, such as women consumers, as well as trades and industries. They would have local organizers and traveling organizers, and subsidize local boycott committees nationwide. The third section would provide consumers with information about goods they could purchase in place of German ones. This section would be responsible for contact with American manufacturers through local chambers of commerce, contact with foreign consulates and foreign chambers of commerce, as well as with the World Economic Federation. The fundraising department would solicit contributions by mail campaigns and campaigns by local committees and individuals, as well as through speaking tours of movement leaders.[20]

The American Jewish Congress joined the boycott movement at its meeting on August 20, 1933. It was there that the organization admitted that it did not appear Nazi Germany could be de-

terred from its course of persecuting Jews, and that the only re-
course was boycott of German products. A resolution adopted at
that meeting read as follows:

> The American Jewish Congress has come to the conclusion
> that no mercy can be expected from the savage tyrants now
> in the seat of the German Government, and that it is the duty
> of the American Jewish Congress, which stands for the de-
> fense of Jewish rights, to use all its available resources for the
> promotion of a vigorous and relentless nationwide Boycott
> movement for the self-defense of outraged humanity against
> the orgy of brutal persecution by the present masters of Ger-
> many.[21]

Among the other groups to join the boycott movement was the
American Federation of Labor, led by its president, William Green,
who, as indicated, was not Jewish but was distressed by the Nazi
harassment and incarceration of German labor leaders, both Jewish and Christian. (Green was among those who spoke in the early
rally at Madison Square Garden to protest Jewish persecution in
Germany.) At its convention of October 13, 1933, the American
Federations of Labor officially approved a resolution to

> join with other public-spirited organizations in our country in
> officially adopting a boycott against German-made goods and
> German services, this boycott to continue until the German
> government recognizes the right of other working people in
> Germany to organize into bona fide, independent trade union
> of their own choosing, and until Germany ceases it repressive
> policy of persecution of Jewish people.[22]

Countless others, both Jews and Christians, would later join the
boycott movement, including Norman Thomas of the American

Socialist Party who would use Madison Square Garden as his venue for providing the party's endorsement of a boycott of German goods.[23]

Jewish Americans versus German Americans on German Persecution of Jews: The Debates Begin

German Americans, however, were not universally in favor of the boycott of German products. Many German Americans feared American entry into war with Germany. Indeed, any anti-Nazi display was cause for concern on the part of some that the violence perpetrated against German Americans during World War I would be repeated. In fact, it was in the March 28, 1933, issue of the *New York Times*, which reported on the American Jewish Congress rally, that readers might have been first apprised of some friction between the German American and Jewish American communities over how to deal with German-Jewish persecution. The *Times* had printed, along with stories about the rally, the text of a speech that Bernard Ridder had planned to give, but which had been rejected by the organizers of the rally. Bernard Ridder was one of the Ridder brothers who edited *The New Yorker Staats-Zeitung*, the leading German American newspaper of its day. He was the brother of the Victor Ridder who a few months later would kick Heinz Spanknoebel out of his office for demanding that he print only stories sympathetic to the Nazis. The text that Bernard Ridder wanted to deliver at the Madison Square Garden rally was turned down by the organizing authorities, said Ridder, because it wasn't strong enough. In point of fact, Ridder's text was equivocal in its recommendations. Ritter explained that he understood persecution because he, like thousands of other German Americans, had suffered persecution simply for being of German descent during World War I. His intended speech went on to warn Jewish Americans that loudly announcing German persecution of

Jews might bring upon German Americans persecution similar to that which German Americans suffered during World War I. Ritter warned American Jews to be wary that "in protesting against the injustice of the persecution of the Jews that you do not permit yourselves to be guilty of the very same sins of racial persecution."[24]

Those who read the *Staats-Zeitung* would become familiar with Germany's rather weak rationalizations that Bernard Ridder would repeat in order to explain away German persecution of Jews. On June 8, 1933, having recently returned from a trip to Germany, Ridder tried to justify Hitler's efforts to remove Jews from government posts by arguing that 62 percent of all government offices had been occupied by Jews. "The dismissal of these Jews," he continued, "was merely a partisan political measure, precisely as most of the Republicans here have to walk the plank when the Democrats come into power, and vice versa." However, according to the German Statistical Yearbook for 1931, government posts in Germany numbered 1,638,000. Of the approximately 600,000 Jews in Germany, about 250,000 were adult males who might be eligible for jobs in the government. The 62 percent figure was very obviously bogus and would have been understood as such by anyone who looked into the statistic. Even if one included women and children, there were simply not enough Jews in Germany to fill 62 percent of the government offices in Germany. The data were simply more Nazi propaganda for those who were eager to listen.[25]

That Bernard Ritter could warn Jews in 1933 that stories of German persecution of Jews could bring down persecution upon German Americans is important for this study. The fear that stories of German persecution of Jews in Germany might lead to persecution of German Americans, or at least stereotyping of Germans and German Americans as Nazis, remained a major concern of German American organizations throughout the remainder of the twentieth century (and into the twenty-first). Indeed such fears on the part of German Americans contributed to the sentiment that existed in the United States against U.S. involvement in the Second World War. In the 1980s, that same fear would be the basis for German American sentiment against commemoration of the Holocaust. The German American community would argue against the establishment of a U.S. Holocaust memorial museum, largely because it felt that the additional publicity of the Holocaust would encourage strong anti-German and anti–German-American response in the United States.

American Nazi Boycott of Jewish American Businesses and the German American Response

In 1933, Ridder was only one among many German Americans who felt that Jewish American protests against German persecution were injurious to the German American community, and required some form of response. As the boycott of German goods began to impact German American retailers and businessmen who traded in providing German articles to the public, the Nazi organization in the United States saw its opportunity. It was the Nazi-sponsored Bund (Bund der Freunde des Neuen Deutschland, or League of the Friends of New Germany) that in March 1934, instigated a new boycott of Jewish businesses in the United States to counteract the Jewish boycott of those who did business with Germany. The organization under whose auspices the boycott would be conducted was the more reputable umbrella organization, United German Societies (UGS), which had recently been infiltrated by the Friends of New Germany;[26] and the branch of the UGS that would conduct the boycott was DAWA, the Deutschamerikanischer Wirtschaftsausschuss (and sometimes translated as the German American Protective Alliance). This organization is sometimes confused with the Deutscher Konsum Verband (also often translated as the German-American Business League), a boycott organization also formed by the Friends of the New Germany. After the more moderate faction of the UGS regained control of the organization from the Bund in 1935, the Bund left the UGS, and left its subsidiary, the DAWA, as well. The Friends at that point developed their own new umbrella organization, the League of German Societies, of which the new boycott committee, the Deutscher Konsum Verband (DKV), was a branch.[27]

The goal of the DAWA was to enlist German Americans to stop doing business with Jews. German Americans were to do business only with those shops that displayed the blue DAWA trade label, which consisted of the letters "DAWA" with a rising sun underneath and the German eagle above. Jews were not permitted to purchase the label,[28] which German and German American shopkeepers paid five dollars or more for, depending on the size of the establishment. The larger German American establishments that did not want to alienate their Jewish customers would purchase the blue eagle in order not to offend the Bund, but would not display it. Many smaller shops, on the other hand, were very enthusiastic about displaying the eagle and maintained that it brought in more business than their National Rifle Association decals and was well worth what they paid. Consumer members of the DAWA, who agreed to patronize only concerns that displayed the blue eagle, paid one dollar for the privilege of wearing a pin on their lapel as a "badge of honor."[29] The role of the Bund was primarily as "sandwich men" who carried advertising boards hung from their shoulders up and down the street. The signs displayed statements such as, "Tell me, where do you shop and we'll tell you who you are!" On occasion, however, the Bundists were more aggressive, performing virtual shakedowns of Jewish shop owners. The overall effect, however, was to endear American Nazis to German nationals and German American shopkeepers who had been selling German *Apfelmus* (applesauce) and discovered that they were being boycotted by anti-Nazi sympathizers. In many instances, they believed that they were simply compensating for loss of one patron with the addition of another. The Bundists, in their turn, gained a degree of respectability by association with well-regarded, German American businessmen who might otherwise have had nothing to do with Nazism.[30]

Like the DAWA, the intention of the DKV was to encourage the purchase of German goods from German Americans and discourage patronage of Jewish businesses.[31] The method employed by the DKV, however, differed from the DAWA. The intention of the DKV seems to have been to develop a cooperative along socialist lines. Discount stamps were issued that could be obtained by German American businesses from central League offices, which then listed these stores or service centers in their Trade Guide. Consumers could then consult the Trade Guide to find out which businesses were offering the special discount stamps. The stamps were handed out to the consumer according to the amount of money spent. At the end of the year, the consumer was entitled to a cash rebate, which was supposed to be divided proportionately among the members of the "cooperative." Participating businesses were assured that their patronage thereby would be increased among "Anti-Semites, Germans, Nazi Bund members, Roosevelt-haters, 'Keep-out-of-war' fanatics and Native fascists of all kinds, from Joe McWilliams' to Father Coughlin's supporters." The types of businesses that participated in the program ranged widely and included infants' wear stores, chocolate stores, chiropractors, cement workers, bologna stores, barber shops and beauty parlors, accountants and art weavers, purveyors of cuckoo clocks and elastic hosiery, electrical contractors and natural food stores, laundries and refrigerator manufacturers, optometrists and pharmacists, poultry markets and pork stores, restaurants and shoe stores, summer resorts and tea stores, travel bureaus and trucking companies, and wholesalers and wheel chair purveyors. The DKV was, of course, put out of business when America entered the war; its managing directors Willi Luedtke and Max Rapp were put in prison when it was discovered that the League had also been conducting subversive activities on behalf of the German government.[32]

Other German American organizations also protested the Jewish boycott of German products, but not by boycotting Jewish businesses. The Board of Trade for German-American Commerce, for example, in June 1934, opened a campaign to end the boycott of German goods. The Board of Trade was a ten-year-old organization dedicated to fostering trade relations between Germany and the United States. A resolution had been passed the previous month condemning the boycott of German goods as "un-American and un-economical, and tending to affect adversely the friendly relations between the United States and Germany." The group denied that they were in any way associated with DAWA.[33] In fact, the statements presented to the public and the U.S. government, even by the Bund, focused on efforts to stop the boycott of German goods and not on the boycott of Jewish businesses. At a mass meeting of 20,000 held in Madison Square Garden and sponsored by the Bund, a resolution was adopted denouncing the boycott as illegal and in restraint of trade. The president of the United States was called upon to direct the Department of Justice to prosecute those responsible for promoting and advertising the boycott of German products.[34]

The relationship between U.S. boycott of German goods and U.S. interventionism in the war against Germany did not escape the attention of Americans. As early as May 15, 1933, the *New York Post* recognized that the boycotting organizations were assuming a role that might more appropriately belong to the U.S. government. Referring to the boycott action of the American League for the Defense of Jewish Rights, the *Post* explained that "[t]his action by American Jews may well tend to drag America into a form of opposition to Germany that it might not care to take. That matter should be left for Government determination in some such manner as the announcement of the establishment of the French-British-American bloc."[35] Public opinion in favor of boycott of German goods grew throughout the decade as Nazi persecutions of Jews and others became more well-known, and as boycott fervor grew, those opposed to the boycott began to express more openly the view that the boycott would ultimately bring America into war with Germany. The development that was perhaps most centrally responsible for bringing Nazi horror to the attention of the American public was the riot and terror of Kristallnacht on November 8, 1938, when German synagogues throughout Germany were set ablaze and Jewish shops looted. It was at that point that President Roosevelt issued a public condemnation of the Nazi terror against the Jews and recalled the American ambassador to Germany. Also, a few days later another major boycott organization was born, the Volunteer Christian Committee. According to a Gallup poll for December 1938, 61 percent of Americans were actually prepared to join in a boycott movement and stop buying German-made goods. In April 1939, 65 percent were prepared to join a boycott movement, and 78 percent, according to the Gallup poll approved of a special tax on German-made goods being brought into the United States. The Gallup poll also disclosed that those who opposed the boycott did so because they believed that ultimately the boycott was an act of war and would lead to physical combat between Germany and the United States. Typical of the responses of those who opposed boycott was, "Boycott is an act of warfare. It would be the first step toward war with Germany."[36]

Isolationism, Interventionism, and the Senate's Hollywood Hearings

Isolationism, of course, has a long history in the United States, extending as far back as George Washington's caution against foreign entanglements. And there is no question but that the isolationist movement in the United States prior to World War II consisted initially and perhaps primarily of individuals—German

Americans and others—whose motivations were not political, but ideological. These individuals, however, were soon joined by German Americans whose isolationism was political, who did not want America to enter the war because it would be entering on the side of England against Germany. It goes without saying that many of the more prominent Jewish Americans who supported boycott of Germany would become the target of isolationists for what would be perceived to be the pro-war movies they made. In effect, the debate between pro-boycott Jewish Americans and anti-boycott German Americans, which was actually a struggle over whether Americans would be killing Germans or Germans would be permitted to continue to kill Jews, continued in the debate between interventionists and isolationists. Hollywood was perceived by isolationists, and German American isolationists in particular, as being Jewish and interventionist. One of the most conspicuous arenas in which the interventionist–isolationist debate was waged was the U.S. Congress, in particular during the Hearings of the Senate Moving Picture Screen and Radio Propaganda Subcommittee of the Committee on Interstate Commerce, held between September 9 and 26, 1941. These hearings were in many respects the precursors to the Holocaust debates in America that took place in the latter half of the twentieth century.

The Senate subcommittee was chaired by D. Worth Clark of Idaho, and included Homer T. Bone of Washington State, Ernest W. McFarland of Arizona, Charles W. Tobey of New Hampshire, and C. Wayland Brooks of Illinois. Senate Resolution 152, which the subcommittee had been formed to carry out, called for the creation of a subcommittee to investigate and report on Hollywood's "propaganda" efforts to bring America into war with Germany through its release of pro-war movies. The resolution was sponsored by Senators Gerald P. Nye of North Dakota and Bennett Champ Clark of Missouri, who also, in effect, *brought charges* against Hollywood at the subcommittee's hearings. The "defendants" called to testify and answer questions about the movies being released by Hollywood included Barney Balaban, president of Paramount Pictures; Nicholas M. Schenck, president of Lowes; Harry M. Warner, president of Warner Brothers Pictures; and Darryl F. Zanuck, vice president in charge of production for Twentieth Century Fox.

Gerald Nye, the senator from North Dakota, was the most vociferous in his attack on the motion picture industry and Jews. Nye was an isolationist, a member of the isolationist organization America First, and the representative of perhaps the state with the most significant German American vote. Nye had come to North Dakota from Wisconsin in 1916, where he bought, managed, and edited the *Fryburg Pioneer* in agricultural Billings County. A year later he married Anna Margaret Munch, a nurse from St. Joseph, Missouri, with whom he had a child. As a household head, he was not drafted into the military during World War I, but spent a great deal of his time in war-related activities—as county director of the Liberty loans and war savings drives, for example—for which his newspaper suffered, but which purchased a great deal of goodwill. In 1918 and 1919, Nye grew closer to the Nonpartisan League, an organization that advocated for the North Dakota farmer who was being exploited by interests outside the state. The Nonpartisan League proved to be successful organizing agrarian interests and capturing state offices and huge majorities in both houses of the state legislature. When a U.S. Senate seat became vacant due to the death of Senator Edwin F. Ladd in 1927, Governor A. G. Sorlie appointed Nye to complete the term. In 1941, Nye was still holding that same Senate seat, staunchly promulgating the isolationist views of his German American constituency. The 1940 election, however, was his last successful run for the Senate. America's entry into the war following the bombing of Pearl Harbor marked the beginning of Nye's political decline.[37]

North Dakota has been called "the most isolationist state in the nation," and Nye's North Dakota constituency epitomized German American isolationism in the United States. Even though

German Americans were actually only the fourth largest group in North Dakota, the second largest group was comprised of Russians of German descent who had migrated to America and had doggedly maintained their "Germanness" while traversing the continents.[38] These Russian Germans are said to have been "the backbone of Senator Nye's political strength." Together, these two groups—the German Americans and the Russian Germans in the United States—formed a considerable force in the state for isolationism. Moreover, North Dakota isolationism was not entirely motivated by pacifist principles. Although they strenuously argued against fighting the Nazis in World War II, they showed little reluctance to go to war later against the communists in Korea. To some extent, the isolationism was motivated by the insularity of certain of these groups, such as the Russian Germans who identify themselves as Mennonites. But the chief reason that German Americans in North Dakota wanted the United States to stay out of the war was what was referred to as *Deutschtum*, the sense that all individuals of Germans ancestry, regardless of where they live, are bound together and that their fate is shared.[39] For America to be at war with Germans in Germany was tantamount to America being at war with German Americans in America. The persecution of German Americans during World War I proved that point. Indeed, it has only rarely been the case that an ethnic American group has not been persecuted by other Americans—including other ethnic Americans—when hostilities of one type or another have broken out between the United States and the parent nation of that ethnic group.

Senator Nye of North Dakota Testifies against Hollywood

Nye's testimony initiated the hearings and encapsulated the arguments that would be brought forward against the motion picture industry. Certain of his complaints charged the industry with indulging financial self-interest in its pro-British, anti-Nazi propaganda films. According to Nye, 10 percent of the industry's wealth—its entire profit margin—came from England; and the industry's pro-British films were part of an effort to hold on to that market. England, in its turn, was more than happy with the anti-Nazi, pro-British propaganda being produced by Hollywood. England was, in effect, sponsoring pro-British war propaganda in the United States, said Nye.[40] Nye also complained that the entire industry was run by just a few individuals—it was a monopoly. In fact, the question of whether the movie industry was a monopoly had been brought up in the past; the question had been dealt with and disposed of in the courts. But the issue was especially relevant in the context of these hearings. Nye charged that not only was the motion picture industry producing pro-British, pro-interventionist films; the industry was in the hands of a few moguls who did not permit others who might have a different view to produce noninterventionist films. Moreover, said Nye, the motion picture industry was being encouraged by the Roosevelt administration whose bidding was being done by the industry through the production of such pro-war movies. Roosevelt was moving the nation into war and the movies were being used to prime the American people.

More important here, however, are the complaints made by Nye which reveal that the relationship between Jewish Americans and German Americans had been strained by Hitler's persecution of European Jews. The movie moguls are Jews, says Nye, and the reason they support intervention is because their relatives in Europe are being persecuted by the Nazis. What the Jews don't realize, he argues, is that the Jews of America are making the situation of German Jews worse by antagonizing Hitler with these prointerventionist films. And anyway, the German people are suffering too.

Further, by presenting the Nazis as evil in these movies, the Jewish movie industry, argued Nye, is creating an anti-Germanism that will spread and produce persecution of German Americans in the United States worse than that which was suffered by German Americans during World War I. What is more, Stalin is doing things to his people as horrible as what Hitler is doing to the Jews. Why isn't the industry making movies about the horrors of Stalinism? Most of these complaints would also become staple arguments of those Germans and German Americans who later in the twentieth and twenty-first centuries would attempt to forget or whitewash the history of Nazi Germany.

Nye's attack on the motion picture industry—and, some argued, on Jews—actually began before the Senate hearings, on Friday, August 1, 1941, when Nye addressed a gathering of the America First Committee at the Opera House in St. Louis. According to a Dr. John H. Sherman, president of Webber College in Florida, who reported the event, the

> principal effort of the evening was a Hitleresque attack upon the American Jews. Deliberately, adroitly, with every trick of timing and inflection of voice, Nye accused the motion picture industry of fostering pro-British sentiment, and then called a list of Jewish names associated with the motion picture industry, drolly exaggerating their most Hebraic sounding syllables, with pauses to encourage his enflamed hearers to shout and hiss. He did not see a complete list, which would have included many honored gentiles. Nor did he mention the fact that some of our best and most convincing motion-picture appeals have been produced by the people he names. His attack thus was not truly an attack on the motion-picture industry, but merely an attack upon Jews because they were Jews, in typical Nazi style.[41]

One would no doubt had to have been there to form an opinion of Nye's pronunciation of the Jewish sounding names of Hollywood's movie producers. However, it is clear—despite Nye's protests—

that he had in fact blamed the "Jews" for what he believed to be the interventionist policy being promulgated by the film industry. In response to Sherman's statement that, had Nye produced a complete list of Hollywood producers, that list would have included many gentiles, Nye responded, "had I continued with the names of those in the motion-picture industry, using those of lesser consequence in the industry, the proportion of Jewish names would, if anything, have increased." Nye was intent on blaming Jews, in what was indeed "typical Nazi style."

The particular films that Nye objected to and thought would "bear investigation" were *Convoy*, *Flight Command*, *Escape*, *I Married a Nazi* (changed to *The Man I Married*), *That Hamilton Woman*, *Man Hunt*, *The Great Dictator*, and *Sergeant York*.[42] It might be useful here to refresh the reader's memory concerning the plot of at least some of these films before discussing the objections that Nye raised to them. The most famous of these films is of course Charlie Chaplin's *The Great Dictator*, a satire of Hitler. The story is the classic one of mistaken identity. A barber who is a Hitler look-alike is mistaken for the Fuehrer, who in Chaplin's film is named Adenoid Hynkel. The film mixes humor with realistic scenes of Jews being mistreated, and ends with the barber, still mistaken for Hitler, delivering a speech on radio declaring he has no intention of conquering the world. Another was the outspokenly interventionist, or certainly antipacifist film, *Sergeant York*. Still being regularly shown for decades after World War II, *Sergeant York* is the true story of Alvin York, who was originally a pacifist but fought in World War I and proved himself a hero.

The movie *Escape*, a World War II movie, focuses on civilians and tells the story of an American of German descent who rescues his mother, an eminent German actress, from a German concentration camp where she faces certain death. The film displays the cruelties of the Nazis, but is also interesting for its portrayal of the "good German," the German doctor who helps the American rescue his mother. Nye confessed to not having seen all of these films.

In fact, he apparently saw very few of them. His opinion regarding their interventionist bias—the pro-British or anti-German sentiment expressed in these films—seems to have been largely based on hearsay.

The chief accusation introduced by Nye was that Hollywood producers—because they believed war with Germany would end the persecution that their relatives were experiencing at the hands of the Nazis—were making films that portrayed Nazis as evil and thereby were steering public sentiment toward war with Germany. Nye conceded, as any skillful demagogue would, that regrettably the Nazis were indeed persecuting Jews, although Nye did not speak long or with any specificity about the sufferings being experienced by Jews in Germany. But despite the persecution of Jews, said Nye, Americans had to act in their own best interests. Regardless of how much the Jewish producers—largely foreigners—might want Americans to come to the aid of the British against the Nazis, there was no point aiding the British in a war they couldn't win. According to Nye,

> Those primarily responsible for the propaganda pictures [the Jewish producers] are born abroad. They came to our land and took citizenship here entertaining violent animosities toward certain causes abroad [the persecution of Jews in Europe]. Quite natural is their feeling and desire to aid those [the British] who are at war against the causes which so naturally antagonize them. If they lose sight of what some Americans might call the first interests of America in times like these, I can excuse them. But their prejudices by no mean necessitate our closing our eyes to these interests and refraining from any undertaking to correct their error.

The cavil of course is an old one: Jews cannot be loyal to the country in which they live because their allegiance is always elsewhere with the nations that are home to their relatives. They are forever foreigners. In fact, in a moment of anger Nye goes so far as to refer to Hollywood as not only comprised of foreigners, but as actually comprising a "fifth column" in the United States that was making every effort to bring America into war and destroy it. According to Nye, the foreigners in Hollywood were "the most potent and dangerous 'fifth column' in our country."[43]

Another accusation leveled by Nye was that Jews had a persecution complex, evidenced, said Nye, by the fact that they thought he was antisemitic and had been persecuting them. Nye cites a Jewish paper, *The Sentinel*, which accused Nye of scapegoating Jews in his address to the America First Committee. "That is what Nye did," complained *The Sentinel*, "unjust, demagogic, Goebbel[s]-like. . . . We believe that Senator Nye deliberately named the Jews." Nye of course denied that he had been scapegoating anyone. He does not, however, offer any explanation of why or how his emphasis on specifically Jewish filmmakers was *not* an act of scapegoating. Instead, Nye accuses the Jewish writers of *The Sentinel* of suffering from a persecution complex. "If ever there was need for outstanding proof of how a persecution complex seems uneasy in its search for more persecution upon which to sharpen its complex, I should refer to this August 14 issue of the *Sentinel*." Particularly disconcerting, however, is the manner in which Nye goes on to threaten Jews, in truly antisemitic—indeed Nazi—fashion. Unless these Jewish producers stop trying to bring America into the war against the Nazis, says Nye, Jews will indeed be scapegoated by unemployed and angry individuals for whatever misery they might be suffering at the time. In Nye's words,

> Whether we get in or stay out of war, when the full burden of these very costly months come to rest upon the people of our country, it is but natural to expect that a perplexed, angry, burdened, unemployed people will be ready to respond to the agitators who will want to help them find the scapegoat responsible for it all, someone upon whom to place the blame

for every misery that grows out of this present world mad-
ness. Organized forces and leaders will find a goat.[44]

One will recall that in similar manner Hitler had warned American Jews that unless they ceased their criticism of Germany, the
Jews of Germany would indeed pay the price. All the while, of
course, German Jews were already being persecuted in Germany.

Nye's accusation that the Jews of Hollywood were suffering
from a persecution complex, curiously, was accompanied by the
accusation that Jewish filmmakers portrayed Nazis as evil in order
to take revenge on the Nazis for what the Nazis were doing to
Jewish relatives in Germany. The inconsistency in these views—
that Jews were only imagining that their relatives were being persecuted, and that Jews were taking revenge on Nazis for persecution that had really taken place—was somewhat mitigated by the
statement that, according to Nye, he was not the individual charging the Jews with being vengeful. The culprits were other Americans who confided in Nye. "More and more every day," said Nye,
"I find the Americans bitterly charging that the pictures seem to be
in control of men entertaining vengeful spirits, born in the pain
being visited upon their own people abroad."[45] The charge of revenge is one that would be brought up again of course and continue on into the twenty-first century. Holocaust commemorations
and memorials of all types would be identified as efforts by Jews
to take revenge on Germans—and German Americans—for what
the Nazis did to the Jews of Europe. Commemoration of the Holocaust, according to some German Americans, simply stirred up
hatred against Nazis who were identified by most people with
Germans and anyone of German descent. There is no thought giv-
en to the possibility that acts of memorialization are designed to
prevent such horrors from occurring in the future toward not only
Jews but other peoples as well.

The movies, in Nye's opinion, were saturated with hatred for

Nazis, and this hatred was unfair. Nye explained that he had not seen a great many of these movies and that he was not very good at remembering the ones that he had seen. He had heard recently, however, of a film being made in Hollywood about a ship carrying British children and pregnant British mothers being attacked by a Nazi submarine. On board were Nazi officers gleefully anticipating the opportunity of killing two generations of British people at one time. What stood out in Nye's mind was the "feeling of how the picture must have made people hate a whole people, a class of people, a race of people."[46] Nye was of course referring to the way in which the film's audience would, in Nye's opinion, leave the theatre hating Germans. The view that an American audience was incapable of separating Nazis from Germans, or even separating Nazis from German Americans became a staple of anti-Holocaust commemoration sentiment later in the century as the Holocaust became more prominent in the minds of Americans. One of the main arguments against the construction of the United States Holocaust Memorial Museum was that it would foster anti-Germanism by virtue of the fact that it would house pictures of Nazis.

Moreover, in Nye's view, the British were not the only victims of the war; the Germans were victims too, as were the people of the other Axis powers.

> The British are portrayed as a nation of people suffering and standing courageously and with determination against the violent bombardment by a hideous enemy. But we only learn of the British suffering. That kind of propaganda never lets us see and feel that maybe the people of Germany or of Italy or of Finland are also suffering.[47]

While it is no doubt true that there were German soldiers, as well as others, suffering during the war, the argument presented by Nye is a red herring. It distracts the reader from the real issues. The Germans were persecuting Jews. What is more, the Germans started the war and were benefiting from a wartime economy. The argument that the Germans were victimized as much as anyone else is another argument that would appear later in a slightly altered form. During the Bitburg controversy of 1985, President Reagan would compare the Nazi soldiers in the graves at Bitburg to those who died in the concentration camps.

Lastly, Nye made the argument at the hearings that the motion picture industry was biased against only the type of horror being perpetrated by the Nazis. The Nazis weren't the only ones murdering innocent people. If the public really wanted terror, why wasn't the motion picture industry showing the public what was going on in Russia? If the public really wanted someone to hate, why wasn't the industry showing the public what Stalin was doing to people? According to Nye, there were 17,000 theatres in the United States devoted "to the creation of hatred of the people of Germany and now of France. . . . Does anyone see a pictorial representation of life in Russia under 'Bloody Joe' Stalin? They do not."[48] The effort to de-emphasize the horrors of Nazism by diverting the audience's attention to Stalin—who was of course a madman of the same order as Hitler—is also a tactic that would continue to make its appearance later in the twentieth century. Ernst Nolte in the German historians' debate of the early 1980s would be among the more prominent individuals to employ the comparison between Hitler and Stalin as he avowedly attempted to make German history more palatable to Germans and the world. And of course it was not just Stalin but other criminal leaders as well—Pol Pot, for instance—who would be called upon by Germany's apologists in their efforts to suggest that Hitler wasn't really all that bad.

Harry Warner's Defense of the Hollywood Film Industry against the Accusations of Senator Nye

Of the testimonies that followed Nye, none was bolder or conveyed more humanity than that of Harry M. Warner, president of

Warner Brothers Pictures. Harry Warner had lived the American dream. He and his brothers had pulled themselves up by their bootstraps. Born in 1881, he was sixty years old when he testified before the Senate subcommittee on propaganda in the motion pictures. He had started work at age eight, shining shoes and selling papers. Had he not worked, there would not have been enough food on the table for himself and eight younger brothers and sisters. Harry Warner, to use his own words, "had no opportunity for a schooling." In 1903, he started work as a film distributor; in 1905, he and his brothers opened their first nickelodeon in nearby New Castle, Pennsylvania, with a secondhand projector and chairs borrowed from the mortuary next door. His sister Rose played the piano, brother Jack sang, brother Sam ran the projector, and brother Albert sold the tickets. By 1912 the Warners had a string of nickelodeons and turned their talents to making movies. Their first success came in 1917 with a film called *My Four Years in Germany*. The proceeds were used to create Warner Brothers Studios. In 1941, at the Senate proceedings, Harry Warner would proudly point out that by 1920 Warner Brothers had produced film versions of such literary classics as Sinclair Lewis's *Main Street* and *Babbit*, and Charles Norris's *Brass*. For an individual who had never had "a schooling," Harry Warner intelligently set the standards of taste for his time. But the Warner brothers made movie history when they gave the world the first full-length "*talking* picture show," *The Jazz Singer*, starring Al Jolson. Harry Warner recounted for the Senate subcommittee the afternoon he had been invited to Bell Laboratories to witness the Vitaphone, the machine that made it possible to synchronize sound and film. "I tell you frankly," said Warner, "that afternoon in the Bell Laboratories thrilled me. I thought I had seen the most important development since moving pictures were first thrown on the screen."[49] In retrospect, it seems odd that other studios and businessmen would not have recognized the potential of "talking pictures," but in fact Warner Brothers had to go it alone, at least initially. As

Warner pointed out, "the larger motion-picture companies, directed by men more successful than I, had already turned down the new contrivance." Curiously, only Harry Warner—among these men who purveyed the pleasures of the imagination—had the vision or courage to venture into the future.

Nor was Harry Warner one to be intimidated or bamboozled by the sly old senators of the U.S. Congress. His opening statement was designed to answer some of their allegations, while at the same time placing the subcommittee on the defensive. Warner responded to Senator Nye's accusations that Warner Brothers was producing pictures that incited people to war, and that they were doing so in coordination with directives from the White House. Warner started by making clear his view of the Nazis. They were criminals who terrified their population and committed unspeakable atrocities. As Warner explained, the Nazis were fighting to create "a world revolution whose ultimate objective is to destroy our democracy, wipe out all religion, and enslave our people—just as Germany has destroyed and enslaved Poland, Belgium, Holland, France, and all the other countries." By verbalizing in very clear terms the abhorrent nature of the Nazis in this public forum, Warner challenged the senators to express their own abhorrence for the Nazis, thereby forcing the senators to tacitly acknowledge the need to take action against the Nazis and support the Allies with U.S. resources, if not with U.S. soldiers. Warner also made clear, of course, that he was a patriot, whose love for America was unequaled. His humble origins and his successful career were recounted to the Senate as proof of his indebtedness to the United States and reason for his love of country. Warner Brothers did indeed make patriotic films, but they were a product of their sense of duty to the country and not any encouragement from the president. In response to the accusation "[t]hat, in some mysterious way, the Government orders us to make this or that type of picture," Warner answered,

> This we deny. We receive no orders, no suggestions—direct
> or indirect—from the administration. It is true that Warner
> Bros. has tried to cooperate with the national-defense pro-
> gram. It is true that Warner Bros., over a period of 8 years,
> has made feature pictures concerning our Army, Navy, and
> air force. It is true that we have made a series of shorts por-
> traying the lives of American heroes. To do this, we needed
> no urging from the Government and we would be ashamed if
> the Government would have to make such requests of us. We
> have produced these pictures voluntarily and proudly.

If Warner Brothers pictures had in the past presented themes that
echoed the president's sentiments, it was purely a coincidence.
Moreover, while patriotism was a significant factor in the decision
of Warner Brothers to make these war films, the major consideration of course was profit. It was the American way. Warner Brothers was a business, and their business was to produce films that
pleased their customers. Movies about the Nazis, in particular,
were a natural outgrowth of individuals' concerns about what was
happening in their world.[50]

In the course of his statement to the Senate subcommittee and
the questions that followed, Harry Warner answered certain other
allegations by Senator Nye as well. To the charge that Jews wanted
America to go to war with Germany to rescue their relatives from
the Nazis, Warner responded that Jews were not the only ones being persecuted by the Nazis; moreover, he, Harry Warner, was not
certain whether the time had come for the United States to enter
the war on England's behalf. As Warner explained, "[S]hortly after Hitler came to power in Germany[,] I became convinced that
Hitlerism was an evil force designed to destroy free people, whether they were Catholics, Protestants, or Jews." Other peoples, apart
from Jews, were being persecuted by the Nazis. All of these
peoples—virtually all the peoples of the Western world—had an

interest in seeing the Nazis defeated. But whether the United States should immediately enter the war on behalf of the Allies was not a question that Warner felt competent to answer. "Frankly," said Warner, "I am not certain whether or not this country should enter the war in its own defense at the present time. The president knows the world situation and our country's problems better than any other man. I would follow his recommendation concerning a declaration of war." Until such time as the president felt it was time to go to war, it was the duty of Americans to support the Allies. In fact, supporting the Allies with American goods and products, in Warner's view, was the way to ensure that Americans would not need to fight. As Warner explained, "either we help the people over there and give them material with which to fight, or our children are going to have to fight. What I am interested in is to prevent our children from fighting." If the Allies were able to win the war on their own, if they were given American weapons, there would be no need for assistance from American soldiers.[51]

Senator D. Worth Clark of Idaho versus Harry Warner on Anti-Germanism in Hollywood Films

Warner was not arguing for intervention. He was arguing for support of the Allies, and in so doing he forced some of the noninterventionist senators to reveal their true sentiments. A number of these senators were not against war—they were *not* pacifists— they simply did not want to fight on the side of the Allies against Germany. These senators were not really interested in keeping America out of the war; they wanted to see Nazi Germany win the war against the British. Harry Warner's movies, they complained, produced hatred of the Germans and encouraged Americans to go to war against Germany. To these accusations Harry Warner responded that Warner Brothers films were not anti-German; they were anti-Nazi. Warner took as an example the film called *Under-*

ground. Directed by Vincent Sherman and released by Warner Brothers in 1941, the movie told a story of German resistance to Nazi terror. At the center of the movie are two brothers, one a radio operator for the underground, the other a wounded soldier still dedicated to Nazism. Eventually the Nazi brother is won over to the side of the resistance. The film was low budget and included none of the stars of the period; however, Martin Kosleck appeared as head of the Nazi secret police and was so good at the role that he went on to make a career of appearing in films as the evil Nazi villain. The picture portrayed the German citizen in a favorable, and indeed heroic, light. In response to Senator Clark of Idaho, who charged Warner with presenting only the evil Nazi, Warner responded that "*Underground* showed the sympathy for and the struggle of the German people who are trying to come back and live like human beings."[52]

Senator Clark, however, continued to question Harry Warner regarding the hatred for Germans that might be spawned by a film like *Underground*. Clark had read a review that described the film as "so depressing and harrowing that it leaves one, not only in an extremely unhappy frame of mind, but in a nervous state as well. The scenes of torture inflicted on human beings by the Nazis are terrifying and a bit sickening." Clark asked Warner, "[D]o you think that a picture like that, assuming that that is a fairly accurate portrayal, tends to inflame the American mind to hatred for Germany?" Warner's initial response was that the picture was true to life, however offensive it might be. But then Warner shifted the focus from who might be hated after watching the film to who would be doing the hating, and provides an unanticipated answer. The film, said Warner, inflames Nazi sympathizers who might be watching the film because it presents the Nazis in a bad light. At first, Clark did understand how Warner shifted the subject of the conversation. When Warner stated, "I think it would incite a Nazi," Clark responded, "It would what?" And Warner answered,

"Incite a Nazi, any man believing in nazi-ism. It would incite him." Others would appreciate the film, implied Warner. Warner was of course attacking Clark for his Nazi sympathies, but Warner checked himself and decided he really did not want to call Clark a Nazi sympathizer. Speaking directly to Clark, Warner stated, "I say [the film] will not incite you. It will only portray to you what actually exists. You will see, for one thing, what you have kind of missed. . . ." Warner did suggest that Clark would feel differently after watching the film and learning about things that he's "missed"; that is, he would learn about the horror committed by the Nazis against even other Germans.[53]

What Senator Clark of Idaho was really concerned about, of course, was a resurgence of a World War I type of anti-Germanism in America. Clark's argument here, however, proceeded from a larger premise. Clark argued that national unity was desirable (a premise that Warner had earlier introduced into the discussion), and therefore any action that bred contention between different groups of people in the United States was undesirable. Warner's films, said Clark, turned ordinary Americans into German haters. Clark asked Warner, "Do you think that the production of these pictures that tend to stir race against race—and by that I mean and point to the fact that we have a tremendous German population or of German extraction, people who have the German heritage. . . . Do you think that the production of pictures like *Underground* and the *Mortal Storm* tend to create unity among our people or disunity?"[54] Again Harry Warner replied by pointing out that Warner Brothers' films were not anti-German. This time Warner pointed to the fact that Warner Brothers had produced films about great Germans. He mentioned specifically the 1940 film *Dr. Ehrlich's Magic Bullet*, which dramatizes the accomplishments of the German chemist as he sought a vaccine for syphilis and introduced it to the civilized world, despite attacks from critics who pretended moral outrage. The film was directed by William Dieterle and starred Edward G. Robinson as Dr. Ehrlich. Such films, maintained Warner, helped the public form a balanced portrait of Germans and militated against any anti-Germanism that might appear in the United States.

Just as Senator Nye had indulged in comparisons (complaining that Stalin was just as bad as Hitler, but Hitler was receiving all the bad press; and the Germans were suffering as much the British were, even though all the sympathy in the press was extended to the British), so too did Senator Clark indulge in comparisons in the course of his criticism of Warner Brothers. The film that his criticism focused on was *Confessions of a Nazi Spy* (1939), directed by Anatole Litvak and again starring Edward G. Robinson. The story, written by FBI Special Agent Leon G. Turrou, is based on fact and tells of a Nazi spy ring that operated in New York. Clark's comparison was actually derived from a statement made by Nye. Nye's statement extolled the virtues of *Confessions of a Nazi Spy*, but asked for pictures about the "propaganda emanating from all foreign lands." Both Nye and Clark were asking for media coverage of not only German propaganda, but also England's efforts to influence opinion in the United States, as if to suggest there were a basis for comparison between what the Nazis were doing and British activity in the United States. Warner responded, "I do not agree with that part of the [news story], and that is as to propaganda of all nations. You see, we were at that time discussing the picture *Confessions of a Nazi Spy*. That dealt with a specific subject, namely, Nazi sabotage in America, right in our own home, at our doors."[55] There was a difference between what the Nazis were doing and England's efforts to enlist support from the United States. There was a difference between sabotage and propaganda, assuming that England was propagandizing the people of the United States, a matter that would first require some agreement as to what the term "propaganda" meant and how it differed from influence peddling or, simply, advertisement.

Senator Clark would not let the matter rest. He wanted to know why Harry Warner was producing pictures showing Nazi propagandizing and Nazi brutality toward individuals, and was not showing British propagandizing in the United States and British brutality. Clark was insisting on the comparison between Nazi Germany and the British. "Have you made any pictures," asked Clark, "depicting British propaganda in the United States designed to get us into this war, and which in a broad sense, in the view of some of us, might be called sabotage, because it might destroy our country forever? Have you ever made any picture depicting British propaganda?"[56] According to Clark, the British were engaged in the same activities as the Nazis. Warner replied that Warner Brothers had never made a picture depicting British propaganda because there was no British propaganda in the United States that is detrimental in any way to the United States. As Warner replied, "We have not made any picture that I know of showing British propaganda, because I do not think there is any British propaganda here to destroy the principles of America. I think the British propaganda here is to help them fight a war to help us." There is no comparison, maintained Warner throughout the hearings, between the Nazis and the British.

Warner actually indulged in a bit of comparison himself in his efforts to defend Warner Brothers against the accusations that their films were anti-German and produced hatred of German Americans. Warner pointed to the historical films that Warner Brothers produced about the American Revolution in which the enemy was Great Britain. Warner asked whether these films were to be construed as anti-British and whether these films were designed to produce hatred of the English. Warner asked Senator Clark, "Would you say that Patrick Henry, a picture showing a fight against Great Britain, would be inciting the American people against Great Britain?"[57] Warner was probably referring here to the short film about Patrick Henry that Warner Brothers produced in 1936 and that won an Academy Award for Best Short Subject (Color). The film was called *Give Me Liberty* and was directed by B. Reeves Easton. It explains the incentives that induced Patrick Henry to advocate separation from Great Britain. But in fact Warner Brothers produced many such shorts about the American Revolution. Three of them, including *Give Me Liberty*, had the same actor, John Litel, playing the part of Patrick Henry. Litel played Patrick Henry in *The Bill of Rights* and *Old Glory*, as well as in *Give Me Liberty*. If *Underground* produced hatred of Germans, did these patriotic films about the American Revolution produce hatred of the British?

Senator Nye and Harry Warner never actually collided with each other as did Warner and Senator Clark during the hearings, but between them they introduced the important arguments that later appear in slightly altered form as German Americans and Jewish Americans argued about the attention given the Holocaust in America. The key concern for German Americans from 1941 onward was the image of the Nazi being presented to the American public. Although there clearly were German American Nazis who encouraged a rabid Nazism, German Americans were primarily concerned about the anti-Germanism that might appear in America in 1941, and these fears led to the congressional interventionist–isolationist debate, as well as the controversies surrounding the depiction of the Holocaust that followed. As it became more and more clear that the United States would enter World War II, some German Americans feared that they would be identified with German Nazis by other Americans, and so German Americans became defensive when movies were made depicting the hateful Nazi; as the historical significance of the Holocaust became more and more clear during the latter half of the twentieth century, German Americans became defensive about Holocaust movies or memorials or Holocaust publicity of any type for fear that German Americans would be identified with Nazis. The tack used by German Americans to discourage portraits of the evil Nazi in 1941 was in many ways similar to the ways in which German Americans would later attempt to discourage discussion of the Holocaust for fear of raising the specter of the evil Nazi—the specter that had cast such a pronounced shadow over German Americans during World War I. Among the matters raised in 1941 that would appear later in the Holocaust debates is the accusation on the part of German Americans, and those like Senator Nye who took up their cause, that Jewish Americans wanted revenge on Germans for what the Germans were doing to Jews in Germany (and so Jews were egging on the president to go to war against Germans). Later, German Americans such as the president of the German American National Congress would maintain that Jews were publicizing the Holocaust in an effort to take revenge on Germans for what in fact the Germans had done to the Jews.

The most prominent legacy of the congressional hearings, insofar as the Holocaust debates of latter half of the twentieth century are concerned, was the use of comparisons by Senator Nye and others in their efforts to whitewash Nazi activities. Similarly, historians would later use comparison to attempt to whitewash what the Nazis *had done*. They would use comparison to try to whitewash the Holocaust. In 1941, the comparisons were designed to make the Nazis appear less evil so that there would appear to be no moral need for America to enter the war, but in fact some of the very same comparisons were used in 1941 that would again appear in the German historians debate of the 1980s and elsewhere in order to make it appear that the Holocaust was not as great a horror as it actually was. Nye's point that Stalin was just as evil as Hitler, for example, would in the 1980s be used by Ernst Nolte in his avowed efforts to cleanse German history of the blot on its good name created by the Holocaust.

Nye's point in 1941 that the German people were suffering

because of war every bit as much as the British were suffering would, later during the Holocaust debates, turn into the argument that the German people had suffered just as the Jewish people had suffered under Nazi rule. Moreover, Hollywood would continue to be the target of German American groups well into the 1980s. These groups would complain of the image of the German Nazi that appeared in such films as the James Bond thriller *Never Say Never Again* and *Raiders of the Lost Ark* of the Indiana Jones series. Oddly enough, these debates that would occupy scholars and presidents for the next half-century and beyond had started in the U.S. Congress and the ostensible subject was interventionism in the Hollywood film industry.

Three

German Ethnics and the
United States Holocaust Memorial Museum Question

Ethnic America and the German American

Perhaps the distinguishing feature of ethnicity is persecution at the hands of one's own countrymen. What distinguishes ethnicity in the United States is that many groups within the United States are ethnics, that is, many have at one point or another suffered persecution. In fact, the suggestion that there is or was a "dominant" culture in the United States is a myth perpetuated by early nineteenth-century writers who purposely set out to define an America with characteristics they regarded as enviable and that could be transmitted to future generations. German Americans, like many other ethnic groups in the United States, were well-represented during the founding of the nation and have suffered discrimination while residing in the country. The first European peoples to participate in the founding of the United States and be discriminated against were the British. It was of course General Washington of English stock who led American forces against the British during the American Revolution, but it is also important to note that British loyalists—who regarded themselves every bit as much American as anyone else—were the first to be persecuted for their loyalties to a "foreign country." British loyalists were tarred and feathered, and run out of their homes. Nathaniel Hawthorne's short story, "My Kinsman, Major Molineaux," is only one of the best fictive treatments of the subject; it is the story of a young American from the outskirts of Boston who comes to the city expecting to make his fortune with the help of his kinsman, but he abruptly awakens to the fact that he has no expectations, as he witnesses his kinsman being carried off by the Sons of Liberty to be punished for his allegiance to the British. German Americans too had their generals in the American war for independence. For instance, General Steuben brought order to Washington's unruly army. However, it was not until the First World War that German Americans found themselves in the same unenviable position that British Americans found themselves in during the War for Independence.

German Americans were part of a country that was at war with the country their descendants had come from and they—German Americans—continued to identify with that country. But there were of course differences between the situations of the British and the Germans. During the American Revolution, British politicians in America led the revolt against Britain. During World War I, it was a president of English origins, Woodrow Wilson, who was leading Americans into war with the Germans. Had the president been of German descent—a Hoover or an Eisenhower, for example—the persecution that the German American community suffered might not have been or might not have been felt so severely. But then, had the president been of German ancestry, America might never have entered World War I. In a sense, the lesser persecution suffered by German Americans during the Second World War, while unjust, was probably in some measure due to the fact that individuals of German descent were key players in the war abroad. As suggested, General Eisenhower who led the

Allied forces was of German stock, as was J. Edgar Hoover, head of the FBI, which was effectively in charge of monitoring activity in the United States that might subvert the war effort. Hoover was actively interning German nationals in America, as well as a number of American citizens of German descent.

By the 1980s there existed an awareness among Americans that did not exist in the 1930s of the numbers of German Americans residing in the United States. In 1930, the U.S. Bureau of the Census could calculate the number of individuals who were born of German parents, but had little basis for suggesting the number of individuals in the United States who identified themselves as, at least in part, of German ancestry. In 1930, the number of individuals who claimed to have at least one parent born in Germany, according to the U.S. Bureau of the Census, was about 7 million out of the total U.S. population of about 123 million.[1] It is difficult to say how many might have thought of themselves as German by virtue of a grandparent or great-grandparent, but some authors have estimated that in 1900, the German American population composed about one-fourth the total population of the United States, about the same as the Anglo-American population of the United States.[2] By 1980, however, more discerning questions about ethnic identity were being asked by the Census Bureau, which, using a statistical sample, identified about 50 million individuals as having German ancestry out of a total population of about 226 million. The number claiming German ancestry was close to one-fourth the population and almost identical to the number claiming English ancestry. The number of Anglo-Americans claiming "single ancestry," solely English roots, was greater than the number of German Americans claiming solely German roots. About 23.5 million Americans claimed solely English ancestry; about 18 million claimed solely German ancestry. The number of Americans claiming that they were in part German was greater than the number who claimed they were part English.[3] It is difficult to make much of these figures—it is difficult to say how many Americans who had regarded themselves as entirely Americans for generations might have wondered how to identify themselves for the census, and finally remembered a colorful old aunt of Scottish or German stock. The figures are nonetheless important here because they could be used as leverage by German American groups at election time. In the 1980s, German American organizations, as had other ethnic organizations before them, were becoming increasingly more politically sophisticated at the national level.

By the 1980s, moreover, the nativism of the war periods had gone by the board. It was no longer advantageous to be 100 percent American. The 1960s "happened," and ethnics—all of them—became a privileged class. Everyone was an ethnic all of a sudden. John F. Kennedy, for example, was Irish-American; and as pointed out, Herbert Hoover and Dwight D. Eisenhower were now touted as German Americans by the German American community. There were hardly any Americans left, it seemed to some. Those of English descent, always regarded as simply Americans, became Anglo-Americans; and even the indigenous population of the United States became a hyphenated peoples—they became Native-Americans. The Reagan period of conservatism changed all that somewhat, but ethnic identity remained an important factor as political groups, organized around their ethnic origins became players, at least at election time, when their organizations and newspapers could with considerable degree of success issue calls for support of one candidate or another. The key German American organizations to emerge were the Steuben Society of America, which as pointed out had been founded in 1919; and the German American National Congress (Deutsch Amerikanischer National Kongress, or DANK), founded in 1959.

The Steuben Society of America and the German American National Congress: Some Issues of the Early 1980s

The manner in which the Steuben Society is, at least in some instances, a product of the way Germans were treated during the First World War is reflected in a number of the organization's official statements about itself. For example, the Society emphasizes its "Americanness." First among its "purposes" is "to support the Constitution of The United States of America by advocating the proper application of its provisions, inculcate the principles underlying true democratic government, quicken the spirit of sound Americanism and foster a patriotic American spirit among all citizens."[4] While many civic organizations will make similar statements regarding their patriotism, the statement from the Steuben Society becomes poignant as one remembers that German Americans were interned during the war for fear they might be working for the enemy. A more explicit reference to the sufferings of German Americans during World War I is its seal, which is round and bordered by rope, and contains a lighthouse in a field of black. It is described by the Society as follows:

> Round, with the outer limit formed by a rope, signifying unity, the bond of common interests and common future, and the necessity of solidarity and co-operation.
>
> The background of the central field is black, signifying the period that gave rise to the organization and the ominous powers which promoted the prejudice and hatred against United States citizens of Germanic extraction.
>
> The lighthouse is the organization itself, standing squarely in its field. The light-rays stand for enlightenment and are to be looked upon as the promise of hope. The rock upon which the tower stands represents the Germanic element in the United States, against which have crashed the great billows of war passions, and the waves of everyday prejudices.[5]

The platform and program of the Steuben Society concern themselves with today's issues—balancing the budget, government subsidies, education, Social Security, and narcotics and drugs, to take

just a few examples.[6] Headquartered in Patchogue, New York, the
Steuben Society of America consists today of twenty-four units,
most of which are on the east coast—Florida, New York, New
Jersey, Pennsylvania, and the Washington, DC area—but there are
units in Ohio and Missouri as well.[7]

According to the Anti-Defamation League (ADL) of the B'nai
B'rith, the Jewish organization that monitors racism and particularly antisemitism in the United States, "The Steuben Society is a
long-time, legitimate German American cultural and educational
organization."[8] This assessment is probably, for the most part, a
correct one. However, the Washington, DC branch, as of the year
2000, was still named for Austin App, the individual that Holocaust scholar Deborah Lipstadt points out "played a central role
in the development of Holocaust denial, especially in the United
States." App, as Lipstadt explains, formulated the eight central
tenets of Holocaust denial that deniers continue to make use of.[9]
Typical of these tenets and App's denial writings generally is the
antisemitic and absurd statement that "most of the Jews alleged to
have met their death at the hands of the Germans [Nazis] were
subversives, partisans, spies, and criminals, and also often victims
of unfortunate but internationally legal reprisals."[10] One wonders
whether App should be awarded the honor of having the Washington, DC unit named after him in light of the fact that he was a
virulent antisemite. Or is it the case that his name was chosen precisely because of his antisemitism? The Austin App unit was
formed in 1985 upon App's death; the speakers on the occasion of
the founding of the unit were national chairman of the Steuben
Society, Augustus J. Veit, and unit member, E. Stanley Rittenhouse.[11] Rittenhouse is identified by the ADL as "an anti-Semitic
propagandist who has promoted 'Christian Identity' theories and
Holocaust denial." He is the author of *For Fear of the Jews*, which,
among other things, accuses "Zionists" of being "the greatest
force of anti-Christianity this Age will ever experience."[12] When
asked by this author whether ADL staff were aware of the fact

that the Washington, DC branch of the Steuben Society of America is named for Austin App, the reply was that they were not.[13]

The German American National Congress speaks of itself as "the largest organization of Americans of German descent."[14] In 2000, it had thirty-six chapters, most of them located in the Midwest, three in Chicago where the national headquarters are also located. All together, in the Midwest there were ten chapters in Illinois, seven chapters in Indiana, three chapters in Wisconsin, two in Iowa, two in Michigan, and two in Ohio. There was one in Arizona, and the rest were spread between New York, Pennsylvania, New Jersey, and Washington, DC on the East Coast.[15] The German American National Congress also identified itself as the umbrella organization to over one hundred associated member organizations. While these figures tend to impress, it should be remembered that DANK requires only fifteen members to form a chapter,[16] and while the individual chapters were publicly listed by DANK, the over one hundred affiliated organizations were not. On the other hand, there is evidence for the existence of affiliated member organizations that range from local German singing societies to the German American Policeman's Association.[17]

One of the early missions of the DANK was fostering German culture and language, and that mission continues. As of January 2010, there were six DANK schools that provide children and adults with instruction in German.[18] The German American National Congress also sponsors the German American Education Fund, the primary purpose of which is to support German language classes. The fund also sponsors high school and college awards to students who demonstrate proficiency in the German language, and invites donations of scholarships to students studying German. The purpose of the Fund also includes distributing materials related to German language and culture to schools teaching German subjects, as well as support for German heritage studies and research.

The German American National Congress was influential in

the creation of National German American Day on October 6, 1987. Together with the Steuben Society of America and the United German American Committee of the U.S.A.,[19] the DANK formed the German American Joint Action Committee, which promoted the congressional resolution to establish German-American Day. The German American National Congress claims to have effected 18,000 mailings and thousands of telephone calls to Congress in support of Indiana Senator Lugar's resolution proclaiming German-American Day. Elsbeth Seewald, president of the DANK at the time, presented President Reagan with a German translation of the U.S. Declaration of Independence at the German-American Day proclamation ceremony in the Rose Garden of the White House.[20]

The organization's chapters promote lectures, cultural events, and other activities that are German related. Among these activities sponsored by the German American National Congress is the annual "Miss DANK U.S.A." pageant.[21]

According to the ADL of the B'nai B'rith, the German American National Congress appears to be a "mainstream" organization, but it has "taken problematic positions."[22] Given the self-description of the organization provided above, it might be hard to imagine what problematic positions the German American National Congress might have taken. However, these positions will become clear later. For the time being, it will suffice to say that in a number of instances its actions have been publicly seconded by the German-American National Political Action Committee, which the ADL characterizes as "extremist and anti-Semitic."

The newspapers of these organizations are in a number of respects very similar, even though the circulation figures differ significantly, as do, in some respects, their emphases. The official organ of the Steuben Society of America is *The Steuben News*, which had a circulation of 3,500 in 1999.[23] The newspaper of the German American National Congress, *The German-American Jour-*

nal, or *Der Deutsch-Amerikaner* as it was still named in the 1980s (the name by which it will be referred to here) had a circulation of 10,000.[24] Also, *The Steuben News*, having been established in 1919, at the height of a movement to "Americanize" all ethnic peoples, to some extent still reflected in the 1980s a nationalism that was less apparent in *Der Deutsch-Amerikaner*, which was started in 1959, as ethnic awareness was growing. For example, while *Der Deutsch-Amerikaner* encouraged bilingualism and the study of German in its pages, *The Steuben News* promoted the idea that there should be only one official language in the United States. Among the statements to appear in *Der Deutsch-Amerikaner* was one reader's comment in "Letters to the Editor" pointing out that "Switzerland, as the world's oldest democracy, is a shining example of a multi-lingual government."[25] One could of course endorse both views: one could encourage bilingualism and still argue that only English should be spoken in the schools, but neither *The Steuben News* nor *Der Deutsch-Amerikaner* did both. *Der Deutsch-Amerikaner* printed some stories in English and some in German; stories in *The Steuben News* were all in English. An editorial in *The Steuben News* for October 1985 explained that "German Americans, by and large, do not often make reference to their 'roots,' as some ethnic groups do. The German has become so assimilated into the American way of life that he does not usually stand out in a crowd."[26] As the more ethnically oriented of the two newspapers, *Der Deutsch-Amerikaner* is the more likely of the two to take offense at what it thought of as anti-Germanism in America. It was in the fight against perceived anti-Germanism—especially the anti-Germanism thought to be contained in promotion of Holocaust-related events—that the antisemitism of the German-American National Political Action Committee would appear in the pages of *Der Deutsch-Amerikaner*.

In large measure, however, both *The Steuben News* and *Der Deutsch-Amerikaner* were, and continue to be, "family" newspapers, devoted to their membership who had primarily joined these organizations to be with other Germans, to plan and take part in German festivals or lectures by German speakers, and generally share similar cultural interests. The newspapers reported on a regular basis the events taking place at the various chapters of their respective organizations, and members who had won one sort of distinction or another[27]—especially if it was an award that had something to do with Germany or the German language. And of course the newspapers reported the awards given by their organizations, such as the Steuben medal for outstanding achievement in the study of German.[28] Both groups, however, also reported events taking place nationally that affected or might interest German Americans. Not uncommon in *Der Deutsch-Amerikaner* were stories about such events as the first retrospective of German painter, Otto Neumann (1895–1975) at the Goethe Institute in Chicago, or such matters as the more recent concern for preservation of the statue of German folk hero, Hermann the Cheruscan (the largest copper statue in the United States after the Statue of Liberty), which is in need of repair in New Ulm, Minnesota.[29] *The Steuben News*, on the other hand, favored stories about reducing taxes.[30]

Among the more serious matters to be dealt with in both newspapers was World War II. *Der Deutsch-Amerikaner*, in particular, regularly printed stories in the 1980s (and earlier) having to do with the war. Most of these reports detailed the horrors experienced by Germans. Some stories were of soldiers, Germans who had had unusual experiences of one type or another while in uniform during the Second World War.[31] Not untypical, however, were full-page stories with headlines such as "Hamburg-Holocaust—July 1943." Complete with pictures of Hamburg before and after being bombed by the Allies, this particular full-page story described how one beautiful summer evening while people were lingering in their gardens or getting ready for bed, the sirens were heard and terror struck. Exaggerating the numbers, the author wrote that in four nights, 45,000 men, 22,500 women, and 5,400 children were killed by the bombing. The casualties were considerable, but the generally agreed upon total figure by modern scholars is around thirty thousand.[32] Also typical of the war-related stories that appeared were discussions of the suffering experienced by ethnic Germans, displaced from their homes in Eastern Europe after the war. Dr. Karl T. Marx, for example, spoke of "An Overlooked Holocaust," perpetrated against Germans that had taken place. Marx explained for the benefit of a younger generation who were not old enough to remember, that "[a]ccording to the (Bonn) Bundesministerium fuer Vertriebene (Office for Expellees) the victorious powers forced 11,730,000 German ethnics to give up their ancient homes, farms, factories, offices, etc. to Slavic Settlers, without any compensation whatever. All they could take was one single suitcase." From 1945 to 1950, said Marx, "2,111,000 German ethnics were killed or died from exhaustion before or during the brutal trek into burned-out Germany."[33] This figure, again, is something of an exaggeration. About two million German ethnics were unaccounted for at war's end, but it is not clear how many of them died and how many of them made homes for themselves elsewhere.[34] It must be said, however, that considerable numbers of ethnic German refugees did die.

Anti-Germanism in the United States was also an issue, a major issue insofar as *Der Deutsch-Amerikaner* was concerned. One of the complaints most often registered was that German Nazis were constantly being portrayed as evil villains, while other perpetrators of equally cruel and massive destruction had been forgotten. The other perpetrator that most often came to mind was Stalin and the Russians. Typical of such stories about Stalin was one entitled "Stalin Was Grim Reaper in Ukrainian Famine," which appeared in *The Steuben News* for October 1986. The author began his article as follows: "It never ceases to amaze us that certain bestial events in history remain hidden and never discussed while others, such as the Nazi holocaust, are forever the subject of books, plays and movies. . . ." The article went on to explain a plan that Stalin had to starve the people of the Ukraine by removing all their wheat. It was thought that some ten million people had died.[35] More authoritative estimates, however, suggest a figure of six million.[36] The point is not one of denying the horror in the Ukraine, but that articles in *Der Deutsch-Amerikaner* and less often in *The Steuben News* were written to incite and enflame their audiences of German Americans by exaggerating the tragedies suffered by the German population and other peoples at the hands of the Allies.

Another complaint often registered by some German Americans in both *The Steuben News* and *Der Deutsch-Amerikaner* is that Americans identify all Germans as Nazis. In *The Steuben News* for November–December 1977, for example, the remarks of Peter Mueller to the New York State Convention of the Steuben Society were reported. In those remarks, Mueller commented on the view that "Germans have been assimilated by the Anglo-Saxon center" of American culture, and therefore their presence as a group has vanished in places like Manhattan. Mueller's comment on this state of affairs was that action needed to be taken: "We resent being called a Nazi, whenever we defend our heritage."[37] Among the many similar complaints made by Americans was that by Randy Ratje, a student at the time at Hofstra University on Long Island, whose prize-winning essay, "The Plight of German Americans," was published in *The Steuben News* for March 1985. In that essay, Ratje explained how his classmates in elementary school and junior high school would call him a Nazi because he was of German descent.[38]

In his essay, Ratje went on to voice another common complaint. Echoing the congressional debates that had taken place in the 1940s, Ratje complained that the identification between Germans or German Americans and Nazis was being fostered by the film industry. He explained how "some of the most popular films of recent years have had anti-German themes." He cited, for example, "Raiders of the Lost Ark," in which Indiana Jones races against evil Nazi forces to find the lost Ark of the Covenant; the film "Lassiter," in which a jewel thief is hired to steal a collection of priceless diamonds from the German Embassy in pre–World War II London; the James Bond film, "Never Say Never Again," in which the main antagonist has a German accent; and the "Star Wars" trilogy in which the evil Darth Vader wears a helmet that bears a striking resemblance to the helmet worn by German soldiers; and there were others.[39]

More disconcerting to some German Americans, however, must have been the nonfiction films that had appeared over the years about the Nazis. In an article in *The Steuben News* for March–April 1978, the writer complained about the anti-German offerings appearing on television, among which was "Rise and Fall of the Third Reich," which apparently was going through a second showing on television. According to the writer, "it is obvious we are being force-fed hatred against Germans."[40]

The nonfiction film to receive the heaviest coverage in the two newspapers was the NBC miniseries "Holocaust." In fact, the film created what might be regarded as a controversy of its very own, at least insofar as The Steuben Society and the German American National Congress was concerned. When the series aired in 1978, it was said to have had 120 million viewers, better than half the entire population of the United States. It was this film, more so than any other Holocaust-related event, that probably provided the initial momentum for the Holocaust-related activities that continue today.

One reason why the NBC miniseries created such a fury among at least some German Americans is because at about the same time efforts were being made by the Jewish community to introduce mandatory Holocaust education into the schools—a move that

German Americans argued against. As reported in an editorial for *The Steuben News* of November–December 1977, New York City was considering making study of the Holocaust a requirement in the schools for the following school year. Ilse Hoffman, who sat on the New York State Council's Education Committee, argued against the proposed curriculum change because, in her view, teaching the Holocaust amounted to accusing all Germans of having perpetrated evil. "Isn't it time," she asked, "to recognize, along with the futility of wars, the futility of accusing multi-ethnic Americans of the sins of ancestors in their country of origin?" In Hoffman's view, textbooks "should be stressing the positive contributions of all ethnic influences in the building of America."[41]

The Steuben News ran stories denouncing NBC and the Holocaust miniseries, complaining that the series was anti-German by virtue of its presentation of Nazis, and that NBC was biased because it did not show films or documentaries about other tragedies.

Some German Americans complained that the miniseries had served no good purpose. Contrary to the belief of some that advertising the Holocaust to the United States and the world might serve "to galvanize the viewing public against the continuation of such practices as presented in this picture," no such thing had occurred. Wars were still going on without protest. As one writer put the matter in a letter to the editor, "what has 'Holocaust' really accomplished? Nothing more than mixed emotions and hatred against a generation who had no part in 'Holocaust.'"[42]

The miniseries and related issues were among the matters deliberated at the biennial National Convention of the Steuben Society of America on August 24–27, 1978. *The Steuben News* reprinted what appears to be a summary of the report detailing the three resolutions that the convention adopted. The three resolutions asked that (1) Congress pass legislation to reduce the budget by 5 percent each year until the budget is balanced, (2) that Andrew Young, the black U.S. delegate to the United Nations, step down; and (3) that in light of the NBC miniseries, which had maligned the German people, an effort be made to teach not only the Holocaust in the nation's schools but other horrors as well. It was this last issue, according to the report printed in *The Steuben News*, that "was uppermost in the minds of most convention-eers."[43]

Organizing the United States Holocaust Memorial Museum

The United States Holocaust Memorial Museum was fifteen years in the making. The president's commission established to look into the matter of a Holocaust "memorial" was formed in 1978 by President Jimmy Carter at a time when Jewish lobbying groups were especially upset about a number of developments, including the sale of fighter planes to Israel's neighbors in the Middle East, Egypt, and Saudi Arabia. Stuart Eisenstadt, the president's chief of domestic policy had earlier suggested a Holocaust memorial, and the circumstances of 1978 seemed to suggest that this would be an appropriate time to start thinking about it seriously. Eisenstadt, as was true of perhaps most Jews in the United States, had lost relatives in the Holocaust. He mentioned to Carter the impact that NBC's "Holocaust" had, and pointed out that many nations had already built Holocaust memorials. Unless one were started soon, the many survivors who lived in the United States—the United States had more survivors than any country apart from Israel—would not live to see its completion. It was thought that all that was needed would be a gift of land. The Jewish community would raise the funds to construct the memorial. The memorial museum commission was announced at a White House Rose Garden ceremony on May 1, 1978, celebrating Israel's thirtieth birthday. Israel's birthday, according to Carter, was an appropriate occasion to announce plans for a Holocaust memorial. U.S. policy toward

Israel, said Carter, was influenced by these "indelible memories of the past."[44] Carter did not explain precisely what he meant here by connecting the Holocaust and U.S. policy toward Israel. Scholars had theorized that in the murder of the six million and the founding of the State of Israel, one could discern an archetypal pattern of tribulation and redemption similar to that told, for example, in the biblical book of Exodus between bondage in Egypt and deliverance of the people Israel from slavery. Not all Jews were happy with this theory. It may be that to born-again Christian Jimmy Carter, America had also played a role in that redemptive process when it became one of three nations to liberate Jews who had been incarcerated in the Nazi concentration camps of Europe.

In any case, a fifteen-member presidential commission was formed, with Jewish author and survivor Elie Wiesel as its head. Eventually, the commission was expanded to twenty-four and included camp survivors, Holocaust historians, Jewish community leaders, and rabbis, as well as civil rights activist Bayard Rustin, who gave the board an "interracial character." The report of the commission delivered by Wiesel on September 27, 1979, included among its major recommendations the creation of a "living memorial" to include a memorial, a museum, an educational foundation, and a "committee on conscience" to bring to the attention of government and the public ongoing instances of genocide. To that end, the United States Holocaust Memorial Council was formed and began its work on May 28, 1980. The Council consisted of fifty members, apart from the mandatory ten members of Congress. Of these, three-fourths were Jewish, ten were women, two were African American, two were of Polish ancestry, one was Ukrainian American, and one was of Slovenian descent.[45] That individuals of various ethnic backgrounds were included was important, as will be explained. One should note here, however, that absent is any representation from the very large and, as we shall see, not disinterested German American community.

An important date for this study was March 3, 1983, the date on which the transfer of land to the United States Holocaust Memorial Council was announced in the *Washington Post*. The date is important here because it was in spring 1983 that German Americans expressed their views—including many expressions of opposition—to the proposed memorial. Actually, the land had been transferred on August 12, 1981. The location was prime real estate, worth literally hundreds of millions of dollars, but the property had been effectively wasting away. On the land stood abandoned buildings constructed for use by the Bureau of Agriculture at the turn of the century. Included in the transfer was 0.8 acre of land and two of the buildings. The beauty of the location was that it was just off the Mall, near the Washington Monument, centrally located in the heart of the U.S. capital. Council Executive Director Seymour Siegel called it "the most prestigious spot for a museum in the Western world, perhaps the whole world." Why would location have been important for a museum? For Siegel, the prestige that accrued to the museum by virtue of its location spoke to the truth of the murder of the six million. The location itself provided an "unshakeable basis for the truth of our story and the accuracy of the events." The location of the museum was testimony against those who denied that a Holocaust had taken place. The official transfer of land and buildings took place on April 13, 1983, when Vice President George H. W. Bush handed Eli Wiesel the symbolic keys to the museum in a ceremony that took place in front of the Capitol Building.

The official groundbreaking took place on October 16, 1985, but just as the site of the building proved controversial, so too did the design of the building. The plans for the building went through various stages, and various interests on the Council put forward their designs until finally James Ingo Freed of the prestigious firm of I. M. Pei was hired to design what would eventually become the United States Holocaust Memorial Museum. The design of the building is of interest here because a period for public comment followed completion and submission of the final design to the federal Commission of Fine Arts on May 22, 1987. Among the comments heard were some from the German American community. Stanley Rittenhouse, who, as pointed out, was a Holocaust denier, as well as a member of the Steuben Society of America, presented the view that the "essence" of the design was "offensive to Americans of German descent." He explained, "Christianity teaches forgiveness and love while Zionism and this museum . . . will emphasize and represent revenge . . . and an unforgiving spirit." Contrary to what Rittenhouse might have intended, it seems there was something in his presentation that was sufficient to convince the Commission of Fine Arts that the design was in fact the right one.[46] The museum officially opened about six years later on April 22, 1993.[47]

The presidential commission originally established under the Carter administration had experienced difficulties from the start, although these difficulties were not publicized in the national press until 1993. In fact, apart from the disturbance it generated among some German Americans, very little was said in the press about the work of the presidential commission or the Holocaust Memorial Council during the 1980s. Yet there were definitely major issues that both entities dealt with. First, there were location issues. Lucy Davidowicz, prominent Holocaust historian, was seconded by many in her view that the museum should be located in New York where a substantial population of Jews and Jewish survivors lived, and where many survivors landed when they reached safety on American shores. Then, too, there was the question of who should be included in the museum's exhibits. Was the museum to be about Jews exclusively, or were other nationalities/ethnicities who had been victims of the Nazis to be included as well? In fact, an early battle between Elie Wiesel and President Carter developed over this issue, Wiesel insisting that the emphasis should be on Jewish victims, and the president requiring that equal attention be given to the "five million" victims of Nazism who were not Jewish.[48]

Not irrelevant here are efforts by members of the German government to include a statement in the proposed museum regarding the distance that Germany had come since the fascism of the Third Reich, its status as an ally of the United States, and the friendship it had formed with Israel. Helmut Kohl, before becoming chancellor, had sent Peter Petersen, of the German Bundestag, to meet with Wiesel. Together they formed a committee of six Germans and six Americans to study the matter in early 1984. When Wiesel resigned in 1986, the new chairman of the Council refused to meet with Petersen. Apparently, few members of the Council were aware of the fact that such a committee had been formed. On June 17, 1987, the Council voted unanimously against the participation of West Germany or the Soviet Union in creation of the museum.[49] Surprisingly, I have not found any evidence that members of the German American community made any efforts to assist the German government in their efforts to include a German statement in the museum. The efforts of the German government were clearly in what some German Americans would have regarded as their interests, as well as the interests of Germany. It is worth noting, however, that in the course of providing for the concerns of various ethnic groups in America, an exhibit of physically and mentally handicapped Germans victims of the Third Reich was incorporated into the final plans for the museum, and the exhibit is included today.[50] The appearance in the museum of victimized Germans is a far cry from the request for exhibits explaining German resistance; however, given the museum's focus on victimization, it was consistent. It is also relevant here that among the arguments made by Germany in the Bitburg controversy of 1985 was that Germans too were victims of the Third Reich. However, German handicapped people were not viewed as subjects of victimization in such arguments.

Debates that took place about the composition of the Council were also germane to this study. From the outset, but especially when the Council was formed, various ethnic groups—except apparently German Americans—vied for representation in the decision-making body. First were the Poles who argued that they had lost 3 million Christian Poles in the Holocaust, and therefore should be represented in the museum. It became clear, however, that other ethnic groups such as Ukrainian Americans wanted representation on the Council not because they had lost large segments of their population (although that was the case in certain instances), but because they wanted to ensure that their role as perpetrators of some of the horrors would not be emphasized in the museum's exhibits. In effect, they wanted—and got—the same consideration that Germany wanted but had been denied. There was of course a difference in the two groups of plaintiffs. Ukrainians were represented by Ukrainian Americans. For reasons that are not entirely clear—although one possibility will be suggested in the discussion that follows—Germany does not appear to have called on German Americans for support, nor did German Americans offer it.

The Press: The *Washington Post* and German American News of the New Museum on the Mall

Full-scale discussion of the United States Holocaust Memorial Museum did not take place until the museum was completed in 1993. At that time articles criticizing the museum, as well as many congratulatory pieces, began appearing in the popular press nationwide. However, when the transfer of land was announced in the *Washington Post* in March 1983, it became clear that the "Holocaust Museum on the Mall" was to be a reality, and some controversy was generated in the pages of the *Washington Post* itself. The other newspaper in which the matter of a national Holocaust museum became an issue in 1983 was *Der Deutsch-Amerikaner*, the journal of the German American National Congress.

Washington Post staff writer Phil McCombs broke the story on

March 3, 1983, that the land transfer had taken place, which appeared on page one. The estimated cost of the museum, at that time, was between thirty and forty million dollars. The cost when the museum was completed turned out to be in the neighborhood of 180 million dollars. Elie Wiesel, in March 1983 still chairman of the Council, said "my hope is that whoever will enter the museum will leave it a different person." Micah Naftalin, the Council's senior deputy director made the point that the museum was for all Americans. McCombs reported that the 1979 presidential commission findings had stated that the memorial museum would emphasize American liberation of the camps and the American reception of survivors after 1945, as well as the negligible U.S. response while the Holocaust was occurring. [51] The appropriateness of an "American" Holocaust museum was also discussed by George F. Will in a follow-up article in the *Washington Post* on March 10. In Will's view, the United States now had "broader, graver responsibilities" than it had in the past, presumably referring to its role as a world leader. "No other nation," therefore, was more in need of "citizens trained to look life in the face." [52] Presumably, the Holocaust museum would explain to innocent Americans what real horror looked like, as if to suggest that such institutions as black slavery had never existed in America, nor had Native Americans suffered near-extermination by conquerors and settlers. Gerald P. Carmen, of the General Services Administration that performed the transfer of land, stated that the memorial will be "held as a symbol of what can happen when [we] let down our guard." [53]

The first criticism of the museum project to appear in the *Washington Post* came in the form of letters to the editor on March 14, 1983. The first concern was that there were tragedies closer to home that also required memorialization, and the second concern was that a Holocaust museum might foster discrimination toward German Americans. Edward N. Leavy, regional director of the

Anti-Defamation League of B'nai B'rith, thought it was all fine and well to have memorials to the evil of the Holocaust, as well as the memorials to the great men who had built the nation, such as those that had traditionally adorned the nation's capital; but Leavy also pointed to the fact that anyone sensitive to the suffering of the victims of the Holocaust should also be sensitive to the sufferings of African Americans and Native Americans. "It would be fitting," said Leavy, "if there were a tribute to those millions of blacks who suffered from slavery and those who continue to suffer from discrimination, as it would also be fitting to remember the Native Americans, so few of whom survive." Reverend H. Stein-Schneider registered another concern, the concern that "today's Germans are being identified by a number of people with the Holocaust, the horrors of the war and the torture of patriots. Yet, what of the Germans who were themselves victims of the Gestapo?" German Americans would register and address this same concern in *Der Deutsch-Amerikaner*. As it turned out, however, the museum did address in its exhibits at least certain German victims of the Gestapo: the Jehovah's Witnesses, the handicapped, and homosexuals. But the concern that the museum would foster the identification of all Germans with Nazism was not addressed by museum planners and organizers. Stein-Schneider continued, "What about the new generation who were never implicated in any of Hitler's crimes? What of those who protected the innocent and never received a reward?" These questions were ones that the German government would have liked to have addressed with an exhibit about German resistance to Hitler, but no such exhibit appeared.[54]

On April 25, 1983, *Washington Post* writer William Raspberry published a piece in the *Post* that was critical of the idea of a Holocaust museum. Raspberry's concern was, first of all, that a memorial to victims was no memorial at all. Memorials, said Raspberry, "are, to me at least, for heroes and heroism, not for villains and villainy." Raspberry was suggesting, of course, that the Mall, with its tributes to Washington, Jefferson, and Lincoln, was no place to invoke the Holocaust. Second, Raspberry—like many others—did not understand why a national Holocaust memorial should exist when, so far as he knew, neither the perpetrators nor the victims were Americans. Later it was determined that, in fact, some Jewish Americans who happened to be in European countries under German control when war broke out were placed in Nazi concentration camps and mistreated, as were U.S. soldiers. Third, Raspberry's story suggested that a Holocaust memorial was inappropriate in light of the fact that there was no memorial to the slavery experience; and what is more, there were other tragedies that took place outside the United States that involved American ethnics, such as the massacre of Armenians by the Turks, which were as deserving of memorialization as the Holocaust. Fourth, Raspberry found ludicrous the suggestion that a memorial to the Holocaust would help prevent tragedies of a similar scale from occurring again. "It is happening. Right now. In many places. And, in Southeast Asia," said Raspberry. Lastly, Raspberry warned that a Holocaust memorial on the Mall attended by convention visitors out for a good time would only serve to "trivialize the special horror of the Holocaust."[55]

Responses to Raspberry's article from K. Leslie Ackman, John Shaw, and Peter D. Rosenstein appeared in the April 30, 1983, issue of the *Washington Post*. To the suggestion that the Holocaust memorial would be a memorial to "villains and villainy," and therefore there was no place for it on the Mall, Shaw responded that "the memorial is surely not to 'villains and villainy,' but to the victims." Ackman's response to Raspberry was that the Council was not planning a monument, which was in his view what Raspberry seemed to be suggesting, but a living museum that would educate. Raspberry's concern that neither the perpetrators nor the victims of the Holocaust were American—and consequently, there appeared to be no reason for a national monument to the Holo-caust—was also addressed by Ackman with the (by now) familiar argument that many of the liberators and many of the survivors were American.

As for the fact that there were no memorials to other victims, especially the victims of American settlement, on the Mall, Ack-man responded that "the reason why the Lincoln Memorial is so awe-inspiring is precisely that it represents an end to slavery." Shaw's answer to Raspberry's concern that there are no memorials to American tragedies was that "more could be built"; and in fact more have been in subsequent years. In 1989, President George H. W. Bush signed into law authorization for a National Museum of the American Indian (NMAI). Currently, several NMAI facili-ties exist and the full-scale National Museum of the American In-dian is now open on the Mall.[56] As of 2009, plans were underway for a National Museum of the African American. Clearly, had there not been a Holocaust Memorial Museum on the Mall, the NMAI would never have been constructed on the Mall nor would there be plans for a National Museum of the African American. Still more national museums—many more—could be appropri-ately built in a nation that was created and continues to be driven by immigrant dedication and labor. The one key matter that was not addressed by any of the respondents to Raspberry was the question of whether a memorial to the Holocaust would genuinely raise the consciousness of the nation toward tragedies being com-mitted elsewhere and help prevent those tragedies from turning into genocides. However, it is clear that one very important com-ponent of the United States Holocaust Memorial Museum is pre-cisely its mission to stand watch for prospective genocides world-wide.

The German American National Congress and the German-American National Political Action Committee (GANPAC—the denial group), at least as represented by the spokespersons of the two organizations, made their views on the creation of a U.S. Holocaust memorial museum known through channels other than the *Washington Post*, although the letter in the *Post* from the Reverend H. Stein-Schneider, in particular, expressed a concern that other German American representatives would also express. White House staff and the U.S. Holocaust Memorial Council were made aware of the views of the German American National Congress and GANPAC, as were the constituents of these organizations, from virtually the time that the transfer of land to the Council was announced in the *Post* and it was clear that plans for the museum were moving forward. Currently, two items have been made available from the archives of the Ronald Reagan Library identifying German American responses to the museum, one from Seewald, president of the German American National Congress, and the other from Hans Schmidt, national chairman of GANPAC. Both opposed construction of the museum. The original letter written to President Reagan by Seewald is missing from the archives of the Reagan Library; however, evidence suggests that the letter was the same as the one Seewald published in *Der Deutsch-Amerikaner* for April 1983. The White House correspondence tracking sheet dated April 18, 1983, indicates that Seewald's letter was sent to "F. Whittlesley" before being routed to the "U.S. Holocaust Memorial Council."[57] In her published letter, Seewald asks for the opportunity to meet with the president "or Mrs. Faith Ryan Whittlesley, Assistant to the President for Public Liaison." Further, in the response to Seewald by Seymour Siegel, executive director of the U.S. Holocaust Memorial Council, to whom the letter was routed by Whittlesley, he addresses the issues that Seewald raised in her published letter.

Seewald expresses basically three concerns in her letter opposing construction of a Holocaust museum. First, there was the moral concern that the museum would promote the concept of the collective guilt "of all those of German heritage in this country."

To Seewald's mind, Americans equated Nazis with individuals of German descent; and exhibits showing people being murdered by Nazis would promote anger against all German Americans. Second, there was the issue of the location of the museum. Seewald objected to the intention to locate the museum in the center of the nation's capital. It set an "alarming precedent" for memorialization in Washington of "other dark moments" in the history of America's ethnic groups, and would turn the capital into "a veritable museum of horrors." Lastly, Seewald objected to the fact that taxpayers' money, or at least their property in the capital, would be donated to the project. Moreover, complained Seewald, it was simply the wrong time to start up a Holocaust museum. German Americans were celebrating the three-hundredth anniversary of German settlement on American soil and the president of the Federal Republic of Germany was scheduled to be in Philadelphia to celebrate the event with the American president. She therefore asked that the project "be stopped, or at least delayed." She asked also that President Reagan or the assistant to the president for public liaison meet with a delegation of German Americans to discuss the prospective museum.[58]

Seymour Siegel's response to Seewald, dated June 14, 1983, addressed these questions, some more directly than others. The issue of collective guilt and the possible embarrassment that discussion of such a museum might cause West German President Karl Carstens were dealt with together. Siegel assured Seewald that the members of the Council "have no intention of promoting the idea of collective guilt. It was the Nazis and their allies who perpetrated the crimes we commemorate. The present German government has been most cooperative and has expressed interest in the project." As for the location of the museum, Siegel only responded that a year-long study had been undertaken before deciding on the Washington, DC site. And as for the use of taxpayer's monies to fund the project, Siegel pointed out that the museum "will be erected with donated funds, not government funds. Yet as we are a Federal agency, the buildings will continue to belong to the United States Government." That is, the government would pay for maintenance of the museum in perpetuity. Siegel also expressed surprise that the German American National Congress was opposed to the museum. "Many Americans of German ancestry," wrote Siegel, "are very supportive of efforts to memorialize the Holocaust. After all, Germany was touched by the tragedies of World War II and is still suffering the experiences of division and political partition." Siegel did not elaborate about who these "many Americans of German ancestry" were who supported the museum; but it was indeed the case that some German Americans did support the museum, as will be pointed out below. Of interest here also is the suggestion that Germany was "touched by the tragedies of World War II," as were other nations. In other words, Germany was also a victim of Nazism, a sentiment that had appeared in the Hollywood debates and that Germany itself would argue in 1985 in support of the view that Reagan should mourn the German war dead at Bitburg.

Hans Schmidt, head of GANPAC, was clearly aware of the contents of Seewald's letter and seconded it—a very dubious distinction for Seewald. As editor of the *GANPAC Brief*, Schmidt indulged in the same virulent antisemitic propaganda found in the worst of Holocaust denial literature. According to the *GANPAC Brief*, the Holocaust was no more than a myth.[59] In Schmidt's letter to the president, he spoke also of "the mythical six million number of claimed Jewish losses in the 'Holocaust.'" Schmidt went on to threaten that if the U.S. government was unable to stop or delay creation of the museum, then he would have no choice but to join "ethnic groups of (mostly) Eastern European heritage in the establishment of a Christian Holocaust Museum in the capital, and expect equally generous support by our elected representatives." Schmidt did not elaborate on what he meant by a "Christian Holocaust Museum" comprised of "ethnic groups of (mostly) Eastern European heritage." Schmidt's letter indicates that a copy of it was sent to "Captive Nations." The Captive Nations Committee is an anticommunist organization which argued for the rights of peoples under former Soviet rule. Presumably a "Christian Holocaust Museum" would be devoted to, among others, the Christian victims of Stalin. Given Schmidt's references to the "mythical six million," the reply he received from Micha Naftalin of the U.S. Holocaust Memorial Council was remarkably civil, although it contained nothing of special relevance to this study, except insofar as both letters—including Schmidt's comments about the "mythical six million"—were subsequently published in *Der Deutsch-Amerikaner*.[60]

The Steuben News published one article about the creation of the U.S. Holocaust Museum. The article was written by staff writer, Dr. Karl T. Marx, and it opposed the construction of the museum on all the same grounds that were put forth by those who wrote for the *Washington Post* and opposed the museum.[61] Seewald tried to use *Der Deutsch-Amerikaner* as a platform from which to rally support for her drive against construction of a U.S. Holocaust memorial museum. In the April 1983 issue, an entire page was devoted to reprinting her letter to Reagan, along with a plea to members of the German American National Congress to write to their senators and congressmen opposing the museum. Instructions and a list of the names of all the senators and congressmen in the United States were provided. Beginning with the June 1983 issue of *Der Deutsch-Amerikaner*, letters to the editor regarding creation of a U.S. Holocaust memorial museum were published. From April through December 1983, twenty letters were written to the editor of *Der Deutsch-Amerikaner* about the plans for a U.S. Holocaust museum.[62] Of the eighteen letters that opposed creation of a U.S. Holocaust museum, four of the letters to *Der Deutsch-Amerikaner* simply registered their support for

Seewald's drive to petition congressmen.[63] Of the remaining four-teen, six felt that Seewald was correct in stating that federal tax money should not be used for the project.[64] Among the more inter-esting statements made about the use of federal tax money was that made by Stefan Gross in a letter to *Der Deutsch-Amerikaner* in November 1983. Those who had supported the museum had argued that at least the construction and outfitting of the museum would be paid for by private donations. Gross pointed out that those private donations really belonged to all the people in the United States. As Gross explains, "those so-called 'Donations' are tax deductible, taxpayers money that should be paid to the U.S. Treasury but is diverted instead to build a white elephant in Wash-ington which has to be maintained at the cost of millions of dollars after it is built. In short, the memorial is being financed with tax-payers' money."[65]

One of the issues that was not raised by Seewald, but which was raised in the *Washington Post*, and which a number of letter writers addressed was the fact that many other horrors had been committed in the past that have not been memorialized. These people saw no reason why the Jewish tragedy should be singled out for a memorial museum in Washington, DC. Among the hor-rors identified by opponents of the museum were those perpetrated against African Americans and Native Americans within the Unit-ed States. And among the letter writers were one Native American and one African American. The Native-American letter was signed simply "Leroy, a Hopi." It began, "What are you Germans and Jews arguing about where and what kind of a holocaust historical site to build?" The letter ended, "We Indians could advise you where to build the first holocaust memorial. Build it at 'Wounded Knee.' We generously will donate the land."[66] The letter from the African American was more irate. Having read Seewald's letter in the April 1983 issue, Nancy A. Carter "hit the ceiling." She con-tacted "Executive Director Dr. Benjamin Hook of the NAACP, the

Chicago Defender and all black congressmen to stop this nonsense project of whites building Holocaust memorials for other whites." Carter ended her letter, "Build your memorials wherever the crimes occurred. Build our memorials across the White House and name it the Black House!"[67] Since *Der Deutsch-Amerikaner* is the journal of a German American organization, and it is unlikely that either the African American or Native American would have looked upon himself or herself as a German American, one wonders how these individuals would have known enough about *Der Deutsch-Amerikaner* to realize that it had identified the proposed museum as a concern, or that one could write a letter to its editor expressing one's opinion about the United States Holocaust Memorial Museum. The German American National Congress claims to have a number of affiliated organizations, but I have not come across any letter or article in *Der Deutsch-Amerikaner* that would suggest that any Native American or African American group was among its affiliates. In fact, I know of no letters or articles from an African American or a Native American, apart from these two, that have ever appeared in *Der Deutsch-Amerikaner*.

Other letters to the editor were also indignant about the fact that a memorial was being built to commemorate a Jewish holocaust when other mass murders had taken place and continued to take place elsewhere in the world; but they were not concerned about specifically the murder of African Americans or Native Americans.[68] Among the tragedies mentioned by these other letter writers were the British genocide in Ireland;[69] and the slaughter of Ukrainians by communists, of Armenians by Turks, Lebanese by Israelis, and Cambodians by Pol Pot.[70] Still other letter writers explained that among the groups of people to experience mass murder were Germans, some of it at the hands of the Americans. Joseph Stein, secretary of the American Aid Society of German Descendants, apparently speaking of the experience of ethnic Germans after the war, explained that Germans "suffered greatly at the hands of the communists. We were taken to work in Russian labor camps and deprived of all our worldly possessions. More than 50% of our people died in the process. Where are our monuments? Where are our stories?"[71] And it was not only the communists who committed mass murder. As Stefan Gross explains, the Americans also committed their share of murder. "One only has to add up the victims of air raids on Dresden, Hiroshima, Nagasaki, Berlin, Hamburg, Cologne, [and] Tokyo to name only the most important ones. One can easily come close to if not more than a cool million innocent people deliberately put to death."[72]

Lastly, another major concern of the German American letter writers was that a Holocaust museum would stir up additional anti-Germanism.[73] As already pointed out, some German Americans believed that people associate Nazis with anyone of German descent. Films that portrayed Nazis as evil—as was most often the case in both fictional films and documentaries about World War II—created in the minds of the audience hatred for Germans. Among the more verbal presentations of this problem was a letter from Raymond Braun of Nevada. Braun explained that his children had confronted anti-Germanism while growing up:

> When I lived in New York, one day my children came home from school and told me they were called Nazi's [sic] and Krauts just because they told these fellow pupils they were of German descent.

Braun went on to explain that every time he, himself, defended the German people he was called a Nazi. "The reason for this," he said in his letter, "is because of the constant barrage of anti-German T.V. programs . . . that rubs off on the American public, as will this museum."[74]

There were also two other articles that appeared in *Der Deutsch-Amerikaner* between April and December 1983, and that argued that a U.S. Holocaust museum would stir anger against individuals of German descent. What distinguished these two articles is that both suggested, after having warned the reader of anti-Germanism, that the reader write to the Institute for Historical Review to find out about the truth of the Holocaust. Founded in 1978, the Institute for Historical Review describes itself as "a not-for-profit research, educational and publishing center devoted to truth and accuracy in history. . . . The Institute's purpose is to 'bring history into accord with the facts.' The IHR is at the center of a worldwide network of scholars and activists who are working—sometimes at great personal Sacrifice—to separate historical fact from propaganda fiction by researching and publicizing suppressed facts about key chapters of history, especially twentieth century history, that have social-political relevance today."[75]

The IHR is in fact an institute comprised of individuals who pretend to be scholars, but distort and manipulate data—in some instances, they actually lie—in order to further their racist and antisemitic agenda. The Institute also publishes a journal and distributes books by leading Holocaust deniers, who are known to speak at rallies of neo-Nazis and other supremacist organizations. In effect, because *Der Deutsch-Amerikaner* was not notorious for Holocaust denial, as the publications of the Institute for Historical Review were, *Der Deutsch-Amerikaner* could serve as a recruitment tool for the Institute for Historical Review. One might find *Der Deutsch-Amerikaner* in places one would not find publications of the Institute for Historical Review.

It is significant, however, that letters in support of a Holocaust museum also appeared in *Der Deutsch-Amerikaner*, however small the percentage of these letters were.[76] Among the more interesting was one directed to Seewald from Susan Ann Huss of Pittsburgh, a student of German literature, who distinguished between anti-Germanism on the one hand, and memorializing the dead on the other. In Huss's view, creation of a Holocaust memorial "should not be misconstrued as being anti-German. Regardless of whether it should or should not be completed, this memorial commemorates World War II and the needless death of millions (not all Jewish), not negative stereotypes of today's German or German-American." Moreover, Huss took issue with Seewald's characterization of Holocaust memorials and events as promoting a "collective guilt" for the Holocaust among Germans and individuals of German descent. "When you mention collective guilt, that is a personal hang-up that would exist with or without this memorial. I personally do not suffer from this phenomenon, be it for WW II or the slavery question, and I assure you that many people I know express a similar point of view."[77]

The point that Huss makes concerning the large number of German Americans who do not suffer from "collective guilt" for the Holocaust, indeed who like most Americans are hardly aware of the concept, bears repeating. While it might appear from the discussion above of the views regarding creation of a Holocaust museum that most German Americans in the United States opposed it, it is more than likely that most in 1983 did not know of it, and it is difficult to say whether they would have opposed it had they known of it. Those who write letters to the editor are the more outraged of a population, and it is difficult to say whether, for example, the percentage of the outraged who opposed the museum is really in any way similar to the percentage of the total number of German Americans who opposed the museum, assuming again that a significant number of German Americans even knew about a museum in 1983. In any case, when the real debate began in 1993 as the doors to the United States Holocaust Memorial Museum opened, the German American organizations said nothing. Apparently, these German American organizations had already had their say, at least about the museum.

In general, arguments found in *Der Deutsch-Amerikaner* (and in *The Steuben News*) against the creation of a national Holocaust museum were the same as the arguments made in the *Washington Post*. First were the moral arguments. For instance, a Holocaust

View of the United States Holocaust Memorial Museum, from 15th Street, Washington, DC, circa 1993. Photo #N03538. *Courtesy of the United States Holocaust Memorial Museum.*

museum is anti-German and fosters the view that all individuals of German descent are like Nazis. Moreover, there were other victims, in particular the victims in the United States—African Americans and Native Americans—but one should include also the victims of Pol Pot, of Stalin, and others. Lastly, there were the German victims of the Soviets as well. But there was also the political argument: the money of American taxpayers should not be used to pay for a memorial to an event that occurred on foreign shores to people who were not American. Those writing for the *Washington Post* who favored the museum explained that the victims are in fact Americans today, or a good many of them are, and Americans had helped liberate them. As for the moral issue, Huss, writing in *Der Deutsch-Amerikaner* maintained that a Holocaust museum is not anti-German, and that she did not believe that individuals of

German descent would collectively be called upon to do penance for Nazi crimes because of this museum or any other phenomenon. The difference between the presentation against the museum in the *Washington Post* and *Der Deutsch-Amerikaner*, of course, was that there was a far greater percentage of German Americans registering their opposition to the museum in *Der Deutsch-Amerikaner* than there were individuals arguing against the museum in the *Washington Post*.

However, there were also two other distinctive features about discussion of the Holocaust museum in *Der Deutsch-Amerikaner*. First, two of the letters published referred the reader to the Institute for Historical Review, an antisemitic denial organization. Second, it published Hans Schmidt's letter to the president. Schmidt's organization, the German-American National Political Action Committee publishes the *GANPAC Brief*, characterized by antisemitic diatribe that questions the truth of the Holocaust. In Schmidt's letter to Reagan, which was published in *Der Deutsch-Amerikaner*, in fact, a statement appeared referring to the "mythical six million number of claimed Jewish losses in the 'Holocaust.'"[78]

But what is remarkable here is that while the idea of a memorial to the Holocaust (as well as the NBC miniseries on the Holocaust) conjured up in the German American mind thoughts of the way in which Germans have been victimized—thoughts of the bombing of Germans toward the end of the war, thoughts that had appeared in earlier articles without the provocation of a prospective Holocaust museum—there is no mention in this period by German Americans of the sufferings of German Americans during the wars. The issue would be raised only later in the 1990s, after it appeared that Japanese-American efforts to win reparations for their period of internment had been successful. This matter will be discussed further in the conclusion to this study, but it should be said here that the absence of any discussion of what was clearly an embarrassing, and indeed traumatic, experience for the German American community is significant. Much of the defensiveness toward anti-Germanism—in fact the worry on the part of some German Americans, regularly reinforced by the pages of *Der Deutsch-Amerikaner*—that Holocaust-related events produced anti-Germanism that extended to all German Americans was probably in part produced by feelings of shame about the internment of German Americans and an unwillingness on the part of German Americans to talk about it.

The next Holocaust-related issue that German American organizations would become involved in would be President Reagan's visit in 1985 to the German cemetery at Bitburg to mourn for the war dead. Against significant political pressure from Jewish and veterans' groups not to go to Bitburg, the president made the decision to go. German Americans who made their views known in the newspapers of the German American National Congress and the Steuben Society of American unanimously endorsed the visit to Bitburg. By this time, the German American National Congress was far better organized and politically ensconced in the national machinery of state to be more effective at promoting their views. While it is not clear how much influence German American organizations had on the president's decision to go to Bitburg, the organizations themselves, as well as other observer German American organizations, would view Reagan's decision as a victory for German Americans.

Four

The Battle of Bitburg

The Bitburg controversy was an international incident. President Ronald Reagan, in order to provide some small symbolic compensation to German conservatives and Chancellor Helmut Kohl for having successfully managed acceptance of American missiles on German soil—and in order to shore up West German support for his Star Wars initiative—in 1985 suggested that it was time to relieve Germany of "the guilt feeling that's been imposed upon them" for their Nazi past. On April 11, 1985, the White House announced that Reagan, accompanied by Kohl, would lay a wreath at the German military cemetery in Bitburg "in a spirit of reconciliation." At a news conference on April 18, 1985, Reagan explained his desire to commemorate the German war dead in a comparison that has since become famous. These dead at Bitburg, said Reagan, "were drafted into service to carry out the hateful wishes of the Nazis. They were victims, just as surely as the victims in the concentration camps."[1] Subsequent news reports revealed that at Bitburg were buried about two thousand soldiers, including forty-nine former SS, most from the Waffen SS, some from the Second SS Panzer Division, which in 1942 murdered 642 villagers in Oradour-sur-Glâne, France.

The Jewish American community and U.S. veterans were outraged and called upon the president not to go to Bitburg. The military cemetery at Bitburg contained no American soldiers. The thought of the president of the United States paying his respects to the German dead and not the American dead who had died at their hands was repugnant to veterans. The idea of honoring the SS was appalling to many. The Nuremberg International Military Tribunal had branded the SS as a criminal organization.[2] Adolph Eichmann had been in the SS, as had Joseph Mengele, the infamous doctor responsible for experimentation on humans at Auschwitz. Surely some other cemetery or some ceremony at a site other than a military cemetery would be more suitable. Conservatives and Reagan supporters argued that they weren't honoring the SS at Bitburg, only the young soldiers who didn't want to be there but had been conscripted—the German victims of the Nazis. Moreover, Germans had been strong allies for forty years and were key players in maintaining the stability of Europe during the Cold War era. For its part, the German American community was outraged that what was to be a symbolic gesture of reconciliation between Germany and America over crimes committed by the Nazi regime forty years earlier was being thwarted by American Jews and some veterans organizations. On May 5, 1985, Reagan paid his visit to the Kolmeshöhe military cemetery at Bitburg, after first visiting the Bergen-Belsen concentration camp.[3]

Efforts by Jews and veterans' groups to convince President Reagan not to go to Bitburg were reported extensively in the national press, although all these efforts were ultimately unsuccessful. Reported less extensively in the national press was the support received from members of Reagan's party and from Germany in favor of the trip to Bitburg. Some of Reagan's more cynical supporters insisted that Jews, two-thirds of whom it was well-known had voted for Walter Mondale in 1984, were just out to discredit Reagan. Entirely unreported in the national press, however, were the views of German American organizations such as the German American National Congress or their constituency. But German Americans did make their views known to the president directly and in publications of both the German American National Congress and the Steuben Society of America. Like Reagan's other supporters, they too criticized Jews, but for different reasons.

The National Press Says No to Reagan's Bitburg Visit

In the American popular press, there were basically two types of concerns that motivated the various arguments made for and against Reagan's trip to Bitburg. First, there were the political issues: there was, for example, the matter of responding to the request of a devoted ally who was doing America's work and keeping the Soviets in check in Europe. The president's participation at a ceremony that in fact had been taking place for years must have seemed like not much to ask, at least initially. Second, there were the moral issues. There was the matter of reconciliation. It had been forty years since Germany and the United States had fought each other in World War II. For forty years Germany and the United States had been staunch allies. French president Mitterand and Chancellor Kohl had had a well-publicized "moment" together at a German cemetery in France where the two had remembered the World War I dead of both nations, producing what was supposed to have been a catharsis of sorts, a cleansing of the bad blood that might still have existed between the two nations because of the war. Kohl looked forward to a similar experience at Bitburg. However, more important than the issue of reconciliation—some would say that reconciliation had long ago taken place and that it was not an issue at all—there was the issue of forgiveness, hidden in the use of the term "reconciliation." In Germany, the *Historiker-streit* was going on. Ernst Nolte, among others, was arguing—with the blessings of Germany's conservatives—that it was time to rid Germany of the burden of its Nazi past. Reagan agreed, in all likelihood unaware that he was taking a position in what was a major German debate about the way Germans viewed themselves. Because of the Holocaust, said Reagan, the Germans were a guilt-ridden people. It was time they were absolved of the Nazi past.

Sometimes it was difficult to separate the political from the moral issues. Advocates of the president's trip might argue that the reason he was going was to show his political support for a loyal NATO ally. But opponents might mix political and moral issues, and argue, for example, that Reagan's very act of laying a wreath at a military cemetery where German soldiers, indeed SS, were buried—whether or not it was performed only to please a political ally—was tantamount to exoneration of the SS for their crimes, and the president had no authority or moral right to perform any such national act of forgiveness. Further, the views of German Americans, almost universally, was that forgiveness was appropriate, precisely because Germany had been a loyal ally and important bulwark against Soviet aggression, and that it was time to forgive the Germans for the Holocaust, as well as World War II.

Although there were political issues raised by opponents of the president's trip to Bitburg, the opposition in the United States was primarily on moral grounds. The first moral issue, "Reconciliation" between the United States and Germany, opponents argued, had taken place a long time ago; the second, forgiveness of Germany for Nazi criminality in general—and the Holocaust in particular—was, *if possible*, not really the president's to give.

The idea of reconciliation came to be viewed in a variety of different ways by those who remarked on Reagan's Bitburg visit. Some who neither opposed nor supported the president's trip, but merely looked on as impartial observers, viewed forgiveness for the Nazi past as one of the terms of reconciliation between Germany and America. Reconciliation between Germany and the United States could not be complete until Germany was forgiven for the Holocaust.[4] The opponents of Reagan's trip, however, separated Germans from Nazis, and distinguished between reconciliation with Germany for the enmities that had developed during the war, and forgiveness of the Nazis for the Holocaust. For those who distinguished between reconciliation and forgiveness, reconciliation was not a problem. Forgiveness, however, was another matter. Israel's Prime Minister Shimon Peres was quoted in the American press as having said, "Reconciliation in the present is fine between British and Germans, French and Italians, Americans and Japanese." In an effort to control the damage that Reagan had done when he equated the dead soldiers at Bitburg with the Nazi victims of Bergen-Belsen, Secretary of State George Shultz would admit that he shared "the deep conviction that there is no place, within the deep spirit we feel of reconciliation, for understanding for those who took part in the perpetration of the Nazi horror."[5] Lance Morrow, writing for *Time* magazine, would distinguish reconciliation, which he defined as a "transaction" of sorts that might take place between nations, from forgiveness, which was a kind of "moral embrace, a clearing of the books, that is difficult if not impossible in the context of Nazi Germany."[6]

In fact, for many of these opponents, reconciliation was unnecessary since it had already taken place some time ago. Arthur Schlesinger, Jr., writing for the *Wall Street Journal*, would ask,

> Why this sudden need for "reconciliation" with West Germany? One had supposed that reconciliation was achieved 30 years ago when West Germany was permitted to rearm and to enter the North Atlantic Treaty Organization. Twenty-two years ago John F. Kennedy declared that he too was a Berlin-

er. How much longer will West German leaders keep on demanding further evidence of reconciliation? How many more pilgrimages will American presidents be required to make?[7]

Others were similarly baffled. Mary McGrory, writing for the *Washington Post*, felt compelled to point out that "reconciliation has been the official policy of the U.S. government for 40 years."[8] After the ceremonies at Bitburg and Bergen-Belsen, the editors at the *New York Times* still found it incredible that Kohl and Reagan could pretend that reconciliation was the point to the visit. "Yesterday's final travesty," complained the *Times* editorial, "was the pretense that German–American reconciliation still required affirmation—four decades after the Marshall Plan and the Berlin Airlift. This alliance will survive the folly of Bitburg, just as it would have survived the cancellation of Bitburg, because it is now deeply rooted in the democratic politics and prosperity of all its peoples."[9] But it was not really reconciliation that Kohl was after. The issue, apart from the political ones, was forgiveness.

For many who opposed the president's trip to Bitburg, the central concern seemed to be that SS were buried there. In some instances, no further explanation was needed to argue that Reagan should not go to Bitburg. As one *New York Times* editorial explained, "that some of these criminals lie at Bitburg is not just an awkward circumstance. It makes a tribute at their graves indecent."[10] The SS were a criminal group who had committed massive and heinous murder out of all proportion to any act of forgiveness. Others, such as Charles Krauthammer in a *Time* magazine article, explained the issue. The Waffen SS, according to Krauthammer, were created by Hitler in 1938 with the intention of serving as his personal guard. In 1940, their future role was defined: the Waffen SS would be a special state police force to keep order in the once-foreign territories subsumed by the Reich. Forty miles from Bitburg, seventy-one American prisoners of war had been murdered by the Waffen SS, said Krauthammer.[11] The president's place, argued some of the opponents, was not with the SS, but with the innocent, with the victims of the Holocaust. The most eloquent expression of opposition to Reagan's visit to any site with SS graves was probably Elie Wiesel's. On the occasion of receiving the Congressional Gold Medal at the White House on April 19, 1985—the ceremonies at Bitburg and Bergen-Belsen would take place on May 5—Wiesel presented an impassioned plea to the president to give up the visit to Bitburg precisely because the president *now* knew there were SS members buried there, while he did not know that before. Speaking directly to the president with the media present and invoking the image of America as refuge for the persecuted, Wiesel exhorted,

> I am convinced, as you have told us earlier when we spoke that you were not aware of the presence of SS graves in the Bitburg cemetery. Of course, you didn't know. But now we all are aware. May I, Mr. President, if it's possible at all, implore you to do something else, to find a way—to find another way, another site. That place, Mr. President, is not your place. Your place is with the victims of the SS.[12]

In Wiesel's view, the president had a choice to make. He could either mourn for the SS or its victims; he could not do both.

Other opponents of Reagan's visit argued that his attendance at a ceremony for the war dead that included the SS amounted to a symbolic form of forgiveness for their crimes. They argued that when President Reagan participates in a ceremony to "mourn"— that was his word[13]—the war dead at a cemetery where SS are buried, he, in effect, will be forgiving them of their crimes against humanity, the crimes of the Holocaust. Moreover, to mourn the SS, some opponents argued, would be not merely to forgive the SS, but to exonerate them for the crime of the Holocaust—to suggest that the crime itself was not that bad. Dov Hikind, an American who flew to Bitburg to protest the president's appearance at the site where SS lay, is reported to have said, angrily, "I still can't believe I am here to see my president rehabilitate the SS."[14] His mother had survived Auschwitz. His concern that the president's visit to Bitburg was a step in the direction of rehabilitating the SS was echoed by others.[15] In fact, eight hundred former SS meeting in a small Swabian village south of Munich had toasted President Reagan, which seemed to confirm to opponents that the president's visit, regardless of his intentions, would in fact be interpreted by some as exoneration.[16]

There was the argument, also, that forgiveness was impossible; and even if it were possible, it was not the president's place to perform the act of forgiveness. Lance Morrow explained that there are two conditions for forgiveness in Judaism. The first is genuine contrition before the person injured and the second is that one compensate as best as one can for the crime committed. But compensation for killing one's entire family is impossible. Moreover, Reagan is not a party to the injury incurred by Jews or any other victims of the Nazis. Reagan can forgive his own assailant, John Hinckley, Jr., who shot him, but it is no more his place to forgive the SS for their crimes than it is his place to forgive Mehmet Ali Agca for shooting Pope John Paul II.[17] Wiesel, speaking before the president, was still more emphatic. "Mr. President," he said, "you have no right to forgive in our names. We do not hate. We do not seek vengeance. We do not kill our killers. But we cannot allow you to forgive. We cannot allow the world to forget."[18] Others argued that no one, not even Jews, could offer forgiveness for the crimes of the SS or the Nazis in general. "No one can grant absolution," maintained Flora Lewis writing for the *New York Times*, "including President Reagan."[19] Moreover, opponents argued that the president's supporters had created a dualism between Christians for whom forgiveness is a central tenet of their religion and the Jews who seek only vengeance. The president had thereby unwittingly contributed to marginalizing Jews once again.[20]

But why not offer forgiveness for the Holocaust to those Germans who felt they needed it? That question was not dealt with in the popular press. That question received no better answer than the one provided by Jürgen Habermas, one of the key figures in the German Historians' Debate, whose essay about the Bitburg fiasco was published for the benefit of Americans in Geoffrey Hartman's collection of essays, *Bitburg in Political and Moral Perspective*.[21] As Habermas explains, the whole Bitburg visit was too well-staged, too artificially brokered for something that would have the regenerative power of a true and genuine moment of forgiveness. The *Frankfurter Allgemeine Zeitung* was in a sense correct when it suggested that "[w]e Germans cannot demand pardon." It would have to be freely offered by the president in all sincerity in order for it to be effective. And there is every reason to believe that the president was sincere at the outset. There is every reason to believe that Reagan in the beginning genuinely felt that forgiveness was something he should and could provide. But feelings are vulnerable to assault. The Reagan who left the Bitburg cemetery, as a glimpse of the picture of him doing so suggests, was a man whose feelings were in tumult. He no longer had any personal truths about forgiveness to offer. Germans would have to learn to forgive themselves; and it would obviously be many years before all Germans would feel comfortable in the presence of the Holocaust.

There were also political reasons given for Reagan not going to Bitburg. Some opponents detected cynical motives in Kohl's invitation to Reagan at that particular time. Arthur Schlesinger, Jr., for example, thought that Kohl's invitation was politically motivated by the upcoming elections in which the Christian Democrats stood to lose some seats. Helmut Kohl, said Schlesinger, had "shrewdly manipulated the American president into serving as a Christian Democratic fugleman."[22] Schlesinger was not alone in this observation. Kohl's party lost many seats in that election.[23]

Some Reagan administration officials also opposed the visit for

U.S. President Ronald Reagan leaving Kolmeshöhe Cemetery near Bitburg with Ret.
Army General Matthew Ridgeway, May 5, 1985. Photo C28887-25A.
Courtesy of Ronald Reagan Library.

political reasons. They worried about the way Soviet propaganda might treat the image of Reagan laying a wreath at the grave of a Nazi soldier. George J. Church reported that Polish Premier Jaruzelski at a communist block ceremony in Warsaw had already railed against President Reagan's "pilgrimage to . . . the graves of SS criminals and butchers and hangmen." Charles Z. Wick, director of the United States Information Agency and a friend of Reagan thought that demonstrators from all over Europe would converge on Bitburg.[24] Dorothy Rabinowitz, writing for the *New York Post*, echoed Church's sentiments: "Could the Soviet propagandists—those folks who have spent so many years portraying the U.S. as a friend of fascism—have conceived in their wildest dreams such an opportunity: that there would be granted them actual footage of a U.S. President paying homage at the graves of Hitler's soldiers?"[25] In the end, Reagan laid no wreath. He spent all of eight minutes at the Bitburg cemetery.

Another less well-verbalized but significant political argument against Reagan's trip to Bitburg was that it would be used by antisemites to their advantage. Menachem Rosensaft, chairman of the International Network of Children of Jewish Holocaust Survivors, was reported to have said that "the visit will be exploited by revisionist historians, neo-Nazis, and their sympathizers."[26] Apparently, Reagan's trip was indeed supported by some neo-Nazis. Reverend Franklin H. Littell noted, albeit in the *Jewish Times*, which has a limited audience, that neo-Nazis had registered their praise for Reagan—for his "hanging tough" on Bitburg.[27] And as already pointed out here, former SS members who met at the time of Bitburg were apparently sufficiently pleased with the symbolism of a visit to Bitburg to drink to Reagan's health. More disconcerting, however, is the hostility toward Jews generated among average individuals by the Bitburg fiasco. William L. Chaze and James M. Hildreth, supporters of the president reporting after the event, quote Henry Siegman of the American Jewish Congress who complained that the Bitburg visit "has encouraged antisemites to speak out in Germany and in the U.S." Siegman goes on to point out that "I'm getting calls and letters, not just from crazies, but from cultured and civilized people, who say in gentle tones, 'I now understand why Hitler did what he did.'"[28] However, it is also true, as will be shown in a later section, that Holocaust revisionists—those who today are called Holocaust deniers—used the Bitburg debacle, as Rosensaft suggested they would, to wage a small campaign in the German American press for new adherents.

Support from the National Press

Unlike those who argued against President Reagan's trip to Bitburg, those who supported him did so primarily on the basis of political arguments, although moral issues were also addressed. The political concerns of those who supported the visit to Bitburg were of two types. There was first the concern about relations with Germany: Kohl had been passed over when the Allies of the Second World War observed the anniversary of the Normandy invasion a year earlier, and he felt slighted. The ceremony at Bitburg would make amends. Also, the Kohl government had supported U.S. military efforts to contain what Reagan regarded as the Soviet threat. Kohl deserved some consideration. Second, there was the domestic concern. If Reagan did not go, it would look as though he had caved in to pressure from—by and large—Jewish groups and American veterans, when in fact the people of the United States were evenly divided on the matter. The moral issues for supporters of the Bitburg ceremonies were the same as those which were addressed by opponents: reconciliation and forgiveness. Of course, the perspectives brought to these issues of reconciliation and forgiveness by supporters of the Bitburg ceremony were considerably different from those brought by opponents.

Ed Magnuson, who describes the events of the Bitburg visit

with only a slightly discernible bias against it, tells in some detail how supporters had hoped that Reagan's participation in the Bitburg ceremonies might compensate for the slight that Kohl had received the previous year at the hands of the Allies. "The origins go back more than a year ago," he explained. "When plans for the observance of the Normandy invasion anniversary were carefully worked out by officials in Washington, London and Paris. Kohl was not invited to participate, since this was seen as a celebration of the wartime victory over the Germans rather than a time for the victor to join hands with the vanquished." Magnuson goes on to state that Kohl was miffed; and when he realized that Reagan would be coming to Bonn for the economic summit around the time of the Victory in Europe Day anniversary on May 8, Kohl thought it would be appropriate to celebrate the "new bonds" between the United States and Germany at that time.[29] Charles Krauthammer, among the more outspoken critics of Reagan's visit to Bitburg, felt that the "sole reason" that Kohl wanted Reagan to come to Bitburg was to compensate for the slight that Kohl felt he had received by not being invited to the anniversary of the Normandy invasion: "The only conceivable reason for the Bitburg visit in the first place is politics: alliance politics. Kohl had a problem. His exclusion from D-day ceremonies last year gave ammunition to complain that Germany bears equally the burdens of the Western alliance but is denied equal respect. Reagan wanted to use this ceremony to help Kohl."[30] Supporters of Reagan's visit to Bitburg couldn't agree more, and what is more, they argued it was the duty of an ally and friend to help erase the damage done to Kohl's and Germany's image of itself. Even Jody Powell, former press secretary to Democratic President Jimmy Carter, could strongly support Reagan's visit to Bitburg on the grounds that Kohl's request to take part in the Normandy invasion ceremonies had been rebuffed—Kohl had personally been stung—and the ceremony at Bitburg should help compensate for that exclusion.[31]

But there was also the matter of America's Pershing missiles, aimed at the Soviets, that Germany had accepted on its soil. The Bitburg visit from Reagan would also provide some compensation to Germany for that circumstance, supporters argued. The Kohl government, which had not hidden the fact that there were American nuclear weapons on German soil, had been victorious in 1983. The vote for Kohl's government was viewed as a vote of support for American military policy in Europe, and Kohl was to be congratulated. Moreover, Kohl had run up against the Soviet Union when he agreed to permit the missiles to be based in Germany; he ran the risk of having East Germany—where relatives of more than three million West Germans still lived—made less accessible. Kohl and the German people deserved the symbolic gesture that was to take place at Bitburg—this small token of regard from the United States for the friendship that existed.[32] Robert Haeger reported in *U.S. News & World Report* that confirmation of Reagan's plans to visit Bitburg was greeted in Germany with applause. The president had made a decision in favor of the people of Germany, despite the most enormous pressures in the United States. Haeger made a point of the fact that "Reagan's firm position was particularly appreciated by those Germans who saw him as returning a favor to Kohl."[33]

Supporters of the Bitburg visit also pointed to the Office of the President, and the manner in which any retreat would appear as weakness both at home and abroad. According to George J. Church, Reagan had confided to an acquaintance that "[e]verybody said after all this trouble I should have admitted the mistake and dropped the visit. But in my view, it boiled down to walking away from a true friend. If I did that, then there goes the friendship. Now I think we must go ahead or appear weak."[34] What is more, that weakness would be perceived both by Americans at home and the world. According to William R. Doener, "former President Richard Nixon and former Secretary of State Henry

Kissinger advised him to stick with his original itinerary. Canceling the Bitburg visit, said Kissinger, 'would do enormous damage to our foreign policy.' Nixon reportedly warned Administration officials that 'the credibility of future negotiations is at stake."[35] Indeed, Chancellor Kohl himself was reported to have told Reagan that canceling Bitburg might do damage to the official relations between Germany and the United States, and more importantly create bad feelings between the German and the American people. It was apparently during that conversation between Reagan and Kohl that Reagan promised not to give in to pressure groups at home.[36]

The particular pressure groups "at home" most often identified as the opposition were of course the Jewish organizations. But Jewish organizations, according to an editorial in the *Wall Street Journal,* opposed Reagan's trip not because they were concerned about the Holocaust. They were simply out to get Reagan. Jews, according to the editorial, were newcomers to the conservative scene, "torn between their predominantly liberal politics of the past and the modern appeal of hawkish neo-conservatism."[37] The numbers supported the view that in fact Jews were not Reagan Republicans. According to exit polls, only one-third of the Jewish electorate supported Reagan.[38]

Forgiveness was a concern of the supporters of the Bitburg ceremony, as it was of the opponents; but supporters of course argued that in fact it was time to unburden the Germans of at least some of the guilt they felt for Nazi atrocities. Tyler Marshall, writing for the *Los Angeles Times*, pointed out there was some sentiment in Germany that God's forgiveness extended to the SS as well, and that Catholic bishops in the United States should support Reagan's visit to Bitburg. Alois Mertes, member of parliament for Bitburg and a secretary in the West German Foreign Ministry, had asked in a radio interview "where the Catholic Church and other churches are in this debate, especially the Catholic bishops, who have plenty to say about strategic and economic issues but have not brought the joyful news that God's blessing also extends to the buried SS soldiers."[39]

Most supporters, such as McGeorge Bundy, took a different tack and simply argued that it was certainly not the president's intention to condone the crimes of the SS, or the Nazis, or any other crimes anywhere else on the planet by his trip to the military cemetery at Bitburg. It was the decent Germans, the soldiers who were conscripted and had no other choice but to go and fight, that were being mourned by the president and Chancellor Kohl.[40] Reagan himself made the task of forgiveness easier by putting a distance between the average German soldier and the SS. Ed Magnuson, writing for *Time* magazine, described a White House lunch between the president and media representatives at which Reagan "conceded that the SS officers buried at Bitburg 'were the villains, as we know, that conducted the persecutions and all.'" But he described the other German soldiers there as averaging eighteen years of age. "These were those young teenagers that were conscripted, forced into military service in the closing day of the Third Reich when they were short of manpower."[41] West Germans, Americans were told, themselves distinguished between SS who were stationed as concentration camp guards and those, like the ones buried at Bitburg, who were members of combat divisions. A public opinion poll indicated that 94 percent of West Germans considered those buried at Bitburg "Germans," as opposed to "Nazis."[42] The implicit argument here was that forgiveness was an appropriate gesture after forty years of carrying the burden of guilt, at least forgiveness aimed at innocent Germans. William F. Buckley, Jr.'s *National Review* put it plainly—albeit crudely—when it stated that "most people sense that at some point the present population of Germany must be allowed to stop groveling morally. This was Reagan's healthy instinct in agreeing to go to Bitburg."[43]

Perhaps the most moving and convincing argument for forgiveness and for Reagan's visit to Bitburg was June Tierny's in the *Washington Post*. Tierny had grown up in postwar Germany and recalled for her readers the manner in which her classmates would bow their heads in shame when Hitler was mentioned and how they would accept responsibility for the crimes committed by a different generation. Students learned nothing about the Nazis until the seventh grade, at which point *Kriegesschuld*, guilt for the war crimes of the Nazis, was conveyed from teacher to student, from one generation to another, apparently as official German policy. Students read about the Nazis, and teachers explained, always ending with a reminder that Germany alone was to blame for the war. It was at that point that, Tierny explained, "my classmates would bow their heads and stare at their desks while I would look around, unable to identify with their guilt, but aware that an oppressive mood had settled over the classroom." Never had she seen anything comparable on the part of Americans, who had every bit as much reason to feel ashamed for the mass murder of the Native Americans and the horrors committed against African Americans during the slavery period. But the important point in her story is when she is told by one of her student friends that her father doesn't believe "all that stuff about the Jews." He didn't believe that there really were such things as concentration camps. Tierny makes the point that it is the kind of repressive guilt experienced by the children she grew up with that can make for Holocaust denial. "Whenever you build a mandatory guilt feeling into a conscience, be it individual or national, you are creating a situation that demands release—release from the tension of always being guilty, of being irredeemable. Ultimately it leads to denial, because denying the point is easier than bearing the guilt."[44] In Tierny's view the Bitburg trip symbolized forgiveness, the source of release from the burden of guilt that produces denial.

But there was another type of argument being used by supporters of the visit to Bitburg to suggest that forgiveness was warranted, and therefore the president would be doing the right thing by offering it. Some supporters argued that what the victims of the Holocaust experienced was no worse than what other persecuted peoples experienced, suggesting that therefore forgiveness should be offered. The *National Review*, for example, while admitting that among the "unique" characteristics of the Holocaust was the fact that it had taken place "in a country theretofore considered among the advanced and civilized nations," took issue with the suggestion that the experience of the victims was any worse than that which others endured. "Many others have been slaughtered in this century: Armenians, Ukrainians, Gypsies, Tibetans, Afghans, Chinese, Vietnamese, Cambodians, whole tribes of Africans."[45] As pointed out, this type of argument had been used in the past and would be used frequently by German Americans when arguing that forgiveness was in order, and therefore the president should go to Bitburg; but German Americans would also argue that not only had Armenians, Ukrainians, and others experienced horrors, Germans had experienced horrors also. Needless to say, there was no discussion in the national press of any concerns that German Americans might have had about the proposed visit to Bitburg by the American president.

German American Views of Jewish Antagonism toward the President's Visit to Bitburg

The opinions of the Steuben Society of America and the German American National Congress in the *Steuben News* and *Der Deutsch-Amerikaner* were universally in favor of Reagan's visit in Bitburg. As had Reagan's other supporters, some members of the German American community expressed anger at Jews who opposed the president's trip. The reasons given by the German Americans, however, differed from those of his other supporters. German Americans were angry at Jews not because they suspected that Jews were opposing the trip only because they wanted to discredit Reagan politically. Some German Americans believed that

Jews opposed this opportunity for Germans to be relieved of some of the burden of guilt felt for Nazis crimes. They believed that Jews were trying to avenge themselves.

So sprach Ilya Ehrenburg, Stalins Propagandist:

"Wir sagen nicht mehr guten Morgen oder gute Nacht! Wir sagen morgens: 'töte den Deutschen,' und abends: 'Töte den Deutschen!'

Es geht jetzt nicht um Bücher, Liebe, Sterne, es geht jetzt nur um einzigen Gedanken: die Deutschen zo töten. Sie alle zu töten. Sie zu vergraben. . .Es gibt nichts Schöneres fur uns, als deutche Leichen. Schlag den Deutschen tot.—bittet Dich die alte Mutter. Schlag den Deutschen tot!—so fleht Dich das Kind an. Deutsche sind keine menschen, Deutsche sind Zweibeinige Tiere, widerliche Wesen, Bestien. Sie haben keine Seele. Sie sind eizellige Lebewesen, selenlose Mikroben, die mit Maschinen, Waffen Minenwerfern ausgerüstet sind. Wenn Du einen Deutschen ershlagen hast, schlage noch einen anderen tot, es gibt für uns nichts Lustigeres als deutsche Leichen!"

Thus spoke Ilya Ehrenburg, Stalin's propagandist:

"The common expression among us is no longer 'good morning' or 'good night'! In the morning we say 'Death to the Germans' and in the evening we say 'Death to the Germans.' We interest ourselves not in books or love or stars; our thoughts are only of killing Germans, burying Germans. There is nothing that is more beautiful for us than German corpses. Beat the Germans to death—the elderly mother asks it of you. Beat the Germans to death—so begs of you the small child. Germans are not humans; Germans are two-legged animals, disgusting creatures, beasts. They have no soul."

I quote the above not from a newspaper of the Stalinist era, but from the May 1985 issue of *Der Deutsch-Amerikaner*. This issue, like the June 1985 issue, was almost entirely devoted to discussion of the controversy surrounding President Reagan's trip to Bitburg. A notable exception was page four, which was devoted entirely to an article entitled, "Rette sich wer kann: Ein Augenzeugenbericht vom Untergang Berlin 1945" [Save Yourselves You Who Can: An Eyewitness Account of the Fall of Berlin, 1945]. Inset in the article was a box with the Ehrenburg quotation from above in it. The quotation was titled, "Haben wir Schon vergessen?" [Have we already forgotten?][46] On page two of the same issue a telegram appeared by Seewald, president of the German American National Congress at the time of the Bitburg controversy, which she sent to President Reagan. The telegram acknowledged that Germany had a "dark past" that "must be overcome," and continued as follows:

> It almost seems as if Jewish people are attempting psychological murder of the German people and the German nation in order to avenge. Is this any different from the physical murder during World War II? One method is as deadly and unsavory as the other.[47]

Jews were trying to psychologically murder Germans for what the Germans did to their relatives during World War II. And in case anyone had forgotten, *Der Deutsch-Amerikaner* was there to remind them that some Russian Jews of the Stalinist period had an intense hatred for Germans and called for their annihilation.

Equally alarming, however, is the possibility that the anger generated by Bitburg among some German Americans might have made it easier for the Steuben Society to condone the renaming of one of its chapters after Holocaust denier, Austin App. It is perhaps no coincidence that the renaming took place in 1985.[48]

The German American National Congress had a different agenda. In *Der Deutsch-Amerikaner* for May 1985, one of the two issues in which the Bitburg controversy was discussed at length, a letter to the editor was published advertising the Institute for Historical Review for those who wanted to know the *real* history of Germany and the Allies. As indicated earlier, *Der Deutsch-Amerikaner* had also published letters referring the reader to the Institute for Historical Review in its issues discussing the creation of the United States Holocaust Memorial Museum in 1983. Anger in the German American community over Bitburg had produced the conditions under which Holocaust deniers were able to get a hearing in the official journal of the German American National Congress. Moreover, statements flirting with Holocaust denial appeared in *Der Deutsch-Amerikaner* from supporters of Reagan's visit to Bitburg, just as earlier statements of denial had appeared in *Der Deutsch-Amerikaner* from opponents of the United States Holocaust Memorial Museum. In the case of the museum, the denial appeared—almost predictably—in a statement from Hans Schmidt, head of the antisemitic GANPAC organization. In the case of the Bitburg trip, the statement came from the president of the German-American National Congress.

German American Influence in the White House

Among the political factors that might have contributed to President Reagan's decision to visit the Bitburg military cemetery and which have not been given any attention is the influence of the German American community. As explained earlier, the influence of the German American community in the 1980s was growing. A national German-American Day was instituted; a German-American Friendship Garden was created in Washington, DC; politicians courted the community if only for the strength of its numbers of voters; and leaders of the community such as the president of the German American National Congress were invited to the White House when German dignitaries were in town. Letters to the president such as the telegram written by Seewald accusing Jews of trying to psychologically murder Germans might very well have actually reached the president. It is clear, however, from correspondence and interoffice White House memos that are available that one of Seewald's letters supporting Reagan's visit did make it as far as the desk of Pat Buchanan, arch-conservative, communications director, and head of the Reagan team of speech writers. What is more, with that letter came a memo explaining the large numbers of German Americans for which the German leaders presumably spoke.

Pat Buchanan was one of those people chosen by the president because of pressure from the right wing of the predominantly conservative Republican Party. He was not so much an advocate of the president as he was an advocate of rightwing politics. But as communications director he participated in some of the more critical meetings to take place in the White House. After the news broke that SS members were buried at Bitburg, Jewish leaders, primarily Republicans, were brought to the White House on April 16, 1985, to discuss possible solutions to the dilemma confronted by the president's upcoming visit. Buchanan, of course, participated. As the meeting proceeded, Buchanan could be observed scribbling on his notepad. It was discovered that Buchanan had been writing over and over again, "Succumbing to the pressure of the Jews."[49] On April 18, 1985, Linas Kojelis, sent Buchanan an interoffice memorandum, accompanied by three telegrams. The memorandum said,

> Pat, I thought you might be interested to see the attached copies of telegrams we have received from German American organizations supporting the President's intention to visit Bitburg. Of course, these groups are not especially well organized and do not constitute a powerful lobby in Washington, a factor worth considering. On the other hand, there are 49 million German Americans, they vote, and 68 percent of them voted for the President last November.
>
> I thought this information might be of interest to you.

The allusion here to the Jews, who were "well organized" and did "constitute a powerful lobby" is fairly obvious. Kojelis knew, given the Jewish opposition to Bitburg and developments at the recent meeting of Jewish leaders at which Buchanan had been present, that the memoranda, as well as the numbers of German Americans, would indeed be interesting to him. It is likely that Kojelis was correct in suggesting that the German American vote made up a substantial proportion of those who had elected Reagan. Both the German American National Congress and the Steuben Society had supported Reagan, and their newspapers publicized the fact. Moreover, German Americans, as pointed out earlier, had by and large voted Republican since the world wars when German aliens and at least some American citizens of German descent had been interned by two Democratic presidents. Kojelis was obviously providing Buchanan with additional reasons that the president should go to Bitburg.

The telegrams that Kojelis sent to Buchanan were from Hans W. Eberhard of the German American Business Association of Van Nuys, California; John Schank from the German American community in Orange County, California; Siegfried Reinke, president of the Chicago North Chapter of the German American National Congress, which claimed four thousand members; and Seewald, National president of the German American National Congress. Seewald's telegram to President Reagan that Kojelis sent to Buchanan was far more subdued than the telegram she sent to Reagan, which was published in *Der Deutsch-Amerikaner*. The surprise contained in the telegram by Seewald that Buchanan saw might have been the news that the Germans, as opposed to the Nazis who fought in World War II, were not fighting against democracies but only against communist expansion, just as NATO was today. "This symbol"—the visit to Bitburg—as Seewald explained, "would be an acknowledgment, particularly for the young West German NATO soldiers that their fathers—some of whom might be buried at Bitburg—were also fighting Communist expansion while giving their lives for their country (not for the National Socialist party). It is in the interest of the United States to emphasize this aspect for the end of World War II."[50] As indicated earlier, supporters of Reagan's visit in the national press had distinguished between SS officers and the average German conscript. Seewald distinguished similarly between those fighting for national socialism and those who gave their lives for their country. However, in Seewald's view, these last were "also fighting Communist expansion" as their sons in NATO did at present alongside Americans. The suggestion that the German soldier was only fighting communist expansion was of course ridiculous. The German soldier of course was fighting not just Russia in the East, but also England, for example, and later the United States. But Seewald was not alone in her view that the Nazis were simply fighting Communism. *Der Deutsch-Amerikaner* for June 1985 published a letter to Reagan from Dr. Dung H. Phan of "The World Anti-Communist Alliance," which insisted that "Germany (let us not forget) was the first nation who went to war against communism—[i.e., the] Soviet Union."[51] The view that the Nazis were simply fighting the communists just as the West was in the 1980s—suggesting that Americans should have joined the war on the side of the Nazis— was not new. "Post World War II revisionists," explained Deborah Lipstadt in *Denying the Holocaust*, "contended that Nazi Germany had also been an excellent defense against Communism but that the Allies had been blind—or blinded—to this fact."[52]

The German American Claim to Victory: Their Arguments for the President's Trip to Bitburg

Seewald's argument that Germans during World War II were fighting communism, and therefore should be mourned at Bitburg by President Reagan, was only one of several arguments made on moral grounds by German Americans. Indeed most of the arguments by German Americans associated with the Steuben Society and the German American National Congress were about issues designated here as "moral" ones. The argument was that the president's trip was the "right" thing to do, as opposed to the most politically advantageous, although at times the two overlapped. Moreover, while many of the arguments made by German Americans in the German American press were similar to those found in the national press, the differences were significant. Arguments for forgiveness in the national press were rarely made from personal experience. June Tierny's argument for forgiveness, based on her account of her experience growing up in Germany, was the exception. Arguments from personal experience among German Americans seem to have been the rule, only it was not individuals' experiences in Germany that were being presented. It was the experience of German Americans in the United States—although not their experience during the wars—that was being presented to argue that forgiveness for the Nazi past was necessary, and, therefore, so was Reagan's trip to Bitburg.

This is not to say that the political issues were ignored. On the contrary, German Americans were at least as well aware of the political reasons in favor of the president's trip to Bitburg as most individuals writing for the national press. In fact, the Bitburg controversy was viewed by German Americans as one of their first victories in the political arena. The German American National Congress, which had argued that German Americans should be more politically active on matters that affected them, had launched a campaign to urge German Americans to support the trip to Bitburg; and as far as they could tell, they had been successful. Seewald, in an address to the Milwaukee chapter of DANK reported by *Der Deutsch-Amerikaner*, explained that the German American National Congress "fully supported" Reagan's trip to Bitburg. "As you all know," she went on, "this was done through letters by all of you, telegrams, articles and advertisements in various newspapers and telephone calls. I do not need to elaborate on this here." However, later in her address, Seewald does elaborate, quite eloquently:

> Past happenings affecting the Germans living in America, have put us into a corner and we have been [there] for a long time, a majority . . . existing on the rim of happenings only. Nobody asked us for our opinion, nobody was interested in how we felt about this. . . . When we talked to the mass media, or to the news media, we received polite but definite nods and answers, but no action. When we talked even to our German American Societies and Clubs, we almost received the same answers. Yes, silently and in the company of friends there was great clamoring about the treatment which our ethnic majority received. But nobody really wanted to stand in the limelight of approval and criticism and tell our side openly. Fortunately, lately we changed this attitude, and I report with pride that all the letters, etc., mentioned before, and our paid ads—yes, we had to pay for them—did suddenly arouse the interest of the nation, our ethnic compatriots, and the press.[53]

The campaign that Seewald alludes to included, for example, a letter to the editor of the *Arizona Republic*, applauding the president's trip to Bitburg as an effort toward reconciliation between the United States and Germany. The letter concluded that "vindictiveness and vengeance are elements foreign to the American way of thinking," an allusion, of course, to those who opposed Reagan's visit to Bitburg.[54] Seewald also wrote letters to the agencies that she felt had presented only the arguments against Reagan's visit to Bitburg. For example, she wrote on behalf of the German American National Congress to the chairman of the Federal Communications Corporation complaining that the television networks, namely CBS, NBC, ABC, as well as the National Public Radio Corporation are in violation of their licenses, because of their undue attention to only one section of the American society. Our organization has repeatedly asked for the opportunity to express our view in support of President Reagan's plans to visit the soldier's cemetery in Bitburg, Germany. Instead of bringing news objectively and representing total community opinion, they have concentrated on the opinion of only one small minority segment of the American population, namely the Jewish protesters. Please acknowledge our communication and provide us with information how this unacceptable situation can be remedied in the future."[55]

Published in *Der Deutsch-Amerikaner* and the *Steuben News* were also letters from other members of the German American community to the White House and, sometimes, the replies that they received. These included a reply from Vice President George H. W. Bush pledging to strengthen the ties between the United States and Germany while never forgetting the Holocaust; a letter from Dr. Marianne Bouvier, National vice president of the German American National Congress, to the president, and a response from Gail W. Ledwig, staff assistant to Michael Deaver, who apologized and explained that Deaver had asked her to write because he was in Europe; and a letter to the president from Gert Wegner, who identifies himself only as "a proud U.S. citizen of German origin," applauding the president's willingness to pay his respects to fallen German soldiers.[56] It is difficult to say at this point in time how much influence Seewald's campaign really had on the president's decision to go to Bitburg, but it is clear that the White House was aware of her views and the views of at least a few other German Americans.

As in the case of the national press, the German American societies concerned themselves with such political issues as the strength of the NATO alliance. The president's trip to Bitburg should be supported, they argued, because Germany was America's "strongest ally, both militarily and economically."[57] But the role that Germany plays in the military and financial arena is not appreciated, as criticism of Reagan's trip to Bitburg demonstrates. Staff writer Karl T. Marx explained on the front page of the *Steuben News* after Reagan's visit that "the West Germans try desperately to please the USA." According to Marx, they willingly assumed a subordinate role and allowed their country to be covered from one end to the other with American atomic missiles, which if placed anywhere else would not be effective against the Soviets. At the same time it is clear to Germans that if atomic war did start, the Federal Republic—because the Federal Republic houses these missiles—would be one of Russia's first targets, and the entirety of both Germanies would be turned into cemeteries. Nothing would please the "Russophiles" in the United States more than a neutral Germany that could easily be taken over by the Soviets. Compared to the risks taken by Germany because of U.S. missiles on German soil, Marx suggests, the potential risks to Reagan's presidency of a visit to Bitburg were minor. Moreover, while the national press had argued that Germany deserved the small compensation of a symbolic gesture such as the visit to Bitburg, Marx argued that the United States had better wake up to the threat from communists—among whom were those who opposed the visit to Bitburg.[58]

It was the moral argument, however, that occupied the German American press. In particular, the press argued the immorality of the position of those who opposed Reagan's visit, and the morality of the position of those who supported the president's decision. It was moral to forgive the Germans; it was immoral not to. While the German American press was very strongly in favor of the visit to Bitburg, they—like the national press—took the opportunity to express their opposition to other related matters.

German Americans, as was true of Bitburg supporters generally, recognized that chief among the objectives of the Reagan visit was Germany's reconciliation with its own past. Supporters seemed to think that the American president's symbolic act of forgiveness might somehow further that process of reconciliation between the forgiving and unforgiving portions of the German nation's psyche. But even if U.S. forgiveness had been generously forthcoming—as it was in other, dissimilar circumstances—the numbers and outrages of those who were victimized by Nazism were simply too stark for forgiveness, once one has decided that, for any reason, he or she is, if only by some awful fate, to blame. An affront to a person's character might be forgiven. But murder is more difficult to forgive, especially when it involves entire families, and virtually whole populations, and is of the more gruesome sort. Helmut Kohl understood this. In his remarks during the Bundestag debate on Reagan's visit to Bitburg, delivered April 25, 1985, Kohl explained:

> I do not venture to judge those who experience[d] all the horror and barbarity of the Third Reich at Auschwitz, Treblinka and Bergen-Belsen, who are unable to forget those occurrences, what they suffered and what their next of kin suffered, and who are unable to forgive.

Kohl did not want forgiveness from the Jews. Jews had nothing to do with it. He wanted forgiveness from a third party—not a neutral third party, but one that had lost soldiers, just as Germany had lost soldiers.

> The idea underlying our discussions and the visit was and continues to be that President Reagan, our friend, and I will jointly commemorate the victims of the war and pay reverence to the soldiers' graves. . . . If one looks around this chamber, one will discover many members on all benches

who lost their fathers, brothers or—in the case of older members—even their sons and who feel this noble gesture is directed towards them.

Kohl did not mention his own brother who had died on the front. Kohl wanted parity, he wanted to feel he was free to express his sorrow for his brother's death, just as others outside Germany who had a relative die in war were free to feel sorrow—that is, without the shame of thinking that his brother had died as an evil individual fighting against the forces of God. These passages from Kohl's speech were reported in the German American press. [59]

Like William F. Buckley, Jr., writing for the *National Review*, German American authors supported forgiveness of the Germans because, among other reasons, the Nazi persecution of their victims was no worse than any of the other many horrors perpetrated in the twentieth century by other peoples. "How many humans were slaughtered by Stalin," asks Karl T. Marx:

> [H]ow many by China's Mao, or by the killers during the French Revolution in the 18th century? How many were massacred in Cambodia by the communists, how many Armenians were killed by the Turks, how many communists were executed in Indonesia? How many Huguenots were slaughtered in 1572 in France? How many Swedes were murdered by Danes in 1520? How many women, children and aged died in brutal, British concentration camps during the imperialistic Boer War 1899–1902?[60]

And Marx's list goes on and on, his point being that relatively few of the perpetrator nations listed are still remembered exclusively for the atrocities they committed. President Reagan, said Marx, would certainly not be criticized were he to express condolences at a British cemetery that contained some of the soldiers who fought in the Boer War.

This type of argument that insists on the comparability of the Holocaust to other horrors that have taken place was being argued in Germany during the time of Reagan's visit to Bitburg. The discussion that took place among German academics has come to be called "The German Historians' Debate" (or the *Historikerstreit*), but the arguments were similar. For example, Ernst Nolte during the *Historikerstreit* had discussed the comparability of Stalin to Hitler, of Pol Pot of Cambodia to Hitler, of the massacre of the Armenians to the genocide of the Jews, among other comparisons.[61] In fact, the comparisons in the paragraph above were not the only such instances of comparison between the victims of the Holocaust and other victims to emerge during the Bitburg controversy, whose authors suggested either that the Nazis too were worthy of forgiveness, or that the victims should forgive their killers, or both. Comparisons arguing for forgiveness for the Holocaust began, insofar as the American version of the Bitburg controversy is concerned, with Reagan's comparison of the dead of Bergen-Belsen concentration camp and the dead buried in the Bitburg military cemetery. Both, according to Reagan, were victims.

Indeed, some German Americans argued, German soldiers of World War II were in fact victims of Nazism; the American president need have no compunction about visiting their graves. German Americans were apprised after the ceremonies, if not before, of the fact that Kohl, like Reagan, believed that the soldiers buried at Bitburg were victims. An article published in the *Steuben News* in September 1985 included a synopsis of West German President Richard von Weizsäcker's address to the Bundestag on May 8, 1985. According to the author of the synopsis, Kohl "seeks, in a sense, to revise history. He (as well as German TV) has pictured Germans under Hitler as victims of Allied bombings and the SS troopers buried at Bitburg as victims of the Nazis and the war."[62]

In addition, some German soldiers—and even some SS officers—were actually anti-Nazis or even heroes in the battle against Hitler and some saved Jewish lives. In a letter originally printed in the *New York Times* for April 25, 1985, and reprinted in the *Steuben News*, Sabina Lietzmann, correspondent for the *Frankfurter Allgemeine Zeitung*, made the point that her brother, who was killed in battle at age nineteen, was not a Nazi, and that her boyfriend, who died at Stalingrad, was an ardent anti-Nazi. In fact, says Lietzmann, "many a German who got into trouble with the Nazi Party sought refuge in the army, where he felt—and was—protected (a member of my family among them). It was common knowledge that the army offered a kind of underground escape route for the politically persecuted."[63] George Beichl, president of the German Society of Pennsylvania, reiterated the point made by Lietzmann that there were many among the German soldiers who were anti-Nazi. In fact, Beichl pointed out, "at least one SS man is memorialized in the Yad Vashem, the institution in Israel dedicated to the Holocaust."[64] It is worth noting that the article in which this comment appeared became probably the most well-published piece of the controversy. Apart from appearing in *Der Deutsch-Amerikaner*, it also appeared in the *Philadelphia Inquirer*, where it was first published, the *New Yorker Staats-Zeitung und Herold*, and twice in the *Philadelphia Gazette-Democrat*.[65]

But it was not just German soldiers who were victims of the Nazis. Equally apparent to German Americans was the fact that German civilians had also been victims of the Allies. Indeed, members of the U.S. Holocaust Memorial Council had made the point just two years earlier. As indicated in an earlier chapter, Elsbeth Seewald had written to President Reagan opposing the museum; and Seymour Siegel, executive director of the U.S. Holocaust Memorial Council, responded by pointing out that "Germany was touched by the tragedies of World War II and is still suffering the experiences of division and political partition." In addition, Siegel's letter had been published for German Americans to see in *Der Deutsch-Amerikaner*.[66] From the point of view of some German Americans, the victimization of Germans compensated for the victimization of other peoples by the Nazis and therefore forgiveness was in order. Karl T. Marx in his column for the *Steuben News* explained how,

> according to the (Bonn) Bundesministerium fuer Vertrie-bene (Office for Expellees)[,] the victorious powers forced 11,730,000 German ethnics to give up their ancient homes, farms, factories, offices, etc., to Slavic Settlers, without any compensation whatever. All they could take with them was a suitcase. From 1945 to 1950, 2,111,000 German ethnics were killed or died from exhaustion before or during their brutal trek into burned-out Germany.[67]

Marx argued that, in fact, the president should not only go to Bitburg to mourn for the German war dead, he should also go to Dresden to do penance for the deaths of thousands of Germans by American bombers. Marx explains:

> I had suggested to our President that he visit Dresden and there do penance for a vicious, allied crime against Europe's most beautiful city, totally undefended, and filled with refu-gees from the advancing Russians. There was not one anti-aircraft gun in place when the Holocaust from the air start-ed and caused—within a matter of two days and incessant bombings and strafings—the massacre by mostly fire-bombs of about 300,000 German civilians.[68]

It was not only the Germans who needed to be reconciled with their actions during the war; it was also the Americans who need-ed to be reconciled. They needed forgiveness for their crimes as the Germans did for theirs. Forgiveness of the Germans by the Ameri-cans would take place at Bitburg, and forgiveness of the Ameri-cans by the Germans could take place at Dresden.

The support in the national press for President Reagan's trip to

Bitburg, while it appears to have been relatively minor compared to the unanimous support that his trip received in the German American newspapers examined here, was similar insofar as some of the arguments were concerned. With regard to relations between Germany and the United States, supporters in the national press argued that Kohl deserved this visit from Reagan because he had been slighted at the Normandy invasion ceremonies and because he had convinced Germans to accept U.S. missiles. Also, it wouldn't look good if he bowed to Jewish and veterans' pressure groups. Arguments in *Der Deutsch-Amerikaner* and the *Steuben News* also pointed to the fact that Germany had been a very good ally to the United States, but some writers were more critical of the president's people for even considering canceling Reagan's visit. Their view was that the hardships and dangers that Germany faced because it had accepted the U.S. missiles were not appreciated. Also, like the national press, the German American newspapers here expressed their concern about the pressure groups attempting to exert their influence on the president. But the concern expressed in the German American newspapers was not for the president's image as a strong or weak leader.

So too, on the moral issue, the issue of forgiveness, the arguments made by supporters in the national press were by and large similar to those made in the two German American newspapers. Examples were arguments that forgiveness was appropriate since other people who had perpetrated similar horrors were no longer identified as villains, and it was necessary to prevent further instances of Holocaust denial. To the argument that no forgiveness was possible for the vicious SS troopers, supporters argued that the president would not be mourning the SS, only other soldiers; and that God's mercy extended to all mankind, including the SS. Some writers for the German American papers also argued that it was not the intention of the president to go to Bitburg to mourn the SS, while other writers argued that some SS officers had been heroes and were memorialized at Yad Vashem, and therefore the president could go ahead and mourn for all the dead at Bitburg. Writers for the German American papers argued, just as the national press had argued, that forgiveness on the part of the victims was appropriate since others had also suffered equal horrors. But writers for the German American papers also argued that forgiveness was appropriate because the German people themselves had been victims, and indeed German soldiers had been victims as well. The one point that had not been considered by the German American writers—a key point made in the national press—is that accusations of guilt contributed to denial of the Holocaust.

Hostility and Antisemitism in the German American Press

German American writers differed from those writing for the national press in that the antisemites among them were more likely to reveal their biases. Disconcerting, for example, was the portrait of Jews presented by members of these German American organizations during the Bitburg controversy. The national press had not failed to criticize Jews for opposing the president's trip to Bitburg, suggesting, for example, that Jews—two-thirds of whom voted for Walter Mondale—were only interested in discrediting Ronald Reagan and the Republican Party, and therefore had unfairly attacked him as being insensitive to their dead. But the German American organizations went considerably further and attacked Jewish opponents of the Bitburg visit as vengeful. As indicated at the beginning of this section, Seewald in an open telegram to the president accused Jews of trying to psychologically murder Germans in order to avenge themselves for the murder of their relatives. Seewald would later repeat that charge in her address to the Milwaukee chapter on its twenty-fifth anniversary. "Our Jewish fellow men," she said, have since Reagan's visit "shifted to a less confrontational approach." But even so, complained Seewald, why do we "get the impression, even if they say they only oppose 'Nazis' that somehow we, the people of German origin are meant? There is no way that the past can ever be repeated. But there is no way either to avenge by slowly killing Germans and their progeny through loud clamors and protests such as have happened recently."[69]

Karl T. Marx had leveled a similar charge. Jews, he explained, wanted to forever brand Germans as the murderers of the Jews, just as Jews had been branded the killers of Christ.

> What the Nazis did or allowed to be done is now used by the enemies of Germany everywhere to accuse all living and as yet unborn Germans of these enormous crimes against humanity. It is a repeat of the charges against Jews through the centuries for the execution of Christ by Roman soldiers, as demanded by certain fanatical high priests to whom Pontius Pilate, the Roman governor, had to listen.[70]

Instead of the Jews, it is the Germans who are being charged with murder; and instead of being charged with the murder of Christ, Germans are being charged with the murder of Jews. The culprits, however, are the same: "certain fanatical high priests" of Israel, to whom the secular authorities "had to listen."

But the charges of Marx and Seewald were only the tip of the iceberg. There were also the threats. Edward Rubel, who signed his comments as a "Member of the Board of Captive Nations, Inc.," warned that everyone should "let the President himself conduct the diplomacy of the United States." Bitburg was no matter for Jews to be meddling with. "Forces behind today's U.S. 'elite people' hate campaigns are playing with fire."[71] Marx was also one who felt that someday Jews would go too far. Marx wrote, "[L]et us be sure those who keep on producing crisis after crisis are made aware some day that there is a limit to their outbursts and arrogance."[72] It was never clear what was being threatened. However, it was clear enough that the Jews would be the target.

Disconcerting also was the letter to the editor that appeared in the June 1985 issue of *Der Deutsch-Amerikaner*, ostensibly in response to a letter written in an earlier issue, suggesting that the real story of what happened during the war could be found in certain books available from the Institute for Historical Review, and of course the address was provided. The Institute for Historical Review, based in California, is the leading source in the United States for dissemination of antisemitic and denial propaganda.[73] The article was signed only "G.T."[74] It is not clear whether the letter was published at the instigation of the Institute for Historical Review or at the invitation of the German American National Congress. However, it seems to me unlikely that the letter was from a random individual. As indicated in an earlier chapter, a similar letter had appeared when the United States Holocaust Memorial Museum was an issue. Moreover, another similar letter had appeared even earlier in the *Steuben News* after some controversy involving the release of *Playing for Time*, a film thought to be anti-German.[75] A pattern existed. Controversy over Holocaust-related matters was simply too good an opportunity for Holocaust deniers to pass up in their efforts to recruit new adherents. Moreover, the May and June 1985 issues of *Der Deutsch-Amerikaner* should sufficiently have enraged readers to action—at least to pulling out a pen and postcard and writing for more information about what "truly happened" during the "so-called Holocaust."

Then too there were the hints of actual Holocaust denial, the statements in *Der Deutsch-Amerikaner* itself regretting the fact that German politicians had admitted to much more responsibility for the Holocaust than they needed to. German statesmen had "acknowledged probably far greater responsibility for the happening of the past than an accurate account of history might support," complained one editorial writer.[76] Among those who seemed to be flirting in a more obvious way with Holocaust denial was, once again, the president of the German American National Congress, Elsbeth Seewald. In September 1985, Seewald wrote an article, published in *Der Deutsch-Amerikaner*, about the nuclear bombing of Hiroshima by the Americans. She signed the article, and then a note—which appeared to be part of the same piece— appeared about J. Robert Oppenheimer, the American physicist who led the team that developed the nuclear bomb. She states,

> ISN'T IT IRONIC! We always hear and are being told about—true or not—the Holocaust of World War II in Europe and Russia, [and that] Germans supposedly perpetrated it. Now here we have J. Robert Oppenheimer, a person of Jewish persuasion, who worked on [and] helped create the basis for the biggest Holocaust ever foisted on mankind.[77]

This piece by Seewald was the lead story on page one. The reader was invited by Seewald to question whether the Holocaust was "true or not." Germans only "supposedly perpetrated it." It is to the credit of the editors of *Der Deutsch-Amerikaner*, however, that they subsequently published a letter to the editor, not denouncing Seewald, but whoever it was who wrote the "Additional Notes" to the article. The author of the denunciation, Hampton J. Rector, explained that "some people need to stop fooling themselves. The Holocaust did occur, Nazi Germany perpetrated it, and it obliterated more than six million Jews." Hampton went on to state that "millions of Americans of German ancestry are currently awakening to their proud heritage. Those who, from guilt, ignorance, or bigotry, seek to foster renewed antisemitism or to fumigate the Nazi era, do us no favor."

After the president's visit and all the furor it had created had died down, an editorial in the *Steuben News* for July–August 1985 reported that it was time for President Reagan to celebrate "another 40th anniversary," the end of the war with Japan. The Japanese, like the Germans, are former enemies, and had become one of the most prosperous nations in the world and a major trading partner with the United States. The president announced that he had no plans to commemorate Victory in Japan Day (V-J Day) with the Japanese.[78] With one Bitburg behind him, the president was in no mood for another.

Efforts at Reconciliation

On the same page as the above-mentioned editorial about V-J Day, an article titled "Mayor Koch Holds 'Open House' for German Americans" appeared. Koch, who is Jewish, had invited several hundred German Americans to tour Gracie Mansion on the eve of mayoral elections. As the article explained, Koch "welcomed Americans of German ancestry, noting that they are the largest ethnic group in the nation and were here from the beginning." The message had gotten through. The article continued, "Koch said he marches every year in the Steuben Parade and some day perhaps will don his lederhosen to show his affection for the culture."[79]

In his essay, "Bitburg as Symbol," Raul Hilberg spoke of the public debate over Reagan's visit to Bitburg and explained how it presented in simple visible cues that anyone could understand "the deepest psychological conflict between Germans and Jews."[80] Hilberg might have said "between German Americans and Jewish Americans" had he known what was happening in the German American community. But German American views were not publicized in national magazines or journals. For Geoffrey Hartman, as for many others, President Reagan was the antagonist. The president had made American Jews feel "vulnerable," said Hartman, no longer "in control."

In the April 1987 issue of the *Steuben News* appeared another of Karl T. Marx's Random Thoughts columns, "Recognition for

Victims of German Resistance." Marx's story started, "[I]t all began during that (in)famous Bitburg agitation . . . ." Marx was referring to the White Rose Foundation created in the U.S. Senate by the lobbying efforts of the American Jewish Committee. The purpose of the foundation is "to honor the victims of the German resistance movement, especially Hans and Sophie Scholl, who in 1943 were beheaded for having distributed anti-war leaflets." The bill creating the foundation was sponsored by among others, Senators Robert Dole (Republican) and Joe Biden (Democrat). Marx's story concluded, "Every man or woman of good will has reason to welcome this first attempt by Jews and Germans to overcome the frightful image that has been fostered until now."[81]

The self-portrait that German Americans drew of themselves vis-à-vis Bitburg was that of an embattled ethnic group, fighting for their image as a peaceable people who were not Nazis and not belligerents. But on the other hand, they would not be victims, not even at the hands of the former victims of Nazism. Anti-Germanism had turned them into a silent ethnic majority, but they refused to be silent any longer. The tone of their writings, when compared for instance with those who supported the Bitburg visit in the national press, is more defensive, indeed aggressive, and at several junctures threatening. Jews and communists were—to certain people at certain times—the enemy. Bitburg was the first victorious battle that German Americans had fought, at least in modern times. Of course, one must ask whether extensive anti-German sentiment in reality existed. Were Jews intentionally out to psychologically murder Germans by insisting that the president not mourn for German soldiers, especially SS troopers? One can categorically state that was not the case. To Jews, the German soldiers and especially the SS represented the killers, the people who had wantonly murdered their relatives. They found the thought of the president paying his respects to these killers repugnant and morally offensive. The other question that one must ask is how extensive among German Americans was antisemitism or the fear of anti-Germanism expressed here? In all likelihood, neither antisemitism nor the fear of anti-Germanism was very extensive at all. We are speaking here of a very small group. The two major organizations of German Americans consisted of, it bears repeating, no more than about thirteen thousand out of a total population of fifty million who either considered themselves entirely of German ancestry or who regarded themselves as at least part German American. Nonetheless it is worth noting that both groups—German Americans and Jewish Americans, including those who opposed and those who supported the president—presented views that could be understood and should be understood. Both groups declared themselves representative and indeed were thought to be so, and so wielded significant political power. One would think that a compromise might have been developed, but it was not. One would think that the controversy could have been avoided, but it was not.

Five

Browning and Goldhagen—Man and Superman

Ordinary Germans or Ordinary Men?

The Issue

From virtually the time of Hitler's rise to power in 1933, the extent and nature of German victimization of Jews has been argued by relatives, descendants, and friends of both Germans and Jews in the United States. Perhaps the most important development in the evolving political struggle for interpretation of German responsibility was what came to be called by some "The Goldhagen Controversy." Daniel Jonah Goldhagen is an American Jew, trained at Harvard, and was assistant professor of government there when, in 1996, Alfred Knopf published his book, *Hitler's Willing Executioners: Ordinary Germans and the Holocaust*. As the title suggests, the book is about the German perpetrators of the Holocaust. Daniel Goldhagen's father is Erich Goldhagen, himself an emeritus faculty member at Harvard where he taught Holocaust history. Erich Goldhagen is also a Holocaust survivor, having lived through the Czernowitz ghetto in what was then Romania and now is the Ukraine. Daniel Goldhagen's book is dedicated to his father. It is not by any means a disinterested analysis of the perpetrators of the Holocaust. According to *Hitler's Willing Executioners*, virtually all Germans wanted the Jews dead and were pleased with the murders taking place. Virtually all Germans of the Nazi period are to be held accountable for the Holocaust. However, modern Germans are not the Germans of the Nazi past, and modern Germany is a model democratic republic.

Goldhagen's major critic—and he has many critics, as well as some allies—was Christopher Browning who taught at a Lutheran university on the West Coast when in 1992 he published *Ordinary Men: Reserve Police Battalion 101 and the Final Solution in Poland*, which is also about German perpetrators of the Holocaust. Browning's background is no more irrelevant than Goldhagen's here. I had the opportunity one afternoon during lunch at Northwestern University to explain to Browning my distressing experience teaching Holocaust literature for the first time to students, many of whom were of German descent. (I recount that same story of my early teaching experience at the beginning of this book.) I explained that these students insisted Jews themselves were responsible for the Holocaust, the Jews were thieves and natural victims and so on. These half-dozen or so German American students, for one reason or another, had expressed the view that the Jews deserved what they got. Browning then explained to me his experience teaching about the Holocaust to a class of Lutheran students at his university. He explained that the experience of guilt was so overwhelming for the Lutheran students that the university chaplain had to come to "hold the hands" of distraught students.[1] Browning's point, I think, was that the Holocaust is to this day as wrenching an experience for at least some Germans and Americans of German descent as it is for Jews in America and elsewhere.

Browning's book, which appeared before Goldhagen's, is often paired and contrasted with Goldhagen's. They confront the same issues—why did the Germans kill Jews or stand idly by as Jews were being killed? And however hard Browning might be trying to be objective and impartial, his is not a disinterested book either. Browning, as Goldhagen suggests but never quite comes out and says, ultimately turns out—intentionally or inadvertently—to be arguing for that view of the Holocaust which, without being deceitful in any way, makes the Holocaust more palatable to Germans and German Americans, and in particular the youth of both populations who still feel guilt for the sins of their fathers and grandfathers. Goldhagen's book, on the other hand, argues the view of the victims of the Holocaust; it insists on their right to the unmitigated truth about the individuals who inflicted upon them some of the worst horror that any people have ever endured. Both projects, Browning's and Goldhagen's, are, in their own way, noble endeavors. The question, of course, is how does one reconcile the two. Browning's book seemed to be stating that while the German criminals of the Holocaust must be held accountable for their crimes, their crimes were those that anyone in the same type of group situation would commit. This statement, of course, would have appealed to Germans and German Americans; but to some Jews, Goldhagen among them, this was not a satisfactory explanation. The suggestion that anyone under the same circumstances as the Germans during World War II would slaughter innocent Jewish children cheapens Jewish lives, and indeed could perpetuate antisemitism by defining the German attack on Jews not as a historically local evil but as an understandably enduring phenomenon.

Here, Christopher Browning, an individual with a sympathetic understanding of what the Holocaust might mean to German Americans, and Daniel Goldhagen, a Jewish American whose father was a Holocaust survivor, met head on. It is important to note, however, that not all Jews supported Goldhagen (in fact, most American Jews apparently did not) and not all Germans or

German Americans supported Browning. But Goldhagen also had an understanding of postwar Germany that was especially important because it provided a view of history since 1933 that many Germans and Jews could accept: the Germans of the Nazi era were indeed culpable, fully and irredeemably responsible for one of the worst crimes in Western history—this satisfied Jews—but modern Germans had entered a new era and had formed a model democratic republic. Their character had changed. Modern Germans too could be proud, despite what had earlier taken place. In order to understand Goldhagen's book and the controversy it stirred, as well as Goldhagen's solution, it is necessary to understand first Browning's book, which represented the state and direction of scholarship about the perpetrators that Goldhagen challenged. The story of Browning's book is the story of Police Battalion 101.

Police Battalion 101

In 1936, Heinrich Himmler was made chief of the German police and divided the police into two branches: the Security Police, led by Reinhard Heydrich and composed of the notorious Gestapo, as well as the Kripo (Criminal Police); and the Order Police, led by Kurt Daluege. The latter consisted of city, county, and rural policemen. Reserve Police Battalion 101 was a unit of the Order Police. It was formed in the mid-1940s when policemen numbered almost a quarter of a million. In June 1942, Police Battalion 101 was stationed in Hamburg and was ordered to cross the eastern border into Poland to take part in Operation Reinhard, the mass murder campaign against the two million Jews of the general government. The campaign was named for Reinhard Heydrich who had been assassinated by the Czech resistance. The role of Police Battalion 101 was fashioned in part by the lull at the Sobibor killing camp, which, like Auschwitz, Chelmno, Belzec, and Treblinka, was built for the enormous enterprise in mass murder undertaken by the Germans. Odilio Globocnik, chosen by Hitler to head Operation Reinhard, ordered Police Battalion 101 to consolidate the Jews in a single area for the purpose of later transporting them to their death. But by July 11, 1942, Globocnik had apparently grown impatient with the ordeal of collecting Jews, and on July 13, Police Battalion 101 was ordered into the town of Jozefow to kill the Jewish women, children, and elderly of the town. They were to spare only working-age men for relocation to the camps. By night-fall of the same day, some 1,500 of the 1,800 Jews of Jozefow had been murdered. By the end of November 1943, at the conclusion of its murderous participation in Germany's "festive harvest" of Jews in Poland's Lublin district, Reserve Police Battalion 101 had directly participated in the murder of at least 38,000 Jews and had sent an additional 45,000 to their death at Treblinka.[2]

The individuals who formed Reserve Police Battalion 101 were by and large average citizens, but not really typical of the individual one might imagine would take part in a massacre of innocents. In 1938 and 1939 when the war appeared to be not very far off, the Order Police in general attracted individuals who preferred to remain local rather than join the fighting that would take place at the front; however, considerable numbers were eventually ab-sorbed into the German army when war came,[3] and the battalions of the Order Police did play a major role in the German occupa-tion of conquered territories. In June 1942, when reserve Police Battalion 101 was called on to take part in what would soon be mass murders, the vast majority of the rank and file was com-prised of laborers from Hamburg. Many drove trucks for a living or worked on the docks; some worked in construction or in ware-houses, while others were waiters, machine operators, and sea-men. Thirty-five percent were lower middle class. Very few were white collar. Virtually none had any education beyond high school. They were by and large economically, socially, and geographically immobile. They were men who, perhaps more to the point, were considered too old for the army. More than half were between ages thirty-seven and forty-two; the average age of the group was thirty-nine. Reserve Police Battalion 101 consisted of Germans who clearly were not the type of combat material that one would assume had it in them to shoot women and children at close range. They were not by and large toughened, professional soldiers. What is remarkable about these individuals in Reserve Police Battalion 101 is that most of the 500 or so policemen who comprised the Battalion chose to massacre Jews at close range when they were given the opportunity to step out of line and *not* participate in the mass slaughter.

The subject of the debate between Christopher Browning and Daniel Goldhagen is why policemen killed innocent women and children when they were given the option of not doing it. Browning maintained that the factors which motivated these policemen to kill innocent Jews were external and situational: the desire not to appear a coward among one's fellow policemen, for example, or the desire for advancement in the police ranks, perhaps. Goldhagen's view was that the motivation behind the killing—not just the killing that Police Battalion 101 took part in, but all of the murdering of Jews that took place during the Holocaust—was ideology: an especially hardened form of antisemitism that ruled the German heart and mind. What was motivating the murderers was not, as Browning supposed, the external situation, but rather an internal condition. In Goldhagen's view, there were no situational circumstances that might be construed as extenuating. The German murderers were guilty of a criminal act.

Both Browning and Goldhagen considered the opposing view. Browning considered the possibility that antisemitic propaganda or indoctrination might have played a role in the minds of the shooters, but after investigation dismissed the idea as unlikely.[4] So too, Goldhagen considered the extent to which circumstances and situation might have influenced the individuals doing the killing, and concluded that the dominant motive was antisemitism.

Christopher Browning and the Shooters of Police Battalion 101

The title of Christopher Browning's book, *Ordinary Men: Reserve Police Battalion 101 and the Final Solution in Poland*, first published in 1992, reminds one of the title of Hannah Arendt's book, *The Banality of Evil*. Both titles seem to suggest something "ordinary," indeed "banal," about the murderers who were responsible for the five to six million Jewish dead that we today call the Jewish Holocaust. Oddly enough, it is probably not the ordinariness of the Germans who did the murdering that is the major contribution of Browning's book. Many would probably agree that the book's major contribution was the recognition that many of the murderers were not compelled by fear of punishment or disciplinary action to shoot innocent people. Other scholars had made the same point, but Browning's book made the point emphatically and was popularly recognized for having done so.

That the Germans who committed mass murder were not really forced under threat of execution to murder Jews was a concept that Goldhagen had explored before Browning's book appeared in print. In fact, Goldhagen had written an article in 1985 addressing the matter, and using *Einsatzgruppen* (mobile killing units that operated behind the Nazi Eastern Front) as examples of individuals who did not have to shoot Jews. These individuals could transfer out of a killing unit without fear of retribution by claiming that they were unfit to kill.[5] Goldhagen explained that the majority of men in the *Einsatzgruppen* who followed behind the German advance against the Soviet Union were not SS troopers, but were instead "regular policemen," and that these "regular policemen" killed Jews without threat of punishment. Goldhagen focused specifically on the case of one Martin Mundschutz, who obtained a transfer from Colonel Otto Ohlendorf, commander of Ein-satzgruppe D, because he claimed to be psychologically unfit for killing Jews. After an interview with Colonel Ohlendorf, a letter from Gustav Nosske, the leader of Einsatzkommando 12 in which Mundschutz was housed, and a letter from Mundschutz himself pleading to be transferred because of nightmares and hallucina-tions concerning the killing he had committed, Mundschutz was transferred to the rear by Colonel Ohlendorf and recommended for treatment in a sanatorium for the mentally ill in Munich.

Browning does not appear to have known about Goldhagen's article when he published *Ordinary Men*, the book that brought home to an English-speaking population of interested scholars the point that German soldiers or policemen were not liable to any punishment for refusing to kill Jews. And the point that Germans willingly killed Jews came as something of a revelation to an American population that remembered films such as Alain Resnais's *Night and Fog*, which presented the chief Nazi defense of their killing as "we were following orders," the subtext of which was that there were severe consequences for them if they did not kill their victims. Browning's book made plain that at least some of the murderers did not have to follow orders, but did anyway.

Browning had discovered at the Central Agency for the State Administration of Justice in the town of Ludwigsburg near Stutt-gart a cache of documents detailing the investigation and prosecu-tion of Reserve Police Battalion 101. What was remarkable about this find is that, unlike Goldhagen's source, it contained enough detailed testimony from a sizeable sampling of the Battalion po-licemen to begin to ask such questions as why and under what circumstances these individuals killed their victims.[6] By Brown-ing's estimate, 80 percent of the murderers in Reserve Police Bat-talion 101 killed despite the fact that there appears to have been no grave punishment for not killing. There were a number of rea-sons why they might have committed the murders, explains Browning. For example, there was the threat of ostracism by the other members of the Battalion and, if the individual was a career policeman, there might be considerable damage done to one's professional future. But the policeman was not threatened with execution, nor was he physically abused for expressing his wish not to shoot. And it appears that his wish not to shoot the innocent was often granted. Moreover, Browning provides us with explanations for why some policemen killed innocent women and children and others did not.

The title of Browning's book does indicate, however, that the focus is on the "ordinariness" of those individuals who in fact did kill innocent women and children. That Reserve Police Battalion 101 was in fact comprised of what one might consider "ordinary" Germans, in the sense that it consisted of individuals who for one reason or another were not suitable for the Wehrmacht—individuals too old or infirm, for example, for the regular army—appeared to have been the case. Moreover, about 25 percent of Police Battalion 101 (43 out of a sample of 174) were members of the Nazi party. These policemen were not primarily Nazis (or members of the generally more ideologically committed SS), but by and large were ordinary Germans who went about the process of murdering 38,000 innocent, unarmed people. But the idea that somehow these killers in Police Battalion 101 were distinctively "ordinary Germans" is not the conclusion that Browning would have us come to. It is in fact this conclusion that Browning argues so strenuously against in his book. Browning argues that these individuals were "ordinary men." The last thing that Browning wants to suggest is that ordinary Germans were distinguished by their murderous inclinations. He avoids that conclusion by arguing that these ordinary Germans were part of the larger, more inclusive category, "ordinary men." Any ordinary man would have murdered innocent people under similar circumstances. And it is here, I would argue, that Browning's reasoning is not very convincing.

In effect, Browning's book emerges as an unsatisfying effort to explain that these killers did nothing in murdering unarmed men, women, and children that other ordinary individuals would not have done. Under the same circumstances, says Browning, he himself could have been a killer, as well as one who avoided killing.[7] He suggests that there are forces external to the human being— forces of community and culture—that can be sufficiently threatening to the human being to prevent him from exercising those better instincts that value the rights of others to life. The argument is not that base instincts triumphed over the strong sense of humanity and the sanctity of life that would normally prevail. Browning's argument appears to be that, in the absence of the conscientious attention of an individual to his baser instincts or instinctual inhumanity (i.e., in humanity's normal and ordinary state), his conscience or sense of right and wrong is so weak that he is easily coerced by external forces to murder weaker individuals. The members of Police Battalion 101 who murdered innocent men, women, and infants were doing no more than others would have done under similar circumstances.

Browning's presentation does not justify the deeds of the murderers or attempt to whitewash German history, as did, for example, some of Ernst Nolte's writings during the German Historians' Debate. But Browning does in fact present these murderers in a more palatable light than they would otherwise appear. After all, if you or I or Browning might have shot children and infants under similar circumstances, can we really condemn these Germans for having killed children and infants? Are these murderers, because they are just ordinary men behaving as you or I would, any more criminal than you or I? Browning is very much aware of the possibility that his book might be understood as an effort to absolve the German murderers, and in several instances he insists that there can be no absolution for them. But anyone paying attention to the material Browning chooses to include in his book, anyone who is conscious of the impact that the material has on a reader would have to conclude that, at the very least, Browning is conflicted about the matter of whether these Germans should be absolved of their crimes. Even when he tells us they are not to be absolved, Browning's treatment of the murderers in certain crucial instances in his book turns out to be sympathetic toward their situation. Has Browning explained these crimes or, whether intentional or not, condoned them?

Browning's Fairhandedness

It is also true, however, that before Browning published *Ordinary Men*, Browning's writings had taken to task scholars who tried to whitewash what the German perpetrators had done. In 1987, for example, Browning published a review of H. W. Koch's collection of essays, *Aspects of the Third Reich*, in which Browning roundly condemns Ernst Nolte's contribution to the collection, as well as those by Koch himself, which present an apologetic view of the Nazis. Nolte's writings and their role in the German Historians' Debate have already been briefly discussed. Nolte's article in Koch's collection, as Browning points out, blames Hitler's treatment of Jews on Chaim Weizmann's declaration that Jews would fight on the side of Britain.[8] In like manner, Koch's own two articles in the collection, as well as his introductions to each of the five sections of the collection, tend to be exculpatory in their treatment of Hitler's crimes and tend to blame the Jews for the horrors that were committed against them. Speaking, for example, of Koch's analysis of Hitler's assumption of power, in which Koch argues that Hitler's abolition of political parties in Germany was not illegal because the party system was not grounded in the constitution, Browning states that "the tone turns nauseatingly apologetic in Koch's attempt to cleanse the events of the following months of any taint of illegality."[9] Browning was very clearly sensitive to the efforts that had taken place during the *Historikerstreit* to make the Holocaust appear as something less than the criminal horror that it was and thereby to exonerate the German perpetrators of their crimes. One cannot therefore simply suggest, as one might otherwise, that Browning's sympathies are with the German perpetrators or their descendants who live with the Nazi past, and that he has no understanding of what the relatives and descendants of the victims experience. Instead, one must recognize that Browning, insofar as he was able, in all likelihood tried to render the history as honestly as he possibly could.

In fact, Browning's book, in many instances, provides a damning portrait of the killers. He explains that he condemns the killings while at the same time trying to understand the killers. Browning describes, for example, the deterioration of Lieutenant Hartwig Gnade, commander of the Second Company of Police Battalion 101, from an ordinary individual to a merciless murderer. Gnade had been a forwarding agent as a civilian and he was a member of the Nazi party since 1937. He was the oldest of the reservists in Battalion 101 selected to receive officer training. He would have been forty-six in 1942 when he participated in his first action, the massacre at Jozefow where 1,500 Jews were murdered. Gnade was not a career soldier. In fall 1941 he led a party of men escorting German Jews to Minsk where Gnade learned that the Jews would probably be shot by members of a regular German police battalion which had earlier murdered Jews. Gnade decided not to stay the night in Minsk; instead he and his men caught a late train back to his station. By July, Lieutenant Gnade was by all appearances less squeamish. His Second Company participated directly in the Jozefow massacre, shooting the Jews in an unpracticed fashion so that the shots to the head often caused brains and bits of bone to spray in all directions and bespatter the killers. By August 1942, when Second Company was given the assignment of murdering some 1,700 Jews in the town of Lomazy, Gnade had become a straightforward sadist. Not content with watching Jews being murdered, he personally picked out twenty-five of the elderly, had them undress, and made them crawl on their bellies while being beaten vigorously by policemen with clubs.[10] Only then were the victims murdered.

Browning's discussion of Gnade's deterioration as a human being is forthright. We witness degeneration—a degeneration that suggests in fact that ordinary men could turn into murderous shooters. One might stop for a moment and wonder whether Gnade's degeneration isn't intended as evidence of the manner in which war affects all men and so it is another argument for the situational factors that contribute to the making of a murderer, but there is nothing in Browning's presentation of the circumstances that would arouse any sympathy for Gnade or convince the reader that Gnade's wartime experience somehow turned him into a beast. We do not hear of any harm to him or his loved ones, for example, that might have produced the kind of hatred and desire for revenge that would "explain" Gnade's deterioration. There are no mitigating circumstances to justify Gnade's cruelty at the end. We are given the facts and they are damning.

There are clearly instances, however, in which Browning is sympathetic to the dilemmas that some of the members of Police Battalion 101 appear to have confronted at the prospect of killing. Browning speaks of Captain Hoffman, commander of the battalion's Third Company, who saw no action while he served under Major Trapp. Hoffman was almost always ill whenever an action was scheduled to take place, and therefore unable to take part in person. It is not clear whether Hoffman suffered from an irritable colon, as his doctors supposed, had no stomach for killing innocent Jews, or both. However, when he was relieved of his company command for unsatisfactory behavior, he was transferred to Russia where he distinguished himself. Browning speaks of him as conflicted, as the "bedridden Captain Hoffman, whose body rebelled against the terrible deeds his mind willed."[11] Hoffman certainly doesn't sound like a killer. But the fact that he might not have been a willing murderer does not absolve him, says Browning. On the other hand, the portrait of Hoffman does skew the larger picture a bit. Captain Hoffman, after all, did not always disobey the orders to kill Jews that Major Trapp gave. He did in fact lead his men into battle to murder innocent civilians in Poland.

Nature versus Nurture

One of the questions that Browning suggests resides beneath the assertion that all men are capable of the same murder is that of "nature or nurture." If only a particular group of individuals—Germans in the case of the Holocaust—is genocidal, then it is nature, an antisemitic predisposition brought about perhaps by centuries of antisemitic propaganda, that is the deciding factor in the murders that took place. If anyone is capable of brutal murder, then it is a matter of circumstance (a type of nurture, perhaps short term) that brings alive this latent tendency in all men and produces killers. Browning's title for chapter 18, "Ordinary Men," is entirely given over to discussion of this question of nature versus nurture. Were the Germans the product of a genetic devolution that had created a pool of individuals with a killer's will? Or were their actions a result of the environment—circumstances that combined to turn average people into murderers? Browning, as might be anticipated, dwells on the way in which the environment can provide the circumstances under which any ordinary individual might commit murder.

Browning does take into consideration the possibility that "brainwashing"—ongoing, German antisemitic propaganda—might have played a role in turning the men of Police Battalion 101 into murderers; but this consideration, as one would expect, extends only as far back as the beginning of the Nazi regime.[12] It is not Browning's intention in this discussion to consider the manner in which centuries of German New Testament antisemitism and its charges of Jewish deicide might have produced a predisposition to murder Jews, or might have made such a predisposition "second nature." Browning is entirely concerned here with the manner in which nurture, the short-term situation and circumstances of the killings, motivated the shooters of Police Battalion 101. And his conclusion insofar as antisemitic propaganda is concerned is that the Nazi effort failed to prepare the shooters to murder Jews. I emphasize this point because it is sometimes suggested that Browning considers antisemitism a major motivating force behind the murders.[13] He does not really take up the matter in *Ordinary Men*.

Browning is impressed with John Dower's study of the battlefield, *War without Mercy: Race and Power in the Pacific*, and Stanley Milgram's infamous psychological study of obedience in an academic setting where a subject's willingness to inflict pain is tested. And while these are interesting and, in their own way, important studies, Browning only briefly mentions that these studies do not discuss circumstances similar to those of the Holocaust and that they do not prove Browning's view that peer pressure was the major consideration of these killers. Instead, Browning discusses these studies in laudatory terms and presents them as if they in a significant way added credence to his argument that all individuals, in general, have within them the latent ability to murder innocent people. It is therefore important to present Browning's reading of these books.

John Dower's study of the Pacific theater explains that all too often the mass carnage and the frenzy of war in itself will turn civilized men into murderous savages. Browning goes on to comment, however, that such was obviously not the case of Reserve Police Battalion 101, which did not see "action" until it started its methodical mass murder of unarmed civilians. Of course, the reader might well ask why Dower's study is being presented and discussed if it does not in any way explain the actions of Police Battalion 101. For one thing, it is suggestive; it presents the reader with a series of horrors such as the My Lai massacre that the reader can and, one might argue, typically will, compare with the Holocaust, even if no real basis for comparison exists. The reader's sense of the horror of the Holocaust is mitigated by the proximity of horrors like My Lai in Browning's pages, even if they are presented and identified as not really relevant by Browning. The horror of the Holocaust is undermined and perhaps the horror of My Lai as well. Of course, there is no way of knowing except from Browning himself what exactly he intended by introducing Dower's book, but the effect is compromising. The Holocaust is relativized.

Browning presents the Philip G. Zimbardo study at Stanford University in which ordinary individuals were divided up into guards and prisoners, and the guards became increasingly more brutal in their efforts to control the far larger number of inmates. Browning suggests that the Zimbardo study interestingly parallels his own data about Police Battalion 101. Browning points out that one-third of the guards displayed sadistic tendencies; most simply followed the rules and regulations governing constraint; and about 20 percent displayed some leniency and kindness to the prisoners. Similarly, says Browning, about twenty percent of Reserve Police Battalion 101 refused to kill or avoided killing, while the Battalion consisted of two larger groups of increasingly zealous shooters and individuals who followed orders but displayed no particular appetite for murder. There is obviously no basis for comparison between the Zimbardo study and the behavior of Reserve Police Battalion 101, except for the 20-percent figure itself; and as explained below, that figure is in itself suspect. Zimbardo produced a study in which individuals were play acting at being guards and prisoners. To some extent, such playacting might have been relevant for discussion of the situation that existed at certain concentration camps. But these "play" guards were not called upon to shoot individuals as were the policemen of Reserve Battalion 101. Why does Browning present the reader with this study?

Somewhat more relevant is the Milgram study, which has been refuted as flawed and unethical,[14] but still maintains its place on a shelf of specimens of like historical value, largely because of the controversy in ethics that the study generated concerning the use of human subjects. Milgram's study, one will recall, consisted of experimental subjects selected at random who functioned as "teachers," asking "learners," who were actually actors, to remember certain word pairings, and administering fake electrical shock to these pretend "learners" when they did not answer correctly. The randomly selected subjects/teachers did not realize they were actually the subjects of the study when they administered shocks to the learners, or that the "learners" were only actors and were not really experiencing pain when the subject/teacher, administered the shock. There was also an authority figure present, the "experimenter," who was also an actor whose role was to coax the subject/teacher to administer ever greater levels of electrical shock when the learner/actor gave an incorrect answer. The experiment was designed to determine the extent to which an individual was willing to inflict pain when coaxed to do so by an authority figure, in this case the "experimenter"/actor who typically stood at the side of the subject/teacher egging him on to inflict increasingly higher and more painful doses of electrical shock. The subject/teacher thought the shocks were being administered for the greater scientific good. After all, it was all taking place at Yale University. One can imagine the subject thinking that the experimenter must believe the electric shocks would somehow strengthen the learner's memory. The experimenter was instructed to tell the actor/learner in the hearing of the teacher/subject, that while the pain might increase, there would be no permanent tissue damage. Nonetheless, while the learner/actor pretended to experience ever greater pain as he answered the subject/teacher's questions incorrectly, the subject/teacher genuinely experienced ever greater levels of anxiety as he was encouraged by the experimenter to inflict what he thought were genuine electrical shocks. While Milgram himself suggested that there might be findings in his work that are relevant for understanding the perpetrators of the Holocaust, one of the chief problems with that correlation is, of course, that there is a significant difference between individuals administering shocks that they are told are non-lethal in the academic setting in which the Milgram experiments took place and individuals shooting people and brains splattering on them in the killing fields of Jozefow.

In *The Anatomy of Human Destruction*, Erich Fromm takes issue with the suggestion that the Milgram experiments might somehow translate from the laboratory to the German camps or mass murders. Fromm is very explicit. He states the following:

> I do not think this experiment permits any conclusion with regard to most situations in real life. The psychologist [experimenter] was not only an authority to whom one owes obedience, but a representative of *Science* at one of the most prestigious institutions of higher education in the United States. Considering that science is widely regarded as having the highest value in contemporary industrial society, it is very difficult for the average person to believe that what science commands could be wrong or immoral.

Apart from the criticism of Milgram's conclusions, many also criticized his ethics. Encouraging subjects to commit acts that they had every reason to believe were sadistic might well take its toll on the subjects themselves. As Milgram himself explains in his original 1963 publication,

> In a large number of cases the degree of tension [experienced by the subjects/teachers] reached extremes that are rarely seen in sociopsychological laboratory studies. Subjects were observed to sweat, tremble, stutter, bite their lips, groan, and dig their fingernails into their flesh. These were characteristic rather than exceptional responses to the experiment. . . . On one occasion we observed a seizure so violently convulsive that it was necessary to call a halt to the experiment. . . .[15]

It is no wonder that the ethics of the Milgram study have been questioned. Indeed, Milgram himself takes an almost sadistic pride in the state to which his subjects were reduced by the dilemma into which he thrust them. In fact, the major contribution of the Milgram obedience experiments are sometimes thought to be the new era of concern for the well-being of the experimental subjects stimulated by Milgram's mistreatment of his subjects in the course of his obedience experiments and, of course, the criticism of those experiments by others who study authority such as psychologist Diana Baumrind.

Again, it is not really clear why Browning brings up the Milgram study at all, since he rejects the suggestion that "authority" was the significant reason that members of Police Battalion 101 murdered people, and the Milgram study is about nothing other than authority. The obedience experiments do not really support the view that the men of Reserve Police Battalion 101 were "ordinary" men since, according to Browning, obedience to "authority" was not really the reason for the murderous actions of the policemen. In fact, according to Browning, the situation of Reserve Police Battalion 101 revealed that not authority but conformity was a key determinant of their killing. As Browning explains, the response of the policemen to conformity instead of authority was the opposite of what Milgram's experiments would predict. In Browning's words,

Milgram himself notes that people far more frequently invoke authority than conformity to explain their behavior, for only the former seems to absolve them of personal responsibility. "Subjects deny conformity and embrace obedience as the explanation of their actions." Yet many policemen [of Reserve Police Battalion 101] admitted responding to the pressures of conformity—how would they be seen in the eyes of their comrades?—not authority.[16]

Milgram's obedience experiments focus on the role of authority in encouraging punishing behavior. According to Browning, "conformity" to the attitudes and views of the system they were caught up in played the largest role in the willingness of the men of the Police Battalion 101 to kill. However, presentation of the Milgram experiment in positive terms, as well as Milgram's premise that the murderous conduct of Holocaust perpetrators has its roots in the authority figure that virtually all people to some extent will obey, in itself lends persuasive force to Browning's premise that the men of Police Battalion 101 were only doing what "ordinary men" would do when they point-blank murdered 38,000 Jews. Even if Milgram is brought up only to be lightly dismissed—and Milgram is by no means dismissed, as Browning does find correlations between some of Milgram's findings and the actions of Police Battalion 101—still the emphasis given the Milgram experiments provides the experiments with a credibility and applicability that support Browning's thesis that "ordinary men" committed the murders at Jozefow. And of course Milgram also provides Browning with a jumping-off point for reasserting his own views that conformity was the key motivating factor behind the killing, a motivating factor that all men are subject to.

On the other hand, the arguments for "nature," the view that there is some distinguishing genetic component for a propensity to violence, is presented and its flaws demonstrated through use of a variety of authorities. The target that Browning produces is Theo-dore Adorno, particularly Adorno's view, also expressed by a number of other authors, that there is a set of characteristics that will define the type of personality that is fascist and prone to vio-lence.[17] Browning begins his argument by presenting the view of Zygmunt Bauman that Adorno is doing no more than "describ-ing" the personality, rather than searching for its origins. Brown-ing does not discuss the possibility that perhaps such a description of "violence traits" might be useful in early discovery and counsel-ing of violence-prone individuals. Instead he goes on to briefly present the modification to Adorno's theory made by John Steiner who proposed that there were individuals in whom the tendency to violence was latent and that these individuals selected them-selves for activities in which that violence could be expressed. Browning concludes with Ervin Staub's further modification of Steiner's proposal, who suggests that while violence might in fact be a latent trait, it exists in all people. Browning thereby brings the point of view of Adorno around to his own. There are traits that define the violence-prone individual, but they exist, if only in a latent state, in everyone. Environment (nurture) becomes the key factor since it triggers the latent propensity toward violence. It is not only the ordinary German who, under no threat to his physi-cal well-being or that of his family or friends, will murder innocent women and children. All men are capable of the same heinous crime, if only the circumstances are right.

Browning's Literary Technique

It is no secret that all historians betray a bias. However much there might appear to be an effort to present both sides of an argument, invariably a point of view comes across. That particular view might be revealed through a variety of devices. Although an au-thor might present both points of view, for example, he might devote more space to one than another, or he might present that other point of view simply to dismiss it. Another technique is to give one's own view the very last word, and perhaps the first word as well. Browning, not surprisingly, uses all of these techniques to present his view that the men of Police Battalion 101 were "ordinary men," the implication being that what they did was not so terrible, insofar as the really terrible events of history go. Sometimes, it is very easy to simply allow language, in all its imprecision, to appear to say things for you.

In large measure the impact of Browning's book is in his presentation, what he says, how he says it, and when he says what he has to say.

For example, it is not always clear what Browning means by "ordinary." At times, it appears that when Browning speaks of ordinary men he means "most" ordinary men, who would have acted similarly. Given the percentages he presents of individuals who took part in the massacres, Browning would appear to be speaking appropriately—if he indeed does mean "most" ordinary men—when he uses the term "ordinary men" since it is obviously impossible to account for all five hundred or so of the individuals in Police Battalion 101, 20 percent of whom according to Browning's calculations, did not kill or gave up killing after having started. "Most" of these ordinary Germans, who were undeniably ordinary men, did take part in the killings. However, when Browning makes statements that suggest there exists *within* "all" men—"all" *ordinary men*—the willingness to kill when told to, he is clearly mistaken since some individuals—a number of ordinary Germans, in fact—did not. Browning himself will make this same point. He too recognizes that one cannot speak of all ordinary men as potential killers. People have different psychologies and propensities. But Browning only makes such statements about the inability to speak of all individuals briefly and in passing. Browning dwells on the collective, not the individual; and his title chapter "Ordinary

Men" ends not on the caveat that there are individual exceptions but on the general principle, espoused also at the outset of his book in the preface, that "If the men of Reserve Police Battalion 101 could become killers under such circumstances, what group of men cannot?"[18]

The problem in this last statement is a semantic one. By "group" here Browning must mean only "most" of the people in the group since in the previous paragraph he acknowledges that one cannot account for all people. But is that the impression that Browning really wishes to convey by this last statement? Is he instead trying to convey the impression that "all" in the group, any group of men, would become killers? I would argue that, in fact, Browning is presenting a statement that denies responsibility for a generalization while at the same time generalizing. He appears to be avoiding a statement while at the same time making one. His final words leave the reader with the impression that all men (any "group" of them) would become killers under similar circumstances. But the issue is not just a semantic one. Regardless of Browning's sprinkling of statements to the contrary, by leaving the reader with the view that ordinary men would kill as did these Germans, Browning relieves these Germans of much of the responsibility for the killing. They were simply humans behaving as all humans would under similar circumstances.

Browning's final paragraphs of his final chapter, titled "Ordinary Men," require quotation in full:

> The behavior of any human being is, of course, a very complex phenomenon, and the historian who attempts to "explain" it is indulging in a certain arrogance. When nearly 500 men are involved, to undertake any general explanation of their collective behavior is even more hazardous. What then is one to conclude? Most of all, one comes away from the story of Reserve Police Battalion 101 with great unease. This

story of ordinary men is not the story of all men. The reserve policemen faced choices, and most of them committed terrible deeds. But those who killed cannot be absolved by the notion that anyone in the same situation would have done as they did. For even among them, some refused to kill and others stopped killing. Human responsibility is ultimately an individual matter.

At the same time, however, the collective behavior of Reserve Police Battalion 101 has deeply disturbing implications. There are many societies afflicted by traditions of racism and caught in the siege mentality of war or threat of war. Everywhere society conditions people to respect and defer to authority, and indeed could scarcely function otherwise. Everywhere people seek career advancement. In every modern society, the complexity of life and the resulting bureaucratization and specialization attenuate the sense of personal responsibility of those implementing official policy. Within virtually every social collective, the peer group exerts tremendous pressures on behavior and sets moral norms. If the men of Reserve Police Battalion 101 could become killers under such circumstances, what group of men cannot?[19]

One might sense here Browning struggling to put his ideas on paper; and it is indeed a difficult matter to present. Is it possible to say that any ordinary individual would murder under the same circumstances and not exonerate the murderer of his crime? To use an old cliché, is it possible not "to turn a crime against humanity into a crime of humanity" after having said that other ordinary individuals might have performed the same acts of murder in a similar situation? It is very clearly Browning's intention *not* to exonerate the killers. But do Browning's paragraphs ultimately say what he intends?

One might, however, suggest that in the final paragraph Browning is arguing that, given the opportunity that exists in the world for mass murder, it is important to recognize that all men are capable of it in order to be vigilant against it and thereby avoid it. The point of explaining these impulses within human beings is to prevent them from realizing their potential for mass carnage. But is there anything we have learned about Police Battalion 101 that is likely to prevent mass murder in the future? How many dictators are reading Browning's book and are likely to take it to heart and be vigilant over their genocidal inclinations? Is Browning's statement, on the other hand, more likely to provide Germans with the sense that, since all have the same impulses to murder, they thereby have received some absolution for the murder of the Jews? And, of course, one also needs to ask, what is so terribly wrong about providing Germans with absolution and forgiveness? One needs to be reminded that we are not the right people to give it. The people who can rightly offer forgiveness are dead, as Elie Wiesel pointed out.

I would call Browning's position in *Ordinary Men* "conflicted." It would appear to me that he is trying to walk a tightrope between, on the one hand, condemning the murderers, and on the other hand, trying to understand them. And the harder he tries to understand the murderers, the more difficult it becomes for Browning not to exonerate them of their crimes. I think Browning has fallen into the trap that no one understood better than Claude Lanzmann who, when asked to attend a conference of psychoanalysts and comment on a film about the early life of death camp commandant Christian Wirths, refused, explaining that such a film about the birth of the man, his parents, his friends and neighbors, could only serve to make the man's crime incomprehensible, and hence, to the mind of the audience, nonexistent.[20] That is not what Browning wants us to conclude about Battalion 101, or so he says; but it is not really clear from *Ordinary Men* what Browning would have us conclude. I don't think Browning is really cer-

tain in *Ordinary Men* what it is he believes, and that is not necessarily a bad thing, although it can be confusing for the reader.
Despite its title and the final sentence of the book, one senses that
Browning really does not want to exculpate these German murderers but feels he must make them ordinary so that some Germans and German Americans can finally throw off the burden of
guilt that they had been experiencing for several generations.

Very often as we read we tend to forget what we are reading
about. We over-homogenize the events we are talking about as we
analyze and try to abstract the essence of them in order to theorize
about them. It is easy, I think, to forget in certain instances that we
are talking about murder of the most heinous type, especially
when we hear about a murderer shedding tears. Are we, you and
I, really capable of the type of murders committed by the members
of Police Battalion 101? I can unequivocally and without any hes-
itation whatever state that I would *not* under any circumstances or
in any situation kill an innocent woman or child if there were no
threat of physical harm to myself or others. I have had the privilege of meeting Professor Browning, and I don't for a minute believe that he would kill an innocent woman or child either. There
is no question in my mind that most people in this time (2010) and
in this place (United States) would not kill an innocent woman or
child, at least not without physical threat to themselves or people
near and dear to them. The Germans of Police Battalion 101 were
not "ordinary men" by our reckoning, nor for that matter were—
or are—the perpetrators of any genocide—today, yesterday, or
tomorrow—"ordinary men."

Goldhagen's Willing Executioners and Hallucinatory German Antisemitism

If the point to Browning's book was to show that situational factors make killers out of ordinary men, and that any ordinary individual under similar circumstances might have turned into a killer

like the killers in Police Battalion 101, the point to Daniel Goldhagen's *Hitler's Willing Executioners: Ordinary Germans and the Holocaust* is that situational circumstances were *not* the key reasons why Germans became killers. And Germans were not "ordinary men," as we would today characterize an ordinary man. The chief motivation for the killing, according to Goldhagen, was not situation but ideology: a virulent form of antisemitism that developed over centuries. However, insofar as German antisemitism had developed over centuries, what Goldhagen is really talking about is a long-term development, an antisemitism that over the course of years became matter-of-fact for the most part, but festered in the German psyche and appeared virulently during times of trial and duress (when the loss of the First World War came to mind, for example, or as economic hardship was felt). At these times and under such circumstances, scapegoating Jews because of German failures and hardships would become foundations for virulent hatred of Jews and provide incentive to murder when called upon to do so.

Goldhagen acknowledges, as Browning points out, that the immediate situation—the opportunity to move forward in one's career or the need to feel part of the larger group—also played a role in the shootings. Says Goldhagen,

> To be sure, some of the mechanisms specified by the conventional explanations were at work, shaping the actions of some *individuals*. It cannot be doubted that individual Germans became perpetrators despite a principled disapproval of the extermination. After all, not all perpetrators were offered the opportunity to refuse to kill. . . . It is also likely that disapproving individuals, finding themselves in an *atmosphere of general approval*, would, because of group pressure, commit acts which they had considered to be crimes, perhaps finding comforting rationalizations to assuage their consciences. It cannot be ruled out that some individuals, who were them-

selves not beholden to virulent German anti-Semitism, would
have been moved to kill by a cynicism that set the value of
some coveted advantage, material or otherwise, higher than
that of the lives of innocent people. A presumption of coer-
cion, social psychological pressure from assenting comrades,
and the occasional opportunities for personal advancement,
in different measures, were at time real enough; yet they cannot explain, for all the reasons already adduced, the actions
in all of their varieties of the perpetrators as a class. . . .[21]

Despite the situational factors that might have been influential in
some cases, for Goldhagen the long-term development of antisemitism in Germany had produced a predisposition to murder Jews
anyway. Only the right circumstances were necessary to turn the
predisposition into a reality.

Many factors were necessary for Hitler and others to have
conceived the genocidal program, for them to have risen to
the positions from which they could implement it, for its
undertaking to have become a realistic possibility, and for
it then to have been carried out. Most of these elements are
well understood. This book has focused on one of a number of the causes of the Holocaust, the least well-understood
one, namely the crucial motivational element which moved
the German men and women, without whom it would and
could not have occurred to devote their bodies, souls, and
ingenuity to the enterprise. With regard to the *motivational*
cause of the Holocaust, for the vast majority of perpetrators,
a monocausal explanation does suffice.[22]

And that monocausal explanation for the motivation behind the
vast majority of the murders was a virulent form of antisemitism
that erupted when the right economic, political, and social ele-

ments came together in Nazi Germany. Goldhagen's language seems deliberately chosen to suggest an embattled position from which he has emerged victorious. Whether in fact Goldhagen's "monocausal explanation does suffice" is a decision perhaps better left to the reader who might attribute such a statement to sheer hubris; but the gist of the paragraph is that Goldhagen does recognize that something less than the majority of perpetrators might have been ruled by some motivation other than antisemitism.

It is also worth noting that at no point does Goldhagen suggest that Germans had a genocidal gene of any sort. The vast majority of the killers, says Goldhagen, were indeed motivated primarily from within, but only because an especially pervasive antisemitism had persisted for so long that it was virtually in the character of the German to think the worst of Jews. Anti-Semitism was second nature to the German of the Nazi period.

According to Goldhagen, the antisemitism that existed within the ordinary German of the period was profound. It had developed over centuries and was especially enflamed and encouraged to express itself through violence during the Hitler period. Immediate circumstances might have been influential in individual cases—there is no denying that in individual cases the desire not to appear a coward or the felt need to defer to authority, however removed that authority might have been from the locale of the shootings, was a motivating factor for the vast majority of the perpetrators. But the common denominator, the impulse that had been nurtured and now shared by virtually all Germans of the Nazi period was the intense antisemitism that attributed all the social and economic suffering of Germany to the Jews;[23] and it was that hatred of Jews that was the reason why Germans murdered Jews, says Goldhagen.

The German's hatred of the Jews during the Nazi period was so intense as to produce a German vision of the Jew that was, to borrow a term from Goldhagen, "hallucinatory."[24] Given the relatively small number of Jews in Germany, which amounted to about 1 percent of the population, the image of the Jew upon which such intense and widespread hatred was based could only have been a product of the imagination, a mass hallucination something like the one that allowed Americans to intern Japanese Americans during World War II, but far more profound for having simmered over centuries and more lethal to Jews for having been promoted as, itself, life-threatening to Germans. Goldhagen's point is that the blame for the Holocaust lies squarely with the Germans and the social culture that gave rise to the Nazi mentality. Others would *not* have murdered under similar circumstances. Others would not have created the circumstances under which such murders could take place. One cannot attribute the murders to "human nature." One cannot whitewash what the Germans did to the Jews.

Hitler's Willing Executioners also differs from Browning's *Ordinary Men* in format. Goldhagen's scope is larger and more comprehensive. Goldhagen discusses not only Police Battalion 101 and the Order Police; Goldhagen's focus comprises the three major venues of German killing: the massacres in which the roaming police battalions took part, the camps in which Jews were tortured and killed, and the death marches during which the last instances of German brutality and murder took place. Goldhagen's objective is to show that German hatred and cruelty toward Jews— German ideology—was widespread among those ordinary Germans who participated in the killings and, by extension, was prevalent among all ordinary Germans.

Given the thesis of Goldhagen's work, that the Holocaust is the product of an antisemitism that had over time become integral to the German character and combusted when the right elements came together during the Nazi period, it is not surprising to discover that Goldhagen's work demonstrates German cruelty with abundant, graphic examples of German brutality. Indeed, such ex-

Photograph of burned body, victim of fire set by German guards at Gardelegen, Germany, April 13, 1945. Photo #75712A.
Courtesy of the United States Holocaust Memorial Museum.

amples are necessary to prove Goldhagen's point. Among crueler but not uncommon forms of execution employed by Germans was burning large numbers of Jews alive. Goldhagen presents one such example from the testimony of a survivor of the death march from Dora-Mittelbau camp. The incident took place at the end of the war when one might have expected that at least the more gruesome acts of killing might stop for fear of retribution. The survivor of the death march recounts how they stopped at Gardelegen where the German guards forced about 5,000 to 6,000 people into a barn. The pressure in the barn was so great that a wall collapsed and many fled. The Germans then poured gasoline on the barn and set it on fire. Several thousand were burned alive. The survivor describes the screams of the victims as she hid in the nearby wood. The incident took place on April 13, 1945, the day before Eisenhower's troops arrived. When the Americans appeared, the bodies were still burning. Pictures exist of victims frozen in place like statues, seated exactly in the position in which they burned to death—one of a victim seated at a brick, box-like object with his head in the crook of his arm.

The German guards who burned down the barn with the Jews in it knew they had lost the war; the guards knew that the allies were not far off and were bound to come upon the conflagration. Why did they continue to murder Jews? Goldhagen explains,

> Jewish survivors report with virtual unanimity German cruelties and killings until the very end. They leave no doubt that the Germans were seething with hatred for their victims; the Germans were not emotionally neutral executors of superior orders, or cognitively and emotionally neutral bureaucrats indifferent to the nature of their deeds. . . . The Germans chose to act as they did with no effectual supervision, guided only by their own comprehension of the world, by their own notions of justice, and in contradistinction to their own interests in avoiding capture with blood on their hands. Their trueness to meting out suffering and death was not an imposed behavior; it came from within, an expression of their innermost selves.[25]

Moreover, this innermost hatred of Jews did not suddenly appear at the end of the war when Germans realized that the war was lost and were blaming the Jews in their charge; the loss of this war according to German thinking was just one more example of Jewish perfidy. The Germans had been blaming Jews for their troubles for quite a while and their detestation of Jews had existed for some time. For example, when the "shoot to kill" order was issued in 1941, allowing Germans to kill any Jew found outside the Warsaw Ghetto, the bureau chief of the Warsaw district, Herbert Hummel, explained that all Germans "welcomed thankfully" the "shoot to kill" order, regardless of its context. Goldhagen explains that "these same beliefs moved the men of another police unit, ordinary Germans, to shoot Jews whom they found even 'without express orders, completely voluntarily.'" Goldhagen provides the testimony of a policeman from a unit other than Battalion 101 who stated, "I must admit that we felt a certain joy when we would seize a Jew whom one could kill. I cannot remember an instance when a policeman had to be ordered to an execution. The shootings were, to my knowledge, always carried out on a voluntary basis; one could have gained the impression that various policemen got a big kick out it." The stories of Germans shooting Jews for sport are, of course, commonplace. That Germans derived not just satisfaction but joy from killing Jews speaks volumes concerning the enormities of the Jew in the German mind.

The same German who in the passage above confesses to enjoy killing Jews continues: "[t]he Jew was not acknowledged by us to be a human being." Germans had become enthusiastic killers and persecutors of Jews because the Jew had been so demonized that in the mind of the German, the Jew was no longer human. And Goldhagen produces ample testimony to that effect. Walter Buch, the supreme judge of the Nazi party, unequivocally declared in 1938 that "the National Socialist has recognized that the Jew is not a human being." Then there was the Battalion 101 policeman who, speaking for not just himself but apparently also for the men he knew in the battalion, stated that "the Jew was not acknowledged by us to be a human being." Then of course there is the nonsensical remark by Hitler himself to the effect that while "the Jews are undoubtedly a race, they are not human." The sentiment that the Jew was something "other" than human was fully acknowledged by these Germans. Jews were not "ordinary men" in the view of the Germans, which is itself testimony that the Germans were not "ordinary men," not as we would understand the term.

These were individuals who took pride in their accomplishments. A member of Police Battalion 101 took photos of the humiliation of the Jews. These photos show the "tranquil and happy" faces of the perpetrators as they undertake their dealings against the Jews with "pride and joy." These photos, some of which were taken during the massacre of Jews at Lomazy, were festively displayed on the wall of their quarters and offered for sale to other members of the battalion. One member of the battalion testified how he, in fact, purchased some of these photos himself. Several of the officers of Police Battalion 101, Goldhagen points out, had wives with them whom they invited to attend some of the killing operations. And some of these wives in fact did attend the massacres, creating something of a discussion among those who felt that these events were not appropriate for the gentle sex.[26]

It is also important to note that, according to Goldhagen, the murderous hatred that Germans exhibited toward Jews was not generic. That is, the Germans were not a murderous people whose cruelty naturally extended to all individuals of foreign blood. The focus was usually local; it was fixed primarily on Jews. In many instances, only Jews were to be humiliated and brutalized and killed without mercy. Goldhagen points for example to the reprisal killing in which Police Battalion 101 was required to kill 200 Poles as retribution for the murder of a battalion sergeant by a band of resistance fighters. Unable to find any partisans in the local countryside, they selected 78 Polish villagers for death and decided to make up the difference by killing 180 Jews. While the Polish villagers might have been somehow associated with the resistance, there was no relationship, of course, between the 180 Jews murdered by Police Battalion 101 and the death of the sergeant at the hands of the Polish underground. Goldhagen makes the point that the policemen demonstrated in this arena and else-where a lust for Jewish blood born of an intense and deep hatred for Jews. Poles were spared and Jews took their place—more Jews than in fact were needed to make up the 200 Poles that were sup-posed to have been killed. According to Goldhagen, the officer in charge, "[Major] Trapp, moved to tears by the killing of the Poles, turned around and initiated the killing of Jews, Jews whose rela-tionship to the offending act was non-existent, except in the Nazi-fied German mind, in which the Jews were considered to be a metaphysical enemy."[27] Browning also discusses this reprisal kill-ing, but for Goldhagen the selectivity was widespread and a mat-ter of ideology, evidence of the fact that German hatred was cen-tered, for the most part, on the Jew.

To take another instance, since the argument is that the Ger-man lust for primarily Jewish blood was *general*, Goldhagen de-scribes the Helmbrechts death march at which Germans took pity on the Slav prisoners but forced the Jews to continue to their death. The victims of the Helmbrechts death march were in part from Schlesiersee, a satellite women's facility of the Gross-Rosen camp, who marched to Grunberg, where a second group of prisoners joined them. On January 29, 1945, the combined group set off for Helmbrechts, a satellite camp of Flossenburg in Bavaria. On March 6, two months before German capitulation, 621 individu-als arrived in Helmbrechts. A total of 230 had been deposited at other camps along the way, and about 150 to 250 women died due to malnutrition or simply exhaustion. Much of the way was cov-ered with snow. Many contracted dysentery and frostbite. Fifty were massacred by the Germans in a single action. On April 13, 1945, the death march continued. Helmbrechts was evacuated and the camp's unused clothing was distributed to the non-Jewish prisoners along with a ration of bread, some margarine, and sau-sage. The Jews apparently received nothing. There were about 580 Jewish prisoners and 590 non-Jewish prisoners, escorted by an estimated 47 guards, 22 men, and 25 women. On the second day of the march, orders arrived from Himmler forbidding the killing of any more Jews. He was negotiating with the Americans and did not want his efforts impeded. Most of the non-Jewish prisoners, primarily Russian and Polish women, were deposited in the Zwotau camp, most in relatively decent health. Twenty-five German prisoners were kept on the march to serve as jailers to the Jews. Finally, only the Jews were marching to their deaths. Starvation consumed them; grass became a staple of their diet. The objective of the German guards was to kill the Jews and only the Jews, despite Himmler's orders, and the deaths were especially unpleasant ones.[28] One gets the impression that for the perpetrators, the Jews would always be non-beings. Jews were the primary subject of the German hallucination.

Of course, such hallucinations did not develop overnight. Christian antisemitism had been prevalent in Germany and Europe for some time, but Christian antisemitism generally, says Goldhagen, called for the conversion of the Jews or their removal from the Christian country in which they resided.[29] The German eugenics brand of antisemitism defined the Jew as a threatening force that not only was bent on destroying Germany but had as its goal the contamination of the Aryan race through intermarriage. The Jews had to be exterminated. As early as the mid-nineteenth century, Goldhagen explains, antisemites were calling for the death of the Jewish people in Germany rather than only their removal. A content analysis of publications of fifty-one prominent antisemitic writers between 1861 and 1895 showed that twenty-eight of them proposed solutions to the "Jewish problem," and of those, nineteen proposed the physical extermination of the Jews.[30]

In Nazi Germany, hatred of Jews was widespread, maintains Goldhagen, despite what many other scholars have stated. Goldhagen explains:

> It is often said that the German people were "indifferent" to
> the fate of the Jews. Those who claim this typically ignore

the vast number of ordinary Germans who contributed to the eliminationist program, even to its exterminationist aspects, and those many more Germans who at one time or another demonstrated their concurrence with the prevailing cultural cognitive model of the Jews or showed enthusiasm for their country's anti-Jewish measures, such as the approximately 100,000 people in Nuremberg alone, who, with obvious approval, attended a rally on the day after *Kristallnacht* which celebrated the night's events.

The evidence for widespread antisemitism and its centrality to the worldview of the German population has been available for years, maintains Goldhagen, although that evidence has been ignored. The reason why it has been so difficult for scholars and others to believe that antisemitism was so pervasive in Germany and so central to German thinking is because such thinking seems so ridiculous to us; to again quote Goldhagen, it was "worthy of the ravings of madmen." And Goldhagen continues: "[T]he truth that they were the common property of the German people has been and will likely continue to be hard to accept by many who are beholden to our common-sense view of the world, or who find the implications of this truth too disquieting."[31]

It was Hitler, however, who according to Goldhagen was responsible for translating such sentiments into action and actually making the extermination of the Jews a reality. Hitler had intended to murder the Jews from the outset. He was simply waiting for opportune conditions under which to do it. However, he clearly had support for the measure from other sectors of the German population. Gerhard Kittel, for example, who Goldhagen explains was the leading Protestant theologian and biblical scholar in Germany, publicly promoted extermination of the Jews at a lecture on June 1, 1933. It was, however, Hitler who "leaped across the moral chasm that ordinary Germans on their own could not cross." It was Hitler, who, said Goldhagen, engineered the conditions that enabled the exterminationist version of the eliminationist ideology to become a practical guide for action. By bringing people harboring an eliminationist mind-set with exterminationist potential into institutions of killing, by sanctioning their actions with the orders, hence the blessings, of a charismatic, beloved leader, the German state was able, easily, to enlist ordinary Germans in the program of extermination, even though, prior to its implementation, most of them had certainly never imagined that they would be mass executioners. After the years of turmoil, disorder, and privations that Germans believed the Jews to have caused their country, Hitler was offering Germans a true "final solution."[32]

According to Goldhagen, the pre-existing antisemitism among the German people needed only to be activated and its lethal potential realized, and that's what Hitler was able to do. Hitler in effect provided the situational circumstances which triggered the latent propensity for murdering Jews that up until that time had been expressed only by a surface hatred.

That *Hitler's Willing Executioners* was especially successful in Germany is not surprising. Goldhagen struck a nerve. He told the "truth" about Germany and Germans during the Nazi period. And this truth was being told by an outsider, an American, who had penetrated the cover-up being perpetrated by some of the most popular German historians, such as Ernst Nolte, as well as American historians who, with far greater subtlety, were giving the English-speaking world the impression that there was nothing unusual about the Germans who murdered Jews. And then of course there were the few misguided Jewish American historians such as Hannah Arendt and Raul Hilberg (eagerly joined by gentile social historians such as Zygmunt Bauman) who had fallen into the trap of appeasing the gentile German and liberal audiences with modernist views that mechanization was the ultimate culprit. One did not have to put a name or face to technology. It was easy to blame the social machinery, and let the Germans "off the hook" that way. But Germans recognized themselves in the portraits that Goldhagen laid before them. The impact was enormous, and not just because of the hype that the book received by its very distinguished publisher.

In fact, there is no greater testament to the truth of Goldhagen's assessment of ordinary Germans in the Hitler period than the overwhelmingly positive reaction of ordinary modern-day Germans to Goldhagen's book. The enormous success of Goldhagen's book tour through Germany—his success in lecture halls and in the media—is well documented. And despite the initially cold reaction from scholars, he won over a number of German historians and was even awarded a German prize—the Democracy Prize from the *Journal for German and International Politics*—presented in 1997 to Goldhagen by Jürgen Habermas and awarded only once before, in 1990, to the leaders of the democratic movement in East Germany.[33]

Some argue that the Germans who were struck by Goldhagen's book were the young ones who knew nothing about the Holocaust and had therefore no basis for attesting to whether antisemitism was at the core of Nazi ideology, whether "ordinary Germans" of the Nazi period were so heavily indoctrinated over the centuries that they had arrived at a state in which they could easily be convinced to kill Jews. However, whether that objection is correct or not, what is clear is that today's Germans, who are as close as we can get to the stories of the Germans of the Third Reich, are quite likely as good a source as any. It will also be argued that the German population liked Goldhagen's book because, in its German printing, Goldhagen led Germans to believe that they were radically different from their parents and grandparents. In effect, today's Germans were no longer by and large racists but had entered the twenty-first century born anew.

The Quarrel between Browning and Goldhagen

Given the two arguments of Browning and Goldhagen, the conclusion an objective observer might come to (assuming in the heat of the fray which ensued that one could be objective) is that quite likely the fear and loathing of Jews which had been internalized over centuries by Germans and given new expression by the Hitler Reich made killing Jews, whether in cold blood or seething hatred, a perfectly acceptable occupation. It also seems quite likely that most of the policemen not only found killing Jews perfectly acceptable from an ideological standpoint, but they also would have chosen to kill to avoid being considered a coward by their peers and being deprived of the camaraderie fostered in a military or paramilitary culture. And in individual cases, there might have been other reasons as well, such as blind obedience to authority. That is, both Browning and Goldhagen present us with different portions of the larger picture, Goldhagen focusing on the internalization of the antisemitism that had been fostered for centuries and Browning on the more immediate situational sources of motivation for the killing.

So why the debate—which was often acrimonious and unpleasant for everyone, even those of us who watched from the sidelines? To a large extent, the issues were personal and political, and not historical or sociological. And judging from the critical reaction to his book, Goldhagen seems to have been to blame. It should be noted, however, that Goldhagen never—not once—mentioned Browning in the text of his book. There are, though, about thirty footnotes by Browning's count that discuss and often criticize Browning's work. But in this regard Goldhagen observes an old-fashioned scholarly decorum which demands that criticism of another scholar's work not appear in the text but in the notes. Goldhagen's criticism of Browning also appears of course directly in the subtitle of Goldhagen's work. *Ordinary Men* (the title of Browning's book and Browning's characterization of the German policemen who did the killing) become in the title of Goldhagen's book *Ordinary Germans*, suggesting that only Germans could have committed the crimes of the Holocaust and not others. But if the criticism of Browning's work, which was largely a question of interpretation of data, was performed largely in the footnotes, Browning was not the only scholar so attacked. Many of the leading Holocaust scholars were criticized, although, again, only in the footnotes by name. Further, even if the names of scholars appeared only in the footnotes, the text nonetheless suffered from arrogance of a sort.

In typical doctoral student fashion (the book was Goldhagen's dissertation), the book made claims for its own contribution and originality that, even if true, were worded in a manner that chided the scholars that had come before him, most of whom were quite capable and had developed platforms of their own. In a word, Goldhagen "irritated" many of the most influential Holocaust scholars in the country and out. And most of all he irritated Browning, who was not unknown in the profession as Goldhagen was, but in fact had already established not only a reputation but a following for, among other accomplishments, his sensible and knowledgeable approach to the intentionalist–functionalist debate. In fact, Browning was, and continues to be, much admired and respected. Zeb Weise, the former Jewish president of the Institute for the Holocaust and Jewish Civilization, introduced him in 2003 as a "real mensch." The support that appeared for Browning on various Web lists was overwhelming.

Goldhagen, however, was receiving extraordinary acclaim from the public and especially from the German public who did not seem to be very much concerned about Goldhagen's tactlessness. Goldhagen had struck a nerve among the Germans in particular. He was right about antisemitism among the Germans during the Hitler period. It was a given, a premise of the Nazi worldview, that Jews had to be wiped out of the German picture, and that Jewish life was a pestilence in the German world. Today's Germans were being told what they knew all along and had hoped that no one else knew. Germans of the Hitler period had really hated Jews and were happy to see them killed. It was a suitable revenge for all the ills that Germany experienced, all of which the Jews had been responsible for. And lately Goldhagen had revealed in still another publication that those Germans were not the modern Germans, who far from being antisemites, were allies of Israel against a world that seemed bent on destroying the Jewish refuge for those Jews who would confront holocausts in the future.

Goldhagen's Willing Executioners and the New Germany: Cutting the Gordian Knot

In March 1996, *Hitler's Willing Executioners* appeared in print in the United States. It was a bestseller. In that edition of *Hitler's Willing Executioners*, Goldhagen had included a brief note stating that since World War II, Germans "have changed dramatically"; Germans were no longer the antisemites they had once been. But it would certainly have been easy to miss this statement in the English edition of March 1996.[34] On August 2, 1996, a few days before the German edition of Goldhagen's book was scheduled to appear, Goldhagen published an article in *Die Zeit* explaining that contrary to what the German people might have heard about his book, it was not a polemic against the German national character nor did it accuse the German people of a collective guilt that would last into perpetuity. In the August 2 article, Goldhagen plainly and fully revealed his view that modern Germans are no longer, by and large, antisemitic. The antisemitism that afflicted the Germans for at least a century and a half is not transmitted genetically. In fact, Germans have become model citizens of a solid democratic republic. "Germany," said Goldhagen, "is the great success story of the post-war era." The importance to Germans of this statement is that it tells them that not only should they not feel guilty about their antisemitic past, but that, on the contrary, they should feel proud of their accomplishments, and not only the economic accomplishments but the extraordinary social and ideological progress that has been made in Germany.

Shortly after publication of the German edition of Goldhagen's book, on August 12, 1996, there appeared in *Der Spiegel* an interview with Goldhagen by the publisher and journalist Rudolf Augstein. Augstein had argued for the comparability of the Holocaust during the *Historikerstreit* of the mid-eighties. He was clearly on the side of exonerating Germans for Germany's past.[35] Goldhagen announced to Augstein, as he had in his article for *Die Zeit*, that he never proposed anything on the order of an enduring collective guilt and that Germany's modern political culture was different "by 180 degrees" from the direction it was heading in during the Hitler period. Similar statements continued to be issued, the importance of which cannot be overstated.[36]

For instance, the August 1996 German translation of Goldhagen's book, *Hitler willige Vollstrecher*, contained a new foreword, much of which was devoted to distinguishing between the political culture of the Hitler period and that which existed in the modern Germany. That foreword was translated and republished in the February 1997, paperback version of *Hitler's Willing Executioners*. In his new foreword, Goldhagen again made it clear that

> any German born after the war, or who was a child during the war, cannot possibly be guilty, and is in no sense responsible for the commission of crimes.

Modern Germans were in no way comparable to the Germans that had existed during the war and before it. The reason for that dramatic change was the new institutions and teachings in the modern Germany, teachings that were exactly the opposite of the teachings that had been promulgated during and before the war. As Goldhagen explains:

> Instead of political and social institutions of society putting forward and supporting the antidemocratic and anti-Semitic views they did before 1945, the institutions of the Federal Republic have nurtured a view of politics and humanity that rejected and delegitimized the anti-Semitism of the Nazis period and before. German society gradually underwent a change. The young of the Federal Republic have been taught a universalistic creed that all people are created equal instead of one that holds humanity to be composed of a hierarchy of races that are differently abled, owed different moral obligations, and are inexorably in conflict with one another. Since people's fundamental views are, to a great extent, imparted to them by their society and their culture, the creation of a new public political culture in Germany and generational replacement has produced what one would have expected: a decline and a fundamental change in the character of anti-Semitism.

Instead of laws implementing antisemitism, the new Germany had laws criminalizing antisemitism. Instead of being taught fascism and racism, the younger generation had been taught democracy and principles of equality. Germans had much to be proud of and had no reason to feel guilty about the past. Goldhagen had never said anything about "some eternal German 'national character.'" Another, altered version of the *Die Zeit* article of August 2, 1996, appeared in the December 1996 issue of *The New Republic* under the title "Motives, Causes, and Alibis: A Reply to My Critics"; and a translation of that August 2, 1996, article that first appeared in *Die Zeit* was published in a collection of essays called *Unwilling*

Germans? The Goldhagen Debate by the University of Minnesota Press in 1998. Goldhagen's view of the new Germany and the new generation of German people, which in a very important way complemented his discussion of Nazis and Nazi Germany in *Hitler's Willing Executioners*, was well circulated.[37]

The importance of Goldhagen's glowing encomiums to modern Germans and condemnation of the Nazis was that these statements, in effect, not only accomplished what Augstein, Nolte, and others had attempted during the Battle of the German Historians; what Helmut Kohl had asked Reagan to provide by virtue of his visit to Bitburg; what the German government had asked be provided in the new United States Holocaust Memorial Museum; and what all Germans and German Americans wanted for the new generation of Germans: exoneration, the acknowledgment that today's Germans are not the Germans of the past nor should they be confused with the Germans of the past.

Goldhagen had also rent asunder the Gordian knot of Holocaust polemics. The dilemma that plagued Germans and Jews since the Holocaust was how to fully condemn Germany for the Holocaust without making modern Germans feel guilty about the past. Germans and German Americans, primarily, argued against uniqueness and wished to normalize or to relativize the Holocaust; and Jews and Jewish Americans, primarily, argued for the uniqueness of the Holocaust and against relativization. Goldhagen took an entirely different approach. He explained to Jews and Jewish Americans that Nazis were rightly condemned for all eternity for the horrors they committed. However, Goldhagen also explained to Germans that while the Nazis were indeed an evil people, the evil days were over and Germany was a reborn country. Germans had every right to feel proud of the path they had traveled from World War II to the present. It was the Christian story of sin and redemption that Goldhagen, a young Jew no older than Jesus himself at the time of his death, conveyed to the German people. But it was foremost a statement of congratulations coming from the son of a Holocaust survivor and a Harvard scholar, and one that had an enormous, worldwide platform that had been built for him by one of the most prestigious publishers in the world. And it was of course to this statement, not of forgiveness (which Browning might have seemed to offer), but of German self-redemption and worldwide congratulations that the enormous success of *Hitlers willige Vollstrecher* in Germany can be attributed. The old Germans had been monsters and the new Germans had slain the monster within.

As simple and some would say simple-minded—indeed hastily contrived and without foundation—as this solution appeared, it nonetheless rang true and, in fact, continues to ring true. Neither Germans nor Germany bear any resemblance anymore to the people or government of the Nazi period.

Goldhagen, in these writings about the new German citizen, was of course not reacting to Browning. He was reacting to the way in which his book had been greeted by German academicians and journalists before it had been translated into German and gathered a wider audience. In 1998, Robert R. Shandley described the book's reception in Germany as having taken place in three stages, the first of which began before the German translation appeared in August 1996. Virtually all the German academics who had read the book first decided that it was, in the now famous words of Eberhard Jackel, "simply a bad book." Goldhagen had insulted German scholarship by pretending that his work had issued *ab ovo* and was without worthy precedent. The few individuals who praised Goldhagen's work were, understandably, German Jews such as Julius Schoeps who in his article for *Die Zeit* on April 26, 1996, identified the virtues of Goldhagen's book.[38] Yet as even Goldhagen's detractors pointed out, only he and Browning had actually given a face to the perpetrators and entered their personal lives. In the larger effort to understand how the Holocaust had happened, their efforts were singular and very valuable.

But a great many German scholars had explored the questions

of why and how the Holocaust happened from other perspectives. Among the most notable of Goldhagen's critics was the prominent German historian Hans-Ulrich Wehler who pointed out in his discussion of Goldhagen's book that there were numerous relevant questions that others had addressed and Goldhagen entirely ignored in his explanation for the Holocaust. Why did the Holocaust happen in Germany of all countries? Why did so many of the elite cooperate? Why did the bureaucracy continue to run smoothly? Why did industry cooperate with the regime? These and many other questions relevant to Goldhagen's quest had been dealt with by scholars and not taken into consideration by Goldhagen.[39] Yet Goldhagen was essentially trying to answer the same question these other scholars were addressing, "Why did the Holocaust happen?" Goldhagen came at the question from the perspective of the mentality of the perpetrators, which was all well and fine; but Goldhagen failed to acknowledge recent research relevant to the larger question of why the Holocaust happened, or, when he did acknowledge recent research, it was only to explain its flaws, in Wehler's words, "for the sake of talking up the novelty value of his own book." Goldhagen's approach conveyed a hubris that was almost stereotypically adolescent. Goldhagen later explained that these questions were not considered precisely because others had dealt with them at length. But extended acknowledgment of the significance of preceding research is what is expected in a doctoral dissertation and in a first book, especially from Old World scholars who had devoted much of their lives to the same questions that Goldhagen addressed, even if they had not used his approach. Browning had not dealt with earlier scholarship either, but Browning did not criticize the work of others in order to promote his own. What is more, Browning had in his earlier work paid proper respect to his forbearers and had clearly indicated his appreciation for the scholarship they produced.

As important, perhaps, as "territory" was to German academics, so too was the question of the uniqueness or comparability of the Holocaust—the *Historikerstreit* question that some thought Goldhagen had again brought to the table. Hans-Ulrich Wehler, who, oddly enough, had taken a position against the relativization of the Holocaust proposed by Nolte and others during the *Historikerstreit* ten years earlier, seemed to be arguing at certain points in his essay against Goldhagen's view of the singularity of the Holocaust. Although Wehler remained consistent in his view that one should not compare the horrors of the Holocaust to that of other genocides, he did maintain that a discussion of German antisemitism, if antisemitism was to be viewed as a major factor contributing to the Holocaust, had to explain how German antisemitism differed from the antisemitism of other European countries. In effect, Wehler was suggesting that antisemitism in other countries was just as bad as that in Germany, if not worse. Goldhagen addresses this matter in his foreword to the German edition of his book. He points out that the antisemitism of other countries is not really relevant since these countries did not develop the political institutions to support antisemitism that Germany had. Both popular and institutionalized antisemitism were the necessary preconditions to the Holocaust.[40] My point here, however, is that in certain respects Goldhagen's view was one that advocated a singularity for the Holocaust that would not be countenanced even by those German historians who had advocated for its uniqueness during the *Historikerstreit*.

While Goldhagen had allies in Germany, the response before publication of the German edition of his book was largely negative. However, after the publication of *Hitlers willige Vollstrecher*, considerably more appreciation for Goldhagen's position appeared in Germany. The interview with Augstein was important, not only because it gave Goldhagen a platform from which to explain to Germans that they were not eternally guilty for the crimes of their fathers and that their political culture had evolved considerably over the years, but also because it brought Goldhagen face to face with an individual who had been in the Wehrmacht during the war and was among those who felt that the Holocaust needed to be normalized. In earlier articles, Augstein had spoken very harshly of what in his view amounted to Goldhagen's indictment of the German people. He found a number of epithets, including "hanging judge," appropriate characterizations of the author of *Hitlers willige Vollstrecher*. However, this personal interview was relatively subdued and ended, it appears, warmheartedly, with Goldhagen telling a story of having stopped the previous day at an outdoor cafe in Hamburg for a bite to eat. The young Germans with their boyfriends and girlfriends seemed to him as though they might have been young people in Boston. He thought to himself that "young people like this shouldn't have to feel tortured by the past." Goldhagen's final words of the interview are "they shouldn't have to feel tormented any longer." To which Augstein responded, "Professor Goldhagen, we thank you for this conversation." And Augstein's expressions of appreciation did not appear to be perfunctory. Goldhagen might not have singlehandedly brought peace to the conscience of the new Germany with his discussions of the barbarities of the Third Reich and humanitarian institutions of the Federal Republic, but he certainly won some friends. This is not to say that scholars no longer took notice of the flaws in Goldhagen's book. The book remained for many historians such as Gotz Aly replete with the arrogance of a young student; but Aly, to take only one example, was prepared to admit that there was much to Goldhagen's thesis that antisemitism was deeply ingrained in the psyches of many Germans of the Third Reich (a thesis that of course was not new, although long ignored). Aly was not alone among German historians who found much to praise in Goldhagen's book.[41]

Hitlers willige Vollstrecher was a commercial success in Germany as it had been in the United States. In the fall of 1996, five forums took place in Hamburg, Berlin, Frankfurt, on German television, and in Munich. At these forums Goldhagen met with German scholars and the public to discuss his book. In particular, the forums in Hamburg and Berlin presented discussions that clarified some of the flaws in Goldhagen's work, as well as some of its accomplishments and the reasons for its success. In Hamburg, Goldhagen shared the podium with Jan Philipp Reemstma, the head of the Hamburg Institute for Social Research; Gotz Aly; and Robert Leicht, editor of the *Die Zeit*, and Reinhard Rurup, a historian at the Technical University of Berlin. Both Reemstma and Aly presented views on German antisemitism that agreed with Goldhagen. Only Rurup criticized Goldhagen for being selective in his choice of source materials and for limiting German antisemitism to the "eliminationist" variety. In Berlin, Goldhagen met with his harshest critic, dean of German studies Hans Mommsen; Jürgen Kocka of the Free University of Berlin; and Kocka's colleague, Wolfgang Wipperman. The venue was the Jewish Community Center, and Mommsen attacked Goldhagen for unwarranted, sweeping generalizations. Based on the Holocaust, Goldhagen generalizes that German antisemitism was eliminationist; because of the different social strata of the individuals who composed Police Battalion 101, Goldhagen thinks he can generalize from their antisemitism to the antisemitism of the German nation in its entirety. Wipperman seems to have come to Goldhagen's rescue by changing the subject and arguing that Goldhagen's book at least brought the discussion of the Holocaust back to the important question of why the Holocaust could happen only in Germany. Then Kocka's presentation of what "working" meant in the camps and during the police battalion massacres generated some heated discussion from Mommsen and Goldhagen. Kocka did, however, make the important point that the success of Goldhagen's book is probably because it portrays the everyday life of the killers and shows the reader the horrors that these killers committed. It is also important that Goldhagen met with a group of history students in Berlin who asked him whether his views of the transformed modern Germany aren't Pollyannaish in light of German hostility toward foreigners and some of the more hostile reactions to his book. Goldhagen insisted that the antisemitism of modern Germany is nothing like the antisemitism that existed before 1945.

The remaining engagements in Frankfurt, on German television, and in Munich were cordial with relatively little debate, offering little more than an opportunity for the audience to meet the scholars. However, at the roundtable discussion sponsored by the German Second Channel, the German historian Arnulf Baring warns Goldhagen that "you have put your scholarly reputation at peril"—not the first of such warnings to later prove prophetic when Goldhagen left Harvard, which had recently created a chaired professorship for a Holocaust scholar that some believed was supposed to have been young Goldhagen.

The third stage of the Goldhagen controversy in Germany began in October 1996, after the media frenzy had subsided. Peter Gauweiler, Munich chairman of the Bavarian conservative party, the Christian Social Union, accused Goldhagen of reverse racism. It was not true that most Germans of the Nazi period were virulently antisemitic. According to Gauweiler, no more than 50,000 Germans ever participated in the horrors of the Holocaust; and in a country of 65 million, 50,000 did not constitute even a substantial minority. Gauweiler was openly denounced by opposition parties in the German parliament, and a second, if short-lived *Historikerstreit* arose in which those Germans who did not side with Goldhagen ran the risk of being considered "normalizers" or even Holocaust deniers. The issue had become one of German identity and German historians of the generation born between the mid-1940s and mid-1950s recognized the value of the Goldhagen thesis, whatever flaws might exist in the scholarship. Goldhagen had given modern German historians the tools to master the past. Modern Germans and German institutions were every bit as strong and virtuous as the Germans of old were racist and cruel. As noted earlier in this chapter, in December 1996, the *Journal for German and International Politics* (*Blätter für deutsche und internationale Politik*) announced that it would award its Democracy Prize to Daniel Jonah Goldhagen; and that Jürgen Habermas, who had argued during the *Historikerstreit* for an honest assessment of German history, would make the presentation. Habermas, in an article for the *Journal* published in April 1997 (even as he acknowledged the achievements of those scholars who had found fault with Goldhagen's book), defended statements that Goldhagen had made. Habermas explained, for example, how Goldhagen's generalization from the murderous nature of the members of Police Battalion 101 to a murderous impulse in the German people should be read as referring only to "the undisputed and widespread anti-Semitic dispositions in the German population during this historical period."[42] Habermas's reading of Goldhagen's book is one that is especially attentive to detail and the way in which various statements in his book are intended to qualify other statements that might at first appear untenable. Habermas also, of course, identified the importance of Goldhagen's work, which Habermas sees as the individuation of collectivities. According to Habermas, Goldhagen's "real contribution" is that

> [h]e is not arguing for supposed anthropological universals or regularities to which all persons are equally subject. Such regularities may well serve to explain a portion of the unspeakable, as some comparative research in genocide maintains. Goldhagen's work, however, refers to very specific traditions and mentalities, to ways of thinking and perceiving that belong to a particular cultural context—not something unalterable to which we have been consigned by fate but factors that can be transformed through a change of consciousness and that in the meantime have actually been transformed through political enlightenment.[43]

Other studies had assumed fundamental and common human characteristics that Goldhagen did not. Other studies assumed that such common characteristics were eternal. Goldhagen's study did not. The German brand of antisemitism might very well have been different from other types that existed and it had indeed quickly dissipated after World War II.

Making Holocaust History "Judenrein": American Holocaust Scholarship and Goldhagen's Reception

Goldhagen's writings were not a critical success in the United States where nothing could stop the outrage heaped upon Goldhagen's head for having so discounted the writings of his academic forebears. It is also true, of course, that the book contains errors, although few have thought to identify them with any precision. At about the same time that *Hitler's Willing Executioners* was first published, a chair in Holocaust studies was endowed at Harvard, avowedly for a leading Holocaust scholar yet to be determined. Some believed it was for the young Goldhagen whose book was based on his dissertation submitted for his doctorate at Harvard. The chair in Holocaust studies at Harvard was never filled and eventually disappeared. Goldhagen is no longer employed by Harvard. Browning went from a position at Lutheran Pacific University to a chaired professorship at the University of North Carolina at Chapel Hill.

What was Browning's appeal in America? Why was Goldhagen's work disparaged by U.S. academics? As pointed out, Browning was already an established scholar with a following whose reputation rested on scholarship of the first order when, suddenly, Goldhagen appeared as if out of nowhere. Moreover, Holocaust historians in the United States were unhappy with Goldhagen's work for all the same reasons that German academics had at first been and more. Goldhagen's book was naive and arrogant, its success a product of crass commercialism, and so on. The fact that Goldhagen had solved the problem of how to present the Holocaust in German history—a problem that American Holocaust scholars (as well as German historians) were in one sense or another dealing with—did not impress American Holocaust historians as it did German Holocaust scholars. The American scholars were not about to deviate from their agenda because a young upstart historian from Harvard had produced an off-the-cuff and not terribly convincing answer to the dilemma that was so profoundly at the bottom of the Holocaust that few had ventured to even verbalize it for fear that the world might realize it was not facts alone that were most crucial to Holocaust history.

This is not to say that there were no scholars who actually identified error—and not just errors of judgment—in Goldhagen's book. Also, as mentioned previously, Goldhagen was disdainful of the work of historians who came before him. One of the more significant contributions in this regard was by British historian Richard J. Evans, who in his 1997 book, *Rereading German History, 1800–1996: From Unification to Reunification*, included an essay titled, "Antisemitism: Ordinary Germans and the 'Longest Hatred,'" which dealt with Goldhagen's book.[44] Evans, of course, took Goldhagen to task for his indecent treatment of the historians who had paved the way for Goldhagen's study, among whom was Christopher Browning, and identified other lapses in reasoning and language. But Evans also identified what appear to be a number of clear errors of interpretation in Goldhagen's book; and, perhaps more significantly, Evans raises an issue of critical methodology that might render both Goldhagen's work and Browning's work on Police Battalion 101 nonrepresentative, and hence of little or no value for understanding groups of killers in general, whether ordinary Germans or ordinary men.

One of a number of the errors of interpretation that Evans identifies concerns Goldhagen's presentation of an incident involving Captain Wolfgang Hoffman, commander of one of the three companies of Police Battalion 101 and a "zealous executioner of Jews." In the course of the genocidal activities that were taking place at the time, Hoffman received an order commanding that the members of his company sign a declaration ordering them to pay for provisions rather than engaging in theft or plunder to acquire them. Hoffman refuses to sign the declaration on the grounds that it was insulting to him and his men to require a signed oath of honor that they would not steal. Goldhagen assumes that the order requires that the battalion not steal provisions from *Poles* and makes the point that Hoffman apparently thought the Poles worthy of a degree of respect that the Jews were not deemed worthy of. According to Goldhagen, Hoffman thought it a point of honor not steal from the Poles, even though he had no compunction whatever about murdering Jews. Evans points out, however, that there is nothing in the declaration to suggest that the battalion is being asked to refrain from stealing from Poles. In fact, Goldhagen is apparently unaware of the fact that Himmler repeatedly told his SS (of whom Hoffman was one) that they needed to be incorruptible in the performance of their murderous activities, by which he apparently meant that SS must not steal from the Jews that they killed.[45] The point here is that Goldhagen might very well have misinterpreted a situation largely because he lacked the background needed to perform a critical reading of the text. Such an error makes Goldhagen's readings of other texts suspect as well.

Far more important than this error in interpretation is the distinct possibility, raised by Evans, that the individuals who comprised Police Battalion 101 were not representative of police battalions generally; and therefore the conclusions drawn about police battalion members generally and "ordinary men" or "ordinary Germans" by both Browning and Goldhagen simply are not justified. In an unpublished essay, Evans points to the startling fact that research published since the appearance of Goldhagen's book has shown that members of Police Battalion 101 were not representative because most were in their thirties and forties. Only seven of twenty-three police battalions active in the occupied Soviet Union contained individuals in their thirties and forties. The other battalions were composed entirely of younger people.[46]

These older individuals differed from the younger policemen in that many had likely served in the German military during World War I. It was traditionally the case, particularly in Prussia, that police positions and other state jobs were reserved for individuals who had served for a number of years as noncommissioned officers and subsequently retired. After World War I, the Treaty of Versailles reduced the strength of the German army to 100,000, so many former officers and noncommissioned officers turned to the police force. These older officers were individuals who by and large had been hardened by both war and an ideology that viewed the political left with suspicion as consisting of primarily traitors to Germany. From 1936, when Himmler became the Reich's leader of the SS and German police, efforts were made to unify the SS, the Gestapo, and police by sending young SS officers fresh out of SS training school into the police officer corps. Himmler also at this time ordered that police recruits should be drawn from the Hitler Youth. In both instances, these were young ideologues committed to an antisemitic platform, with the young SS eventually dominating the junior rank of officers. On April 15, 1937, Himmler drafted into the police corps educational officers whose job was to indoctrinate the average policeman with antisemitism.

The majority of police battalions—sixteen of the twenty-three—would have been dominated by this younger group of officers and individuals. As Evans explains it, Police Battalion 101 was not really representative of most police battalions. Therefore whether one can generalize from one battalion to all (or most) police battalions is questionable. It is even more doubtful whether one can generalize from Police Battalion 101 to the German population as a whole, as Goldhagen does. I would only add here that it is entirely unlikely, given the nonrepresentational nature of Police Battalion 101, that one can generalize from such a group to ordinary humans in general, as Browning does. In fact, one should also add that if, in fact, Police Battalion 101 was not a representative battalion, the figures that Browning presents must be revisited. One will recall that, according to Browning, 20 percent of the individuals in Police Battalion 101 either refused to kill Jews (and so were transferred to other duties) or after having killed, refused to continue. The remaining 80 percent murdered Jews with a lesser or greater degree of enthusiasm. One will also recall that Browning was impressed by the fact that the Zimbardo study produced data similar to his own. In Zimbardo's study, ordinary individuals were divided up into prisoners and guards, and the guards became increasingly more brutal in their efforts to control the far larger number of inmates. Twenty percent of such guards demonstrated kindness and leniency. But if Browning's 20-percent figure cannot apply to the majority of police battalions because Police Battalion 101 was not representative of police battalions in the vicinity, how significant is Browning's data?

The value of the data for purposes of extrapolation to most Germans or most human beings, becomes still more problematic. According to Evans, about 13,000 of the 26,000 policemen in the east took part in the massacres. They were recruited by the SS on the basis of criteria that included their suitability for service in the SS. The pool from which these individuals were chosen was four times larger than the number of individuals selected. Only one in four was chosen, to some degree based on political suitability for the SS; and then those individuals were subject to political and ideological indoctrination. It does not appear that these individuals could have been representative of German society before they entered the police service, and less so after having undergone a basic training of sorts. These individuals were not, as Goldhagen claims, selected at random from among the German population and were not representative of the larger German population of the time. Nor could these individuals be thought of as being representative of humans in general. In short, according to current research, the entire controversy lacks an empirical base.

However misunderstood the original data might have been and however flawed both projects might have been, the point here is that there really does appear to have been an agenda underlying Browning's and Goldhagen's works. Those are perhaps best explained by two essays written about the Goldhagen controversy, one by Jane Caplan and the other by Omer Bartov. What they explain is that ultimately Browning fit in better with the tendency to attribute the Holocaust to a twentieth-century, mechanistic universe in which human beings had become alienated from that which makes them human. What Caplan and Bartov do not explain is that this interpretation tended to relieve Germans of responsibility for the Holocaust, instead making twentieth-century Western mechanization and alienation responsible for the murder of the Jews. In effect, the zeitgeist was responsible for the Holocaust.

Caplan addresses the question of why the press and popular reaction to Goldhagen in America was generally favorable, while the scholarly community—with a few notable exceptions such as an early review by Gordon Craig—was generally disparaging of Goldhagen's book. She focuses on the favorable reaction in the press and suggests that one of the reasons for the book's popularity is that Goldhagen's version of German history is one of "guilt and redemption."[47] Most Germans might have been virulently antisemitic during the Nazi regime, but now Germans are a liberal, democratic people who are no longer antisemites. Caplan goes on to point out, however, that one could also draw the conclusion that the reason there are few antisemites in Germany today is because there are hardly any Jews. Second, Goldhagen offers a demonic portrait of Germans that serves American readers as a "counterimage" to themselves. The murderous tendencies of the Germans of the Nazi period were not "normal" to the "enlightened" European civilization of that period and certainly are not normal in today's Western societies. American readers, says Caplan, are invited to identify with a normalcy that is, in fact, enlightened and civilized and anything but German. Moreover, since the victim stands over and against the perpetrator in this scenario, the American reader is also invited to identify with the Jewish victim. Lastly, says Caplan, Goldhagen's book was successful because of the publisher's media blitz.

Caplan maintains that the major difficulty of Goldhagen's book (and she fully states the deficiencies in his history of antisemitism) is that he sees the German and the Jew in the abstract; and in the abstract the two seem eternally locked in battle. And in the documents, laws, and propaganda presenting the Jew in the abstract or stereotype, there does appear to be genuine animosity. Real Germans and real Jews, says Caplan, have never been certain about each other. Jews have lived with German acceptance and German rejection. She cites Steven Aschheim who explains that "the whole point about the German-Jewish experience, the source of its enduring fascination and unparalleled creativity, lies in its ambiguous nature, the tension between acceptance and rejection, [the fact that] German-Jewish life was always negotiated in a social field of essentially mixed signals."[48] This tension between acceptance and rejection that Aschheim speaks of may be fascinating and a source of creativity for Caplan and Aschheim, but it was not fascinating to the Jews of Nazi Germany, and, if anything, stifled the creative potential of Germany's best Jewish minds by putting an end to them.

Caplan suggests that one of the central weaknesses of Goldhagen's book is that it deals with the hostility of German for Jew in the abstract, as an "eternal struggle" that must lead to either total victory or total defeat." Goldhagen, she explains, does not understand that in reality the relationship between German and Jew was far more complex and nuanced. That Germans and Jews married, for instance, were business partners, and sometimes socialized, although the scale on which such relationships existed could not have been large, even if antisemitism were not prevalent, given the small number of Jews in Germany. However, Caplan fails to take into consideration that however Goldhagen might confuse myth and reality, the two are in fact inextricably entwined. Abstract myths not only become reality; they are often expressions of a genuinely hostile, indeed murderous reality. As Goldhagen points out—and few historians, if any, refute him on this matter—the German view of Jews was based largely on antisemitic propaganda, as must necessarily have been the case since only about 1 percent of the German population was Jewish. It was to the Jew in the abstract—the myth of the Jew, in Goldhagen's terms—that the Nazis were responding to in 1933 and that to which they continued to respond even as the German perpetrators became more familiar with Jews through the killing operations themselves.

But according to Caplan, the commercial success in America of *Hitler's Willing Executioners* was not exclusively due to Goldhagen and the machinery of the market. Another reason Goldhagen's book succeeded commercially was because of the failure of historians to convincingly explain its faults. That the book did not sufficiently account for the years of Holocaust scholarship that preceded it was not an argument that could be conveyed without somehow convincing the world that a body of scholarship existed that was united in its effort to fathom the reasons for the Holocaust having happened and that this body of scholarship had truly been productive in its efforts. One could not easily describe the historiography of Holocaust scholarship within the confines of even a long article. So there were even some scholars who were skeptical as to whether Goldhagen had committed anything much worse than a faux pas by excluding his elders from serious consideration. Then, too, there was the problem of postmodern skepticism, which, however much one might consciously recognize its negative consequences, nonetheless shapes to some extent our worldview. Isn't one interpretation or explanation as good as another? Is there really any such thing as an objective, unbiased, or apolitical history? Isn't Goldhagen's view of the Holocaust as good, if not more convincing, than most? It has the evidence. It simply interprets the evidence in its own way.

As Bartov would state in his article, Caplan explained that in America, as elsewhere, most Holocaust studies focused on the institutions that had shaped Hitler's Germany. As was generally true of all Western institutions of the period, and as remains for the most part true today, these institutions were mechanistic and alienating, if not entirely dehumanizing. One might also add that T.S. Eliot had written about these conditions in his monumental poem, "The Wasteland," as had Samuel Beckett and the other absurdist playwrights. Modern postindustrial society had made all life emotionally barren, a wasteland of inhuman automaton existence. Browning's *Ordinary Men* fit perfectly into this modernist paradigm that other Holocaust scholars (Arendt, Hilberg, Baumann, etc.) had helped develop. Browning attributed the murderous tendencies of the perpetrators of the Holocaust to similar sociological paradigms that have evolved for mechanistic and alienated times. The difference between Browning's view of the German policeman and, for example, Arendt's view of the bureaucrat, is that instead of a Nazi government institution forcing the disinterested button pusher to commit murder from a distance, social demands—authority, camaraderie, and peer pressure—forced ordinary men in Nazi Germany to shoot Jews at close range. It would seem far more likely, however, that, while the mechanization of the twentieth century made it easy to murder from a distance, intense hatred nonetheless was required of those who actually shot or tortured the innocent on a regular basis. The twentieth century compensated for mechanization with brutality. But antisemitism and German hatred of Jews did not fit as neatly into the modern Holocaust paradigm as did Browning's situationalism.

Bartov explains the history of Holocaust scholarship in America, including how it began with early popular accounts of German antisemitism, which some argued Goldhagen's study echoed. However, those early studies eventually gave way to a scholarship that focused on a number of other factors—impersonal factors such as the bureaucracy that mechanized and dehumanized the process of murder—as well as antisemitism. These studies of external influences on the killing were joined by studies of the complex relationships between Germans and Jews throughout the years leading up to the Hitler Reich. These sociological studies also of course complicated the idea that antisemitism was the prominent determinant in the slaughter of the Jews.[49]

Goldhagen's study did not impress many American scholars, but it did appeal to the American press and to the public. According to Bartov, the appeal of Goldhagen's study was that it came along at the opportune moment, at a time when the public no longer trusted the Holocaust scholars who had lost sight of the central horror of the event. Goldhagen also rallied all the anti-German sentiment in the United States that had lain dormant for so many years. Furthermore, says Bartov, employing a sardonic form of free indirect discourse,

> Goldhagen did not "merely" propose to tell the public why the Holocaust had happened and who was guilty of it; he also led a frontal attack against all those scholars who had apparently become wholly incapable of seeing what the general public had intuitively known all along, that it was "the Germans" who had done it, that they had always wanted to do it, that they did it because they hated Jews, and that once

called up to do it, they did with great enthusiasm and much pleasure. This kind of argumentation played both on the anti-German sentiments of large sectors of the American public and on the growing frustration with academic discourse.[50]

Who these large sectors of the American public might be who harbor "anti-German sentiments" might be a matter of conjecture. Is Bartov talking about the Jewish sector of the American population? However that might be, it is unlikely that there was ever a growing frustration among the public with "academic discourse." There was never a sufficiently significant readership for academic discourse among the American public for there ever to have been a frustration toward it.

Goldhagen felt that sociological paradigms were not entirely relevant, even when they were not entirely wrong. Here is one reason for the antagonism of scholars in the United States and elsewhere toward Goldhagen: Goldhagen challenged the paradigm currently under construction for which debates such as the *Historikerstreit* and the intentionalist–functionalist debate served simply as camouflage.[51] These historians were going to figure out some way of making German history "Judenrein." The key was to depersonalize the killing.

Oddly enough, Goldhagen, whether by intention or as a function of circumstances, came up with a different answer to the central dilemma at the heart of the controversy (how to admit to the crime but avoid the penalty). Germans were no longer Nazis; in fact, they were exactly the opposite. The Germans loved him for his honesty and found his explanations intuitively satisfying in a way that depersonalizing the Holocaust simply was not. Germans still remembered what they felt during the Hitler period, and they knew what they now felt. Goldhagen offered Germans absolution in a way that Reagan could never do. Even if German passions during the Third Reich were of the most evil sort, now their better selves had ascended from the depths and had been realized. American historians were dumbfounded. All they could see were mistakes in interpretation, if not in fact; omissions or, worse, dismissal of solid historical research; and claims to major revelations that amounted to platitudes. Their reasons for the success of Goldhagen were, on the one hand, the media hype, and, on the other, the gullibility of the German people. Goldhagen and his publishers had created a new public platform from which to discuss the Holocaust and sell books. Other historians now had a new platform from which to promote a career of their own that they silently wished to themselves might one day resemble Goldhagen's in its popular acclaim. Holocaust historians in America jumped on board the bash-Goldhagen bandwagon.

As some scholars intimated, Holocaust scholarship since the *Historikerstreit* (and even before) had clearly been drifting in the direction of exoneration of the Germans for the Holocaust, even if such exoneration was not taking place by virtue of comparison with other horrors, many of them earlier than the Holocaust. The tendency to focus on institutions and ideologies instead of people had been turning a "crime against humanity" into a crime of the age in which we live, with no particular blame falling on the shoulders of the individuals who carried out the murders or those who were happy to see the murdering take place. Goldhagen tried to put an end to that. His book made plain to the historians who read it that whatever else might have been responsible for the Holocaust, one could not omit antisemitism. What is remarkable is that while scholars today tend to ignore *Hitler's Willing Executioners*, its influence has been enormous. Today, few books on the Holocaust fail to reflect on antisemitism in Germany when speaking of the perpetrators, and many find it necessary to speak of the horrors committed, a matter for which Goldhagen was roundly criticized.

My key point here, however, is not really about whether Browning or Goldhagen was correct in his assessment of what motivated Police Battalion 101 to shoot, although I think it is obvious here that I favor the view of Goldhagen (and others) that antisemitism played a large role. The point to this section on Browning and Goldhagen, as is true of the current book generally, is that most debates about the Holocaust and genocides generally boil down to two points of view: one view sympathizes with current dilemmas of relatives of perpetrators, and the other identifies with the victims and their experience. It is rare that both of these views do not appear in a work of Holocaust scholarship; but usually one or the other dominates.

Conclusion

German American and Jewish American Views of the Holocaust

Was the Holocaust predominantly due to the psychological state of the perpetrators which had been conditioned by propaganda about the prospective victims? Or was the Holocaust largely the product of the murderous environment in which the killers found themselves? This question is actually a non-question. Reality is rarely virtually black or virtually white, or a matter of one or the other of those two qualified terms. In the case of the Holocaust, the two answers bleed into each other. Individual biases create pregenocidal circumstances and pregenocidal circumstances shape personal biases. Invariably both antisemitism and the environment of murder motivated the perpetrators of the Holocaust, and it is not clear where one begins and the other ends. Antisemitism was apparent, as were the dehumanizing effects of industrialization and peer pressure. Some historians, however, prefer to put a face on the murderers. They believe crimes are caused by criminals. Other historians prefer to attribute the murder primarily to circumstances or even concepts.

Again, my point here is not that Goldhagen or Browning was correct in his view of why Police Battalion 101 murdered innocent men, women, and children, although I confess a bias for the view of young Goldhagen who seemed for a time to have overcome the larger forces of history. Then, too, one must take into account Richard Evans's point that both studies are based on flawed premises, at least insofar as they rely heavily on Police Battalion 101. My point is that both Goldhagen and Browning were emphasizing points of view that, in the common understanding of things, lay beneath antagonisms between Germans and Jews that existed even before the Holocaust actually started. One view identifies with the victim—in this case the murdered Jews of the Holocaust—and the other view demonstrates at least some sympathy with the perpetrators and their descendants—the Nazis of Europe and their relatives in this case. And the dichotomy between victim identification and criminal sympathy is important, not only because it may be said to be at the heart of the Holocaust debates that have gone on at least since the Holocaust and, in a sense, before the horrors of it were taking place. The dichotomy is important because, of course, it exists for all mass tragedies and genocides. There have always been and continue to be those who speak for the victims and those who, after the horror, are prepared to view the criminal perpetrators as victims of history. In fact, postmodernism makes it easier than ever to see "both" points of view.

The debate between German Americans and Jewish Americans over what was taking place in Nazi Germany could be said to have started on the eve of America's entry into the war, during the congressional hearings of 1941, when Gerald Nye, senator from North Dakota, accused Harry Warner of Warner Brothers of promoting interventionism with his anti-German films. Nye was of course correct when he argued that films such as *Confessions of a Nazi Spy* were anti-German, although Warner retaliated with the argument that other Warner Brothers films portrayed good Germans (Germans such as Dr. Paul Ehrlich who discovered a cure for syphilis and whose story was turned into a full-length motion picture by Warner Brothers). Nye, however, was not above accusing Warner of creating anti-Nazi films out of what Nye considered a mistaken and misbegotten concern for Warner's Jewish relatives in Germany. And Nye was probably correct here as well, at least partially. Warner was concerned about the Jews of Germany, although that concern was fully warranted, as Nye well knew. It might very well have been that Warner sensed by 1941 that the only salvation of the Jews of Europe was U.S. intervention and the defeat of Germany by the Allies. Moreover, Warner did not make the obvious point that Nye's concern in this matter was not principled and pacifist. Nye was not concerned about the persecution of the Jews in Germany, but he was concerned about the lives of the Germans that U.S. forces would necessarily have to take in order defeat the Nazis; and Nye was also very much concerned about the eruption of a wave of U.S. anti-Germanism comparable and perhaps worse than the one that appeared during World War I. But Warner never brought up Nye's pro-Nazi bias, which necessarily included antisemitism.

The real issue, however, was never squarely faced during the congressional hearings. The issue was not whether Harry Warner's films encouraged U.S. intervention in World War II. The issue was not interventionism versus isolationism. The issue was Jews versus Germans. Were Jews going to be spared and Germans killed at the hands of German Americans, or Germans spared and Jews persecuted and killed at the hands of Germans because of German American fears? But no one put the real issue on the table and looked squarely at what was going on, and so nothing really relevant to the deaths that would occur took place. No consensus that might have led the U.S. government to a course of action that might have spared Germans and Jews was possible.

German Americans did have much to be concerned about should America enter the war, apart from the fear that they would soon be in Germany squarely faced with an enemy who could turn out to be a relative. There was also the genuine issue of the anti-Germanism that would appear should the United States enter the war. German Americans still remembered the experience of World War I when they were humiliated and several individuals were murdered by mobs because of their German heritage. Six thousand German Americans were interned in camps during World War I. There was less violence toward the German American community during World War II, despite the fact that a fairly sizeable group of 25,000 American Nazis stirred up considerable animosity among the U.S. population in general prior to the nation's entry into the war. During World War II, significant numbers of German Americans clearly demonstrated their support for the United States and the Allies. Approximately 11,000 German nationals and Americans of German descent were interned during World War II in places like Crystal City and Seagoville, Texas. These places did not compare to German concentration camps. While sometimes primitive when first established, camps in which Germans were interned, such as Seagoville, were given the resources to expand and become fairly pleasant communities. The Seagoville internment camp was said to resemble a college campus, and internees' privileges extended to various forms of recreation and health care. Nonetheless, being taken away from homes and jobs and confined for an indefinite period of time behind barbed wire was surely a wrenching experience and one that in a great many instances was not warranted. The experience is an important one here because it helps explain the fear of vengeance that some German Americans would continue to associate with virtually any mention of Nazis well into the future, including of course all endorsement of Holocaust-related projects.

After the war, it was no longer a question of what would happen to whom. The victims and the perpetrators were clearly established, or so one would have thought. Despite the persecution of German Americans at home, the mass carnage of civilian populations by the Nazis in the eyes of many did not have its equal in the annals of history. Never before had so much state machinery been employed to murder a single ethnic group. But in the latter half of the twentieth century, anyone could be a victim—or a perpetrator. When in 1983 it was proposed that a national Holocaust museum be built in Washington, DC—a museum that would serve as a genocide watch as well as memorial to Holocaust victims—there were those outside and within the German American community who viewed the prospective museum as an effort to victimize Germans and Americans of German descent. The largest German American organization, the German American National Congress, tried its best to prevent the museum from being built. It was argued that a national museum dedicated to the Holocaust would create a wave of anti-Germanism that would lead to disparagement of all things German, and German Americans would invariably be identified with Nazis. The journal of the German American National Congress issued a call to its 10,000 members to contact their senators—a list of which was provided—and tell them to stop the Holocaust museum from being built. The Holocaust museum was viewed as a means of Jewish revenge upon not only Germans but American relatives of Germans as well. German Americans would be victimized by the existence of a Holocaust museum. Although the internment of German Americans during World War II was never mentioned, the treatment received by German Americans during the war was likely the basis for German American concern. Jews and those who identified with the Jewish victims of the Holocaust, of course, disagreed that a Holocaust museum would create anti-Germanism in America. The museum was intended to memorialize the victims and serve as a warning to Americans and the world of what might happen when individuals with a murderous ideology are placed in power, even in a civilized Western nation.

But truth had become so twisted by postmodern academic

perversions of reality that even Nazi soldiers could be victims. Such was the contention of at least one unwitting American president. In1985, President Ronald Reagan proposed to visit the military cemetery at Bitburg and insisted that the German soldiers buried there "were victims, just as surely as the victims in the concentration camps." (As it turned out, at the Bitburg cemetery were buried members of the Waffen SS who had massacred 642 civilians at Oradour-sur-Glan, but that did not stop Reagan from making his visit, although he decided to visit a concentration camp as well.) The point to Reagan's visit, as he explained, was to provide Germans with some relief for the feelings of guilt they were experiencing because of the Holocaust. His visit to Bitburg would seal America's forgiveness for the horrors that Germany had committed. German historians such as Ernst Nolte had been promoting a similar agenda at about the same time. This was the period of the Battle of the German Historians when several legitimate historians, such as Nolte, unabashedly insisted that German history should be cleansed of the Holocaust. But for Reagan, there was also clearly another matter that argued for his attendance at Bitburg. It was also the case that the Germans had made major concessions to U.S. foreign policy, including allowing American missiles on German soil, and Reagan was feeling obliged.

It is not clear who informed President Reagan that German soldiers had experienced victimization comparable to the concentration camp victim, but, needless to say, the Jewish American community was outraged, as was a substantial segment of the national press. Reagan should not have laid a wreath for the dead at Bitburg. The SS were officially branded a criminal organization. Veterans groups complained that American soldiers who had died in battle, some at the hands of the SS, were not being considered. Former SS, it was reported, were overjoyed by the prospect of Reagan's visit, and could be seen sitting in German beer halls and publicly drinking to Reagan's health. Neo-Nazis registered their praise for Reagan. Opponents to Reagan's visit, and Jewish Americans in particular, focused, however, on Reagan's forgiveness of the Germans; and among the arguments presented by the opponents was that "forgiveness" for the horrors committed during the Holocaust was not Reagan's to give. According to Jewish law, only the victims could provide forgiveness, and the six million Jews were dead.

There was another segment of the national press that supported Reagan's visit to Bitburg as did the German American National Congress. In fact, the verbal attacks by German Americans on Jewish Americans for standing in the way of Reagan's visit to Bitburg were in some instances harsh and threatening. German Americans claimed that Jewish Americans were victimizing Germans and Americans of German descent by insisting that the American president not go to Bitburg and provide the Germans with the forgiveness that they sought. Others suggested that readers contact Holocaust denial organizations such as the Institute for Historical Review to find out the "real story" of what happened to Jews during World War II. But again, the two communities—German Americans and Jewish Americans—were not really talking to each other. The vituperations just flew by the two groups without either really paying a lot of attention to the other.

To this day, the argument persists. German Americans and those who espouse their views, and Jewish Americans and others who present here what I think of as a Jewish American perspective, continue to argue over the Holocaust, sometimes without awareness that they are doing so or that these views have a history that goes back to a period before the worst horrors of the Holocaust took place. Perhaps no group of professionals—journalists or politicians—has dealt with this issue to the extent that Holocaust academics have. Historians continue to pretend that the subjects chosen for study, as well as the readings and interpretations of those subjects, do not influence the portrait of the Holocaust that emerges from the discipline's collective researches. At the heart of the Goldhagen-Browning debate was victim sympathy, on the one hand, and criminal identification, on the other, as was also the case during the U.S. Holocaust museum debate and the Bitburg controversy. It bears repeating that the issues for both German Americans and Jewish Americans—whether journalists, politicians, or academics—are very real, perhaps more so even than for Germans during the *Historikerstreit*.

Some German Americans believe that the mere mention of the Holocaust is enough to bring to the mind of the average American the horrors perpetrated by the Nazis and will ignite associations of Nazism with all things German and German American. Any suggestion that the Holocaust is somehow unique only further fuels the flames of anti-Nazism and, by extension, anti-Germanism in America. This anti-Germanism, they point out, is unfair, especially toward the younger generation of Germans and German Americans who had nothing whatever to do with the Holocaust. It is time to let the dead rest. Moreover, there were worse atrocities in the history of mankind and, what's more, it is human nature. Evil exists in all humans. It is our duty to recognize that evil so that horrors like the Holocaust do not happen again.

Not all German Americans, of course, hold those views. Most don't. It is only the "professional" German Americans, German American teachers and historians, the politicians and newspapermen who work for German American organizations, and the German American organizations themselves who are especially conscious of these views. And there are also many Jewish Americans who will take up one or another of these views, sometimes fully conscious of the history of what they're saying, but most often probably not.

For Jewish Americans, most of whom have relatives who died in the Holocaust, and who are familiar with Holocaust denial groups, Holocaust memorialization is a necessity. Efforts to suggest that there have been equal or worse horrors than the Holocaust perpetrated upon other peoples in history are viewed as efforts to relativize the Jewish experience, to turn it into something less than the tragedy it was, and to minimize both it and the tragedy that it is being compared with. To suggest that individuals other than the Nazis would have done the same thing under the same circumstances cheapens Jewish lives and perpetuates antisemitism by turning a local and temporary event into a universal and enduring phenomenon. Everyone is not evil. Men and women are essentially good and should be encouraged to do what is right when confronted with evil.

These are what I call here Jewish American views, although not all Jewish Americans hold them. Many do not. Some Jews, in fact, think that there has been too much made of the Holocaust and that it has become too commercial. They advocate a moratorium on Holocaust studies.[1] Further, many who are *not* Jewish American *do* hold these views. Those who do advocate the positions above are, again, the professional ethnics within the Jewish community, those who study Judaism, support it politically and organizationally, and teach about Judaism or the Holocaust. German Americans will sometimes hold one or another of these views characterized here as Jewish American, although they might not always be fully conscious of the larger social context in which these views have appeared.

It is these two views—the one that identifies with the victim, which in the case of the Holocaust may be referred to as the Jewish American view, and the one which sympathizes with the criminal or trials of his children or relatives, which is perhaps most aptly referred to here as the German American view—that inform not only Holocaust debates in America and elsewhere, but are probably responsible for much of the debate that takes place about other criminal acts, including other equally great horrors specific to the United States, such as African slavery and the massacres of

Native American peoples. The point here is that there are arguments that tend to exonerate perpetrators and those that tend to condemn them; and arguments that tend to support the claims of victims to justice and those that tend to disparage the claims of victims. Unfortunately, most genocide-related arguments tend to support either the victim or the perpetrator without being able to do both simultaneously. To a considerable extent, Holocaust historiography is about these arguments. It is also about facts, of course, but sometimes the facts are not available and more often than not there are not enough of them to come to a precise assessment of the reality of the situation.

It is also important to emphasize that there appears to have been in the eighties and nineties an academic agenda that to some extent continues to this day, one wholly suited to the desire among many Holocaust scholars to make the Holocaust more palatable to Germans and German ethnics and, perhaps, young Germans as well, by focusing on objective circumstances and concepts, and explaining away the crimes of the perpetrators. The Battle of the German Historians was only the first *avowed* attempt by academics to cleanse German history of the Holocaust by explaining that there were worse genocides in history and that the Holocaust was not that bad, as genocides go. Insofar as Browning's *Ordinary Men* promoted the point that not all of the Germans who killed innocent women and children were forced to do so, the book clearly did focus on the criminal nature of the murders that were taking place. But Browning also attempted to provide a circumstantial explanation for perpetrator behavior by pointing to external, faceless influences such as peer pressure. In that sense, Browning's study as opposed to Goldhagen's, conformed to the more depersonalized studies of historians that focused on the faceless Nazi machinery of the period. It argued that anyone under the same circumstances would perpetrate the same evil perpetrated by the Nazis when they murdered innocent women and children.

Goldhagen's book was notable for among other reasons its dogged focus on the antisemitism of the Germany of the latter half of the twentieth century and its insistence that only Germans and the circumstances produced by Germans were adequate for a Holocaust to take place. *Hitler's Willing Executioners* emphasized that it was the antisemitism inherent in the Germans of the period that combusted when the circumstances were right to produce murderous actions. The argument that all are born with the same inherent evil as that which was exercised by the Nazis simply is not the case. Some individuals during the Holocaust gave their lives for others. Perhaps there are some who need to be taught that they are evil to prevent them from doing evil. I believe we need to be taught that we are essentially good, so that when the times call for it, we are prepared to perform the heroic.

Notes

Introduction

1. For a fuller account of this development, see Michael Schuldiner, "Teaching Holocaust Literature: The New Revisionism," *Martyrdom and Resistance: Published by the International Society for Yad Vashem*, 21 (May–June 1995), 12–13.

2. Later I learned that this pattern of reasoning about what happened during the Holocaust is common among Holocaust deniers. See Deborah Lipstadt, *Denying the Holocaust: The Growing Assault on Truth and Memory* (New York: Penguin, 1993), 4.

3. See Stanley Milgram, *Obedience to Authority: An Experimental View* (New York: Harper & Row, 1974). However, see also the challenge to Milgram's views in Arthur G. Miller, *The Obedience Experiments: A Case Study of Controversy in the Social Sciences* (New York: Praeger, 1986).

4. See Richard J. Evans, *In Hitler's Shadow: West German Historians and the Attempt to Escape from the Nazi Past* (New York: Pantheon Books, 1989), Charles S. Maier, *The Unmasterable Past: History, Holocaust, and German National Identity* (Cambridge, MA: Harvard University Press, 1988), and Peter Baldwin, ed., *Reworking the Past: Hitler, the Holocaust, and the Historians' Debate* (Boston: Beacon Press, 1990).

5. Christopher R. Browning had based his view that the killers of German Police Battalion 101 were ordinary men performing under extraordinary circumstances on Milgram's experiments, although his arguments were made in a considerably more sophisticated manner than these students. Browning makes the important point, for example, that even though, in his view, anyone under similar circumstances might murder as those in Police Battalion 101 did, those who murdered are not thereby absolved of the evil they committed. See Browning, *Ordinary Men: Reserve Police Battalion 101 and the Final Solution in Poland*, with a new afterword (New York: HarperCollins, 1992), 171–189.

6. Heinz Kloss, in *Research Possibilities in the German-American Field*, by La Vern J. Rippley and Heinz Kloss (Hamburg: Buske, 1980); Michael Keresztesi and Gary R. Cocozzoli, *German-American History and Life: A Guide to Information Sources* (Detroit: Gale Research Co., 1980).

7. Timothy J. Holian, *The German-Americans and World War II: An Ethnic Experience* (New York: P. Lang, 1996); Don Heinrich Tolzmann, ed., *German-Americans in the World Wars*, 5 vols. (Munich: K.G. Saur, 1995–1998).

8. See, for example, Karl John Richard Arndt and May E. Olson, *German-American Newspapers and Periodicals, 1732–1955: History and Bibliography*, 2nd rev. ed. (New York: Johnson Reprint Corp., 1965).

Chapter 1

1. Timothy J. Holian, *The German-Americans and World War II: An Ethnic Experience* (New York: P. Lang, 1996), 16.

2. Don Heinrich Tolzmann, *The German-American Experience* (Amherst, NY: Humanity Books, 2000), 311.

3. La Vern Rippley, *The German-Americans* (Boston: Twayne Publishers, 1976), 126–127.

4. Ibid., 104–105.

5. Ibid., 166, 171.

6. Robert Paul McCaffery, *Islands of Deutschtum: German-Americans in Manchester, New Hampshire and Lawrence, Massachusetts, 1870–1942* (New York: P. Lang, 1996), 132.

7. According to Kathleen Neils Conzen, German Americans were among groups that championed not only their own ethnicity, but also helped create ethnicity as a category within American society. See Conzen, "Ger-

man-Americans and the Invention of Ethnicity," in Frank Trommler and Joseph McVeigh, eds., *America and the Germans: An Assessment of a Three-Hundred-Year History*, vol. 1 (Philadelphia: University of Pennsylvania Press, 1985), 131–147.

8. Tolzmann, *The German-American Experience*, 270–273.

9. Holian, *The German-Americans and World War II*, 12.

10. Sean Dennis Cashman, *America Ascendant: From Theodore Roosevelt to FDR in the Century of American Power, 1901–1945* (New York: New York University Press, 1998), 143.

11. Tolzmann, *The German-American Experience*, 274; see also Daniel M. Smith, *The Great Departure: The United States and World War I, 1914–1920* (New York: J. Wiley, 1965), 41.

12. Cashman, *America Ascendant*, 146.

13. Smith, *The Great Departure*, 18–25.

14. Ibid., 10–11.

15. Ibid., 19.

16. Ibid., 29.

17. Ibid., 14.

18. Tolzmann, *The German-American Experience*, 278–279.

19. Smith, *The Great Departure*, 74.

20. Cashman, *America Ascendant*, 151.

21. Tolzmann, *The German-American Experience*, 279.

22. Cashman, *America Ascendant*, 151–152.

23. Tolzmann, *The German-American Experience*, 281–282.

24. Ibid., 161–162.

25. Ibid., 179.

26. Ibid., 183.

27. Ibid., 280–285.

28. In *The Nazi Movement in the United States, 1924–1941* (Ithaca, NY: Cornell University Press, 1974), 41, 56, Sander A. Diamond identifies this organization as pro-German and composed of two million members.

29. Tolzmann, *The German-American Experience*, 260–262.

30. Ibid., 286–287.

31. Martin Gilbert, *First World War* (London: Weidenfeld and Nicolson, 1994), 2.

32. Tolzmann, *The German-American Experience*, 287–288.

33. Peter Frederick Stoll, "German-American 'Ethnicity' and 'Ego Identity'" (PhD diss., State University of New York at Albany, 1984), 91.

34. Tolzmann, *The German-American Experience*, 313–314.

35. Ibid., 335.

36. Ibid., 312.

37. Diamond, *The Nazi Movement in the United States*, 57–58.

38. Ibid., 60.

39. Ibid., 27–31.

40. Rippley, *The German-Americans*, 198–199.

41. Susan Canedy, *America's Nazis: A Democratic Dilemma* (Menlo Park, CA: Markgraf Publications Group, 1990), 51–53.

42. Diamond, *The Nazi Movement*, 128.

43. Ibid., 137–139.

44. Rippley, *The German-Americans*, 201–202, 210.

45. Diamond, *The Nazi Movement*, 140.

46. Ibid., 158–159, 163.

47. In the winter of 1934–1935, the membership rose to about ten thousand as organizations formerly under the umbrella of UGS joined the Bund because of the organizational disarray created by the Spanknoebel affair (ibid., 169).

48. Ibid., 146–147.

49. Ibid., 154.

50. Ibid., 159.

51. Ibid., 190.

52. Ibid., 181.

53. Ibid., 227–232.

54. Martin Dies to F.D. Roosevelt, cited in ibid., 258.

55. Ibid., 277.

56. Stanislaw Mikolajczyk, "The German Terror in Poland," in *Bestiality . . . unknown*, 44; Brendan Bracken, "Press Conference at the Ministry of Information," in *Bestiality . . . unknown*, 38–39.

57. See Arthur Koestler, "The Nightmare That Is a Reality," *New York Times Magazine* (January 9, 1944), 5; Edgar Snow, "Here the Nazi Butchers Wasted Nothing," *Saturday Evening Post*, October 28, 1944, 18–19, 96.

58. See "The President Denounces the Nazi Murder of French Hostages, October 25, 1941," in Samuel I. Rosenman, ed., *The Public Papers and Addresses of Franklin D. Roosevelt*, 1941 vol. (New York: Harper & Brothers, 1950), 433.

59. "The President Asks That Frontiers Be Opened to Victims of Nazi Oppression and Declares That War Criminals Will Be Tried and Punished,

March 24, 1944," in Rosenman, ed., *The Public Papers and Addresses of Franklin D. Roosevelt*, 1944–45 vol., 104.

60. Don Heinrich Tolzmann, ed., *German-Americans in the World Wars*, vol. 4, *The World War Two Experience: The Internment of German-Americans* (Munich: K.G. Saur, 1995), section 1, part 1, 1498.

61. Ibid.

62. "Prisons and Concentration Camps," in *Bestiality . . . unknown*, 9–19.

63. Ibid., 9.

64. In *Bestiality . . . unknown*, 28–29.

65. "General Sikorski's Protest Speech," in *Bestiality . . . unknown*, 32.

66. Ibid., 33.

67. Ibid., 34.

68. "Press Conference at the Ministry of Information," in *Bestiality . . . unknown*, 38–39.

69. In *The Abandonment of the Jews: America and the Holocaust, 1941–1945* (New York: Pantheon Books, 1984), 26–30, David S. Wyman explains how reports of the mass murders of Jews were met with skepticism. See also Deborah Lipstadt, *Denying the Holocaust: The Growing Assault on Truth and Memory* (New York: Penguin, 1994), 34.

70. "Germans Impose Mass Death on Russian Prisoners," *Life*, February 23, 1942, 26.

71. Koestler, "The Nightmare That Is a Reality," Section VI, 5, 30.

72. See David Cesarani, *Arthur Koestler: The Homeless Mind* (London: W. Heinemann, 1998), 189.

73. Snow, "Here the Nazi Butchers Wasted Nothing," 19.

74. Ibid.

75. Ibid., 18.

76. "This Is Why There Must Be No Soft Peace," *Saturday Evening Post*, October 28, 1944, 18. It is worth noting that the above statement includes one of the earliest appearances of the word "holocaust" to describe Nazi violence. It is also interesting that the context suggests that Germany had in the past perpetrated a holocaust.

77. See "Statement Warning Against Axis Crimes in Occupied Countries, August 21, 1942," in Rosenman, ed., *The Public Papers of Franklin D. Roosevelt*, 1942 vol., 329–330.

78. "Statement Issued by President Roosevelt, Prime Minister Churchill, and Premier Stalin Regarding Atrocities, November 1, 1943," in Rosenman, ed., *The Public Papers of Franklin D. Roosevelt*, 1943 vol., 498–499.

79. "The President Asks That Frontiers Be Opened to Victims of Nazi Oppression and Declares That War Criminals Will Be Tried and Punished, March 24, 1944," in Rosenman, ed., *The Public Papers of Franklin D. Roosevelt*, 1944–45 vol., 104.

80. "The German Terror in Poland," *Bestiality . . . unknown*, 44.

81. Tolzmann, ed., *German-Americans in the World Wars*, section 1, part 1, 1696.

82. Ibid., 1498.

83. Arnold Krammer, *Undue Process: The Untold Story of America's German Alien Internees* (London: Rowman & Littlefield, 1997), 18–21.

84. Ibid., 15–18.

85. Esther Heffernan, "The Alderson Years," *Federal Prison Journal* (Spring 1992), 21–26.

86. Tolzmann, ed., *German-Americans in the World Wars*, 5 vols. (Munich: K.G. Saur, 1995–1998), 4.1.2.

87. Emily Brosveen, The Texas State Historical Association, "World War II Internment Camps," *The Handbook of Texas Online* (available at http://www.tshaonline.org/handbook/online/articles/WW/quwby.html, accessed October 13, 2008).

88. U.S. Census Bureau, Census of Housing, 1940, "Historical Census of Housing Tables, Crowding" (available at http://www.census.gov/hhes/www/housing/census/historic/crowding.html, accessed October 14, 2008).

89. U.S. Census Bureau, Census of Housing, 1940, "Historical Census of Housing Tables, Plumbing Facilities" (available at http://www.census.gov/hhes/www/housing/census/historic/plumbing.html, accessed October 14, 2008).

90. Tolzmann, *German-American*, 4.1.2, 1987, 1995.

91. Employment Policies Institute, "Minimum Wage Statistics" (available at http://www.epionline.org/mw_statistics_annual.cfm, accessed October 14, 2008).

92. Tolzmann, *German-American*, 4.1.2, 1914, 1980, 1986.

93. Ibid., 1987, 1998.

94. Ibid., 1987.

95. Ibid., 1985.

96. Heffernan, "The Alderson Years," 26.

97. Tolzmann, *German-American*, 4.1.2, 1903, 1912, 1917–1918, 1920, 1977.

98. Ibid., 1917, 1918, 1922–1923.

99. Ibid., 1909–1911, 1924.

100. Ibid., 1921.

101. Ibid., 1945–1946.

102. Ibid., 1919.

103. Ibid., 1908, 1922, 1976.

104. Ibid., 1936, 1976.

105. Ibid., 2027–2028, 2031, 2041, 2044.

106. Mitchell G. Bard, *Forgotten Victims: The Abandonment of Americans in Hitler's Camps* (Boulder, CO: Westview Press, 1994), 20–21.

107. Holian, *The German-Americans and World War II*, 138–140.

108. Ibid., 151.

109. Stoll, "German-American 'Ethnicity' and 'Ego Identity,'" 163.

Chapter 2

1. Herbert Dunelm, Bp. of Durham, Introduction, *The Yellow Spot: the outlawing of half a million human beings: a collection of facts and documents relating to three years' persecution of German Jews derived chiefly from National Socialist sources, very carefully assembled by a group of investigators* (London: Voctor, 1936), 34.

2. Deborah E. Lipstadt, *Beyond Belief: The American Press and the Coming of the Holocaust, 1933–1945* (New York: Free Press, 1986), 14–15.

3. Cited in Avraham Barkai, *From Boycott to Annihilation: The Economic Struggle of the German Jews, 1933–1943*, trans. William Templer (Hanover, NH and London: University Press of New England, 1989), 14–15.

4. *The Yellow Spot*, 37–38.

5. Barkai, *From Boycott to Annihilation*, 15.

6. *The Yellow Spot*, 36.

7. Barkai, *From Boycott to Annihilation*, 15–16.

8. Lipstadt, *Beyond Belief*, 18.

9. *New York Times*, March 28, 1933, 1.

10. See Gulie Ne'eman Arad, *America, Its Jews and the Rise of Nazism* (Bloomington, IN: Indiana University Press, 2000), 54–56; and Moshe R. Gottlieb, *American Anti-Nazi Resistance, 1933–1941: An Historical Analysis* (New York: Ktav Publishing House, 1982), 37–38.

11. Cited in Gottlieb, *American Anti-Nazi Resistance*, 31.

12. Ibid., 46–47.

13. *New York Times*, March 28, 1933, 1, 11, 12, 13.

14. Ibid., 1.

15. Ibid., 12.

16. Barkai, *From Boycott to Annihilation*, 17–25.

17. Gottlieb, *American Anti-Nazi Resistance*, 47.

18. Ibid., 53.

19. Ibid., 55.

20. Ibid., 104–105.

21. Ibid., 80–81, 392.

22. Ibid., 129.

23. Ibid., 131.

24. *New York Times*, March 28, 1933, 12.

25. The American Jewish Committee, *The Jews in Nazi Germany: The Factual Record of Their Persecution by the National Socialists* (New York: American Jewish Committee, 1933), 45–46.

26. See "Nazis Here Spur Counter-Boycott," *New York Times*, May 9, 1934, 4.

27. *New York Times*, March 28, 1934, 19; July 4, 1935, 16.

28. "Bias Is Charged to German Group," *New York Times*, May 11, 1934, 11.

29. "Nazis Here Spur Counter-Boycott," *New York Times*, May 9, 1934, 4.

30. See Sander A. Diamond, *The Nazi Movement in the United States, 1924–1941* (Ithaca, NY and London: Cornell University Press, 1974), 137–139.

31. "Nazis Here Launch a Counter-Boycott," *New York Times*, July 4, 1935, 16.

32. Kurt D. Singer, *Confidential Report on 1036 Pro-Nazi Firms Who Believed You Could Do Business with Hitler* (New York: News Background, 1942), iii, 50.

33. "Boycott's End Aim of Germans Here," *New York Times*, June 13, 1934, 11.

34. "20,000 Nazi Friends at a Rally Here Denounce Boycott," *New York Times*, May 18, 1934, 1.

35. Gottlieb, *American Anti-Nazi Resistance*, 57–58.

36. Ibid., 262–263.

37. Wayne S. Cole, *Senator Gerald P. Nye and American Foreign Relations* (Minneapolis: University of Minnesota Press, 1962), 24–41, passim.

38. Ibid., 24.

39. Samuel Lubell, "Who Votes Isolationist and Why," *Harper's Magazine*, April 1951, 33, passim.

40. U.S. Senate, Propaganda in Motion Pictures: Hearings Before a Sub-committee of the Committee on Interstate Commerce, Seventy-Seventh Congress, First Session on Senate Resolution 152: A Resolution Authorizing an Investigation of War Propaganda Disseminated by the Motion-Picture Industry and of Any Monopoly in the Production, Distribution, or Exhibition of Motion Pictures (Washington, DC: Government Printing Office, 1942), 22. (Hereafter cited as Senate Hearings.)

41. Senate Hearings, 9–10.

42. Ibid., 35.

43. Ibid., 11, 48.

44. Ibid, 15–17.

45. Ibid., 37.

46. Ibid., 58.

47. Ibid., 56.

48. Ibid., 71. The suggestion that if Hitler's atrocities are being represented, then Stalin's should be too was also voiced later in the hearings in the testimony of John T. Flynn, chairman of the America First Committee (ibid., 103).

49. Ibid., 341, 381.

50. Ibid., 338, 340, 343.

51. Ibid., 338–339, 364.

52. Ibid., 371.

53. Ibid., 374.

54. Ibid., 386. *The Mortal Storm* (1940) is the story of the Roth family, non-Aryans who lead a quiet life in a small village in the German Alps in the early 1930s. When the Nazis come to power, the family is divided and Martin Brietner, a family friend is caught up in the turmoil.

55. Ibid., 370–371.

56. Ibid., 71.

57. Ibid., 389.

Chapter 3

1. U.S. Department of Commerce, Bureau of the Census, *Fifteenth Census of the United States: 1930 Population*, vol. II (Washington, DC: Government Printing Office, 1933), 27, 268.

2. Don Heinrich Tolzmann, *The German-American Experience* (Amherst, NY: Humanity Books, 2000), 268.

3. U.S. Department of Commerce, Bureau of the Census, *1980 Census of Population*, vol. 1, *Characteristics of the Population, Chapter C, General Social and Economic Characteristics: Part I, United States Summary* (Washington, DC: Government Printing Office, 1983), 14.

4. Steuben Society of America, "Purpose of the Steuben Society of America," 1996 (available at http://www.steubensociety.org/ssap.html).

5. Steuben Society of America, "The Seal of the Steuben Society of America," 1996 (available at http://www.steubensociety.org/seal.html).

6. Steuben Society of America, "1998–2000 PLATFORM and PROGRAM of the NATIONAL COUNCIL STEUBEN SOCIETY of AMERICA, as adopted by the 38th BIENNIAL NATIONAL CONVENTION, Kingston, NY, September 10–13, 1998" (available at http://www.steubensociety.org/ssaplat.html#ENRC).

7. Steuben Society of America, Members page (available at http://www.steubensociety.org/Members.htm, accessed on January 9, 2011).

8. Alan Schwartz, research director, Anti-Defamation League of B'nai B'rith, e-mail letter to author, April 25, 2000.

9. Deborah Lipstadt, *Denying the Holocaust: The Growing Assault on Truth and Memory* (New York: Penguin, 1994), 85–86.

10. Austin J. App, "The Six Million Swindle: Blackmailing the German People for Hard Marks with Fabricated Corpses" [1976] in *No Time for Silence*, 19.

11. "Unit Renamed in Honor of Dr. App," *The Steuben News* (November 1985), 3.

12. E. Stanley Rittenhouse, cited in *ADL Education Pamphlet* (New York: Anti-Defamation League, [1985]), 120.

13. Schwartz, telephone conversation, with author, May 4, 2000.

14. German American National Congress, "DANK: The Voice of Germans from Coast to Coast" (available at http://www.dank.org/index.html).

15. German American National Congress, "DANK Chapters and Presidents" (available at http://www.dank.org/dank_chapters_and_presidents.html).

16. German American National Congress, "Why DANK? United We Are Strong" (available at http://www.dank.org/why_dank_.html).

17. On occasion, an article from the president of the German American Police Association will appear in the newspaper of the German American

National Congress. See Norbert Holzinger, "President's Message," *Der Deutsch-Amerikaner* (June 1985), 9.

18. German American National Congress, "DANK Schools" (available at http://www.dank.org/schools.html).

19. The United German Action Committee of the U.S.A. is an organization established to create a national German-American museum in Washington, DC (see United German-American Committee of the U.S.A., Inc., "Building for Our Future" (available at http://www.ugac.org).

20. German American National Congress, "What Is DANK?" (http://www.dank.org/what_is_dank_.html, accessed April 25, 2000).

21. See, for example, "Patricia Kordas: Miss D.A.N.K. U.S.A.," *Der Deutsch-Amerikaner* (October 1986), 2.

22. Schwarz, telephone conversation with author, May 4, 2000.

23. Jennifer O'Connell, ed., *EBSCO's Serials Directory*, 13th ed., vol. 3 (Birmingham, AL: EBSCO Publishing, 1999), 6069.

24. *Ulrich's International Periodicals Directory, 1999*, 37th ed., vol. II (New Providence, NJ: R.R. Bowker, 1998), 2834.

25. Gilbert Fezer, "Letters to the Editor," *The German American Journal* (January 1993), 9. For promotion of a single official language, see, for example, Marvin Stone, "Bring Back the Melting Pot," Guest Editorial, *The Steuben News* (April 1978), 4.

26. "German American 'Roots,'" Editor's Message, *The Steuben News* (October 1985), 4.

27. For example, Dr. H.G. Kosmahl's $15,000 award from the National Aeronautics and Space Administration for developing the world's most powerful and efficient amplifier of audio and visual signals was discussed in a news story: "Dr. H. G. Kosmahl Received Highest Award," *Der Deutsch-Amerikaner* (October 1980), 7.

28. See, for example, "Steinway Unit Gives Awards and Scholarships," *The Steuben News* (September 1985), 3, which reports about the annual breakfast of the German Honor Society of the Patchogue Medford High School, at which Michael Gilg was presented with the Steuben medal.

29. "The Rebirth of a German Artist in the United States," *Der Deutsch-Amerikaner* (November 1979), 1; "Hermann the Cheruscan: Preserving the Second Largest Copper Statue in the United States," *Der Deutsch-Amerikaner* (June–July 1999), 14.

30. See Robert P. Mollenhauer, Jr., "Monthly Tax Letter: Corporate Tax Tip—Fill in Those Corporate Records," *The Steuben News* (October 1985), 4.

31. See, for example, Lee Schlack, "Ex-POW Living in Washington: Luft-waffe Corporal Recalls War," *Der Deutsch-Amerikaner* (May 1980), 7; or Julie Jensen, "G. Wegehaupt, DANK-Member in Iowa: Captured 3 Times by Russians," *Der Deutsch-Amerikaner* (October 1980), 3.

32. "Hamburg-Holocaust—July 1943; Unter den Bomben," *Der Deutsch-Amerikaner* (August 1985), 8. See also Dr. A. R. Wesserle, "The British Blitz," *Der Deutsch-Amerikaner* (May 1981), 2; and Anna Guagliano, "Dresden Remembered," *The Steuben News* (March 1987), 6. For a more authoritative discussion, see Karl Hecks (*Bombing 1939–45: The Air Offensive against Land Targets in World War Two* (London: Hale, 1990), 205, who identifies the number of dead at 30,000.

33. Dr. Karl T. Marx, "Random Thoughts," *The Steuben News* (July–August 1985), 2.

34. See Hellmuth Auerbach, "Literatur zum Thema: Ein kritischer Über-blick," in Wolfgang Benz, ed., *Die Vertreibung der Deutschen aus dem Osten: Ursachen, Ereignisse, Folgen* (Frankfurt: Ullstein, 1985), 226.

35. "Stalin Was Grim Reaper in Ukrainian Famine," *The Steuben News* (October 1986), 5.

36. See Robert Conquest, *The Harvest of Sorrow: Soviet Collectivization and the Terror-Famine* (London: Hutchinson, 1986), 303.

37. Peter Mueller, "The Vanishing German Americans," *The Steuben News* (November–December 1977), 8; the contention that Germans are identi-fied with Nazis also appears, to take one more example, in Jerry Klein, "The Germans: A People Burdened with Two Stereotypes," *Der Deutsch-Amerikaner* (March 1981), 2.

38. Randy Ratje, "The Plight of German-Americans," *The Steuben News* (March 1985), 7.

39. Ibid., 8.

40. "Public TV Can Also Goof," *The Steuben News* (March–April 1978), 5.

41. "Keeping the Holocaust Alive," *The Steuben News* (November–December 1977), 4.

42. "Reflections on 'Holocaust,'" *The Steuben News* (July–August 1978), 4.

43. "Steuben Convention Adopts Resolutions on Issues Affecting All Ameri-cans," *The Steuben News* (September–October 1978), 1.

44. Edward T. Linenthal, *Preserving Memory: The Struggle to Create America's Holocaust Museum* (New York: Viking, 1995), 17–19.

45. Ibid., 46.

46. Ibid., 99.

47. Ibid., 57–62.

48. A myth had been, and continues to some extent to be perpetuated, that there were 11 million total victims of Nazism. Actually, the figure of 11 million was given by Adolph Eichmann at his trial, but it was not the number of total victims. The figure of 11 million given by Eichmann was the estimated total number of Jews in Europe, the number of Jews who were targeted by the Nazis.

49. Judith Miller, "Holocaust Museum: A Troubled Start," *New York Times Magazine* (April 22, 1990), 42, 47–48.

50. Phillip Gourevitch, "Behold Now Behemoth—The Holocaust Memorial Museum: One More American Theme Park," *Harper's Magazine*, 287 (July 1993), 59.

51. Phil McCombs, "U.S. Donates Two Buildings: Holocaust Museum for Mall," *Washington Post*, March 3, 1983, A1, A5.

52. George F. Will, "Holocaust Museum: Antidote for Innocence," *Washington Post*, March 10, 1983, A19.

53. McCombs, "U.S. Donates Two Buildings," A5.

54. "Letters to the Editor: Remembering the Holocaust—and More," *Washington Post*, March 14, 1983, A10.

55. William Raspberry, "Some Questions about a Memorial to the Holocaust," *Washington Post*, April 25, 1983, A11.

56. Fath Davis Ruffins, "Culture Wars Won and Lost: Ethnic Museums on the Mall, Part I: The National Holocaust Museum and the National Museum of the American Indian," *Radical History Review*, 68 (1997), 90–91.

57. "White House Correspondence Tracking Worksheet," Ronald Reagan Library: A Presidential Library Administered by the National Archives and Records Administration, Simi Valley, CA, item 137357/PA002.

58. See Elsbeth M. Seewald, "Oppose Holocaust Memorial," *Der Deutsch-Amerikaner* (April 1983), 10.

59. Schmidt does not use the word "myth" in a literary sense. He uses the word "myth" to mean an event that did not take place. See, for example, Hans Schmidt, "Realpolitik 1985: The Lessons of Bitburg," *GANPAC Brief* (June 1985), 2.

60. Letters from Hans Schmidt, chairman, GANPAC, to President Ronald Reagan, and reply to Schmidt from Micah H. Naftalin, U.S. Holocaust Memorial Council, Ronald Reagan Library: A Presidential Library Administered by the National Archives and Records Administration, Simi Valley, CA, item 135844/PA002.

61. Dr. Karl T. Marx, "Holocaust Museum Perpetuates Memories of World War II," *The Steuben News* (April–May 1983), 8.

62. I exclude here Seewald and Schmidt's letters and the replies to Seewald and Schmidt from Siegel and Naftalin; letters that were reprinted in several issues, which included Seewald's letter and four other letters that had already been published in previous issues, and which happened to be opposed to the Holocaust museum; letters that simply acknowledged Seewald's request to write to Congressmen; and letters that only expressed irritation at being asked to take part in a political act of any type. However, I include letters that did not focus on the issue of the museum, but in the course of discussing another issue registered opposition to it. Of these, two letters, or 10 percent, favored the creation of a Holocaust museum; and of those two, one favored a Holocaust museum that included exhibits about other atrocities the world over, as well as the one experienced by the victims of the Nazis.

63. See I. Bremer, "Leserbriefe," *Der Deutsch-Amerikaner* (June 1983), 2; Meta Well, "Leserbriefe," *Der Deutsch-Amerikaner* (June 1983), 10; M. L. Wilson, "Back to Germany," *Der Deutsch-Amerikaner* (September 1983), 4; Hedwig Bilger, "Compliment," *Der Deutsch-Amerikaner* (September 1983), 4.

64. See Peter Flinspach, "Leserbriefe," *Der Deutsch-Amerikaner* (June 1983), 2; Hannelore Stocker, "Holocaust Museum Letters," *Der Deutsch-Amerikaner* (August 1983), 8; Erika Radavicius, "Holocaust Museum Letters," *Der Deutsch-Amerikaner* (August 1983), 9; Thomas Seibert, "Holocaust Museum Letters," *Der Deutsch-Amerikaner* (August 1983), 9; Karl H. Kuebler, "Protest Museum," *Der Deutsch-Amerikaner* (September 1983), 5; and Stefan Gross, "Leserbriefe," *Der Deutsch-Amerikaner* (November 1983), 3.

65. Gross, "Leserbriefe," 3.

66. Leroy, a Hopi, "Holocaust Museum Letters," *Der Deutsch-Amerikaner* (August 1983), 8.

67. Nancy A. Carter, "Holocaust Museum Letters," *Der Deutsch-Amerikaner* (August 1983), 9.

68. See Peter Flinspach, "Leserbriefe," 2; Stocker, "Holocaust Museum Letters," 8; Erika Radavicius, "Holocaust Museum Letters," 9; Seibert, "Holocaust Museum Letters," 9; Gross, "Leserbriefe," 3.

69. Flinspach, "Leserbriefe," 2.

70. Seibert, "Holocaust Museum Letters," 9.

71. Joseph Stein, "Holocaust Museum Letters," *Der Deutsch-Amerikaner* (August 1983), 8; see also Seibert, "Holocaust Museum Letters," 9.

72. Gross, "Leserbriefe," 3.

73. See Rosalie Hannemann, "Holocaust Museum Letters," *Der Deutsch-Amerikaner* (August 1983), 9; Inge Beyer-Marambio, "Leserbriefe," *Der Deutsch-Amerikaner* (September 1983), 4; Raymond Braun, "Leserbriefe," *Der Deutsch-Amerikaner* (October 1983), 4; Gustav R. Thim, "Leserbriefe," *Der Deutsch-Amerikaner* (December 1983), 2; Dr. Kurt Peter Scharnhorst, "Leserbriefe," *Der Deutsch-Amerikaner* (December 1983), 2.

74. Braun, "Leserbriefe," 4.

75. "Institute for Historical Review Leaflets: A Few Facts about the Institute for Historical Review" (December 1998) (available at http://www.ihr.org/leaflets/fewfacts.html).

76. See Susan Ann Huss, "Holocaust Museum Letters," *Der Deutsch-Amerikaner* (August 1983), 9; Inge Beyer-Marambio, "Leserbriefe," *Der Deutsch-Amerikaner* (August 1983), 8; Seibert, "Holocaust Museum Letters," 9.

77. Huss, "Holocaust Museum Letters," 9.

78. Hans Schmidt, "Leserbriefe," *Der Deutsch-Amerikaner* (June 1983), 2.

Chapter 4

1. "Remarks of President Reagan to Regional Editors, White House, April 18, 1985," in Geoffrey Hartman, ed., *Bitburg in Moral and Political Perspective* (Bloomington, IN: Indiana University Press, 1986), 240.

2. Raul Hilberg, "Bitburg as Symbol," in Hartman, ed., *Bitburg*, 18.

3. Hartman, ed., *Bitburg*, xiii–xv.

4. Stewart Powell, "Reagan in Germany: Coming to Terms with the Past," *U.S. News and World Report*, 98 (May 6, 1985), 24.

5. Cited in Ed Magnuson, "A Misbegotten Tip Opens Old Wounds: Reagan's Ill-Planned Journey Sparks a Furor on Both Sides of the Atlantic," *Time*, 125 (April 29, 1985), 18 [6].

6. Lance Morrow, "'Forgiveness to the Injured Doth Belong,'" *Time* (May 20, 1985), 90.

7. Arthur Schlesinger, Jr., "The Rush to Reconcile," *Wall Street Journal*, May 9, 1985, in Hartman, ed., *Bitburg*, 182.

8. Mary McGrory, "Decline and Send No Regrets," *The Washington Post*,

April 23, 1985, in Ilya Levkov, ed., *Bitburg and Beyond: Encounters in American, German and Jewish History* (New York: Shapolsky Publishers, 1987), 448.

9. "Bitburg Bears Remembering," *New York Times*, May 6, 1985, in Levkov, ed., *Bitburg and Beyond*, 469.

10. "The False Choice of Bitburg," *New York Times*, April 21, 1985, in Levkov, ed., *Bitburg and Beyond*, 445.

11. Charles Krauthammer, "The Bitburg Fiasco," *Time*, 125 (April 29, 1985), 90.

12. Elie Wiesel, "Remarks of Elie Wiesel at Ceremony for Jewish Heritage Week and Presentation of Congressional Gold Medal, White House, April 19, 1985, in Hartman, ed., *Bitburg*, 243.

13. Ronald Reagan, "Remarks of President Reagan at Bitburg Air Base, May 5, 1985," in Hartman, ed., *Bitburg*, 259.

14. William R. Doener, "Paying Homage to History: Caught in a Storm of Controversy, Reagan Tries to Heal Old Wounds," *Time*, 125 (May 13, 1985), 10.

15. Notably, by Menachem Rosensaft, chairman of the International Network of Children of Jewish Holocaust Survivors (cited in Stewart Powell, "Reagan in Germany: Coming to Terms with the Past," *U.S. News and World Report*, 98 [May 6, 1985], 24 [3]); but see also, for example, Stanley Diamond, "Cemetery Politics," *The Nation*, 240 (May 4, 1985), 516.

16. The meeting of the former SS troopers was reported in the American press by, among others, Martin E. Marty, "'Storycide' and the Meaning of History," *Los Angeles Times*, May 12, 1985, reprinted in Hartman, ed., *Bitburg*, 225; it was also reported by Powell, "Reagan in Germany," 24 [3].

17. Morrow, "'Forgiveness,'" 90.

18. Cited in Mark Krupnick, "'Walking in Our Sleep': Bitburg and the Post–1939 Generation," *The Christian Century*, June 5–12, 1985, in Hartman, ed., *Bitburg*, 188.

19. Flora Lewis, "Another 40 Years," *New York Times*, May 5, 1985, in Levkov, ed., *Bitburg and Beyond*, 465.

20. Krupnick, "'Walking in Our Sleep,'" 187–188.

21. Jürgen Habermas, "Diffusing the Past: A Politico-Cultural Tract," trans. Thomas Levin, in Hartman, ed., *Bitburg*, 45.

22. Schlesinger, "The Rush to Reconcile," in Hartman, ed., *Bitburg*, 182–183.

23. Krupnick, "'Walking in Our Sleep,'" 190.

24. George J. Church, "Scratches in the Teflon: On the Eve of His Trip to Europe, Reagan Catches the Flak at Home," *Time*, 125 (May 6, 1985), 12 [3].

25. Dorothy Rabinowitz, "Bitburg Is a Long Way from Arlington," *New York Post*, April 26, 1985, in Levkov, ed., *Bitburg and Beyond*, 454.

26. McGrory, "Decline," in Levkov, ed., *Bitburg and Beyond*, 448.

27. Reverend Franklin H. Littell, "Despite Bitburg Blunders, Religious Leaders Work for Real Reconciliation," *The Jewish Times*, May 9, 1985, in Levkov, ed., *Bitburg and Beyond*, 472.

28. William L. Chaze and James M. Hildreth, "The Rebound Begins," *U.S. News & World Report*, 98 (May 20, 1985), 26 [5].

29. Magnuson, "A Misbegotten Trip," 18 [6].

30. Krauthammer, "The Bitburg Fiasco," 90.

31. Jody Powell, "Why the President Should Go to Bitburg," *Los Angeles Times* (April 17, 1985), in Levkov, ed., *Bitburg and Beyond*, 440.

32. Powell, "Reagan in Germany," 24 [3]

33. Robert Haeger, "Bitburg: Reagan's 'Magnanimous Gift,'" *U.S. News & World Report*, 98 (May 13, 1985), 26.

34. Church, "Scratches in the Teflon," 12 [3].

35. Doener, "Paying Homage to History," 12.

36. Magnuson, "A Misbegotten Trip," 18 [6].

37. "About Cemeteries," *Wall Street Journal* (April 19, 1985), in Hartman, ed., *Bitburg*, 174.

38. Krupnick, "'Walking in Our Sleep,'" 189.

39. Tyler Marshall, "Germans Decry Bitburg Furor," *Los Angeles Times* (April 30, 1985), in Hartman, ed., *Bitburg*, 221.

40. McGeorge Bundy, "What Transcends Bitburg," *New York Times* (May 2, 1985), in Levkov, ed., *Bitburg and Beyond*, 462–463. Mertes apparently made different arguments at different times. According to Flora Lewis, Mertes argued, along lines similar to those of Bundy, that one cannot hold a people collectively accountable for a crime. He thereby suggested that forgiveness was in order for at least some. Lewis, "Another 40 Years," in Levkov, ed., *Bitburg and Beyond*, 465.

41. Magnuson, "A Misbegotten Trip," 18 [6].

42. Marshall, "Germans Decry Bitburg Furor," 222.

43. "The Bitburg Phenomenon," *National Review*, 37 (May 17, 1985), 12 [2]. Although this issue is dated after the Bitburg visit, internal evidence indicates that the article was written before. Some magazines mark their issues with an expiry date, as opposed to a publication date, in order to maximize sales.

44. June Tierny, "Enough War Guilt," *The Washington Post* (April 28, 1985), in Levkov, ed., *Bitburg and Beyond*, 458–61.

45. Magnuson, "A Misbegotten Trip," 18 [6]. Similar comments are reported by Doener, "Paying Homage to History," 11.

46. "Rette sich wer Kann! Ein Augenzeugenbericht vom Untegang Berlin 1945," *Der Deutsch-Amerikaner* (May 1985), 4; "Haben wir schon vergessen," *Der Deutsch-Amerikaner* (May 1985), 4.

47. Telegram from Elsbeth M. Seewald to President Ronald Reagan, *Der Deutsch-Amerikaner* (May 1985), 2.

48. "Unit Renamed in Honor of Dr. App," *The Steuben News* (November 1985), 3.

49. Lou Cannon, *President Reagan: The Role of a Lifetime* (New York: Simon & Schuster, 1991), 577–579.

50. "Memorandum and Attachments from Linas Kojelis to Pat Buchanan," The Ronald Reagan Library, Simi, CA, item 311527/1110/TR123-01. Linas Kojelis continued to provide Buchanan with information supporting the president's trip (see item 313090/1110/TR123-01).

51. Dr. Dung H. Phan, Letter to the Editor, *Der Deutsch-Amerikaner* (June 1985), 6.

52. Deborah Lipstadt, *Denying the Holocaust: The Growing Assault on Truth and Memory* (New York: Penguin, 1994), 39.

53. Elsbeth Seewald, "Address of National President Seewald," *Der Deutsch-Amerikaner* (June 1985), 8.

54. Elsbeth Seewald, "Reconciliation Attempt Applauded, Overdue," *The Arizona Republic* (May 12, 1985), C4.

55. Elsbeth M. Seewald, [Letter to the Chairman of the Federal Communications Corporation], *Der Deutsch-Amerikaner* (May 1985), 5.

56. George H. W. Bush, "Bush Comments on Reagan Visit," *The Steuben News*, 58 (June 1985), 5; Dr. Marianne Bouvier, "President Reagan's Bitburg Cemetery Visit," *Der Deutsch-Amerikaner* (June 1985), 6; Gert Wegner, "Reagan's Visit to Germany; President's Plan Praised," *The Steuben News* (May 1985), 5.

57. Elsbeth Seewald, "A Message to All Members of the US Congress and Senate," *Der Deutsch-Amerikaner* (June 1985), 1.

58. Dr. Karl T. Marx, "Fallout from the Bitburg Affair," In Retrospect, *The Steuben News*, 58 (June 1985), 1, 6.

59. Helmut Kohl, "Excerpts from Chancellor Kohl's Remarks during the Bundestag Debate on President Reagan's Visit to Germany, Delivered April 25, 1985," *The Steuben News*, 58 (May 1985), 7.

60. Karl T. Marx, "Reagan Plan to Visit German Cemetery Causes Furor in U.S.," *The Steuben News*, 58 (May 1985), 2.

61. See Richard J. Evans, *In Hitler's Shadow: West German Historians and the Attempt to Escape from the Nazi Past* (New York: Pantheon, 1989), 80–88.

62. "West German President Urges Countrymen to Face Up to Germany's Past," *The Steuben News*, 58 (September 1985), 5.

63. Sabina Lietzmann, "The German War Dead," *The Steuben News*, 58 (May 1985), 5.

64. George J. Beichl, "The German Side Should Be Told," *Der Deutsch-Amerikaner* (June 1985), 6.

65. See Beichl, "The German Side Should Be Told," *New Yorker Staats-Zeitung und Herold*, 151 (11–12 May 1985), A-2; Beichl, "The German Side Should Be Told," *Philadelphia Gazette-Democrat* (June 1985), 2, 8.

66. Seymour Siegel, "Holocaust Museum Letters," *Der Deutsch-Amerikaner* (August 1983), 8.

67. Karl T. Marx, "Random Thoughts," *The Steuben News* (July–August 1985), 2.

68. Marx, "Fallout from the Bitburg Affair," 8. These figures are of course exaggerated considerably.

69. Seewald, "Address," 9.

70. Marx, "Fallout from the Bitburg Affair," 6.

71. Edward Rubel, "Holocaust: The Other Side of the Coin," *Der Deutsch-Amerikaner*, (June 1985), 4.

72. Marx, "Reagan Plan," 2.

73. For a discussion of the Institute for Historical Review, see Lipstadt, *Denying the Holocaust*, 137–156.

74. G.T., "'Wo sind die Denker?'" *Der Deutsch-Amerikaner* (June 1985), 4.

75. See Anna Guagliano, "Writer Tired of Turning the Other Cheek," *The Steuben News*, (January–February 1981), 4.

76. "A DANK Editorial: 40 Years after the War," *Der Deutsch-Amerikaner* (May 1985), 1.

77. E.M.S., "40 Years Ago: The First Atomic Bomb," *Der Deutsch-Amerikaner* (September 1985), 1.

78. "*Editorial*: Another 40th Anniversary," *The Steuben News* (July–August 1985), 4.
79. "Mayor Koch Holds 'Open House' for German Americans," *The Steuben News* (July–August 1985), 4
80. Raul Hilberg, "Bitburg as Symbol," in Hartman, ed., *Bitburg in Moral and Political Perspective*, 21.
81. Karl T. Marx, "*Random Thoughts*: Recognition for Victims of German Resistance," *The Steuben News* (April 1987), 2.

Chapter 5

1. The conversation took place in a cafeteria at Northwestern University at the Institute for the Holocaust and Jewish Civilization in summer of 1997.
2. Browning, *Ordinary Men: Reserve Police Battalion 101 and the Final Solution in Poland*, with a new afterword (New York: HarperCollins, 1992), 4–6, 53–55, 142.
3. Ibid., 5.
4. Ibid., 184.
5. Goldhagen, Daniel, "The 'Cowardly' Executioner: On Disobedience in the SS," *Patterns of Prejudice* 19(2) (1985), 19–32.
6. Browning, *Ordinary Men*, xvi–xvii.
7. Ibid., xx. Browning repeats this statement in an article, "German Memory," in Saul Friedlander, *Probing the Limits* (Cambridge, MA: Harvard University Press, 1992), 36.
8. Christopher Browning, Review of *Aspects of the Third Reich*, *Holocaust and Genocide Studies* 2(1) (1987): 161–164.
9. Browning, *Ordinary Men,* 162.
10. Ibid., 43, 64, 82–83.
11. Ibid., 114–120, 188.
12. Ibid., 176–184.
13. Robert Michael suggests this in his otherwise very fine and very important study, *Holy Hatred: Christianity, Antisemitism, and the Holocaust* (New York: Palgrave Macmillan, 2006), 174.
14. Arthur G. Miller, *The Obedience Experiments: A Case Study of Controversy in the Social Sciences* (New York: Praeger, 1986), 2 (see Introduction, n. 3).

15. Cited in ibid., 11, 214.

16. Browning, *Ordinary Men*, 174.

17. Ibid., 166.

18. Ibid., 189.

19. Ibid., 388–389.

20. Claude Lanzmann, "The Obscenity of Understanding: An Evening with Claude Lanzmann," *American Imago: Studies in Psychoanalysis and Culture*, 48(4) (Winter 1991), 478–484.

21. Goldhagen, *Hitler's Willing Executioners: Ordinary Germans and the Holocaust* (New York: Knopf, 1996), 417.

22. Ibid., 416 (Goldhagen's italics).

23. Ibid., 417.

24. Ibid., 118, 121.

25. Ibid., 367–369.

26. Ibid., 241, 246–247.

27. Ibid., 241.

28. Ibid., 346, 357.

29. But see Robert Michael's *Holy Hatred: Christianity, Antisemitism, and the Holocaust* (New York: Palgrave Macmillan, 2006), 182, in which he argues that Christian antisemitism was equally bent on murdering even converted Jews. Michael's book in general points to the extensive and long-enduring Christian antisemitism that was, in Michael's view also, the key determinant of the Holocaust, although Michael's focus is not on the eugenicist variety but on the charges against Jews of deicide that are found in the New Testament.

30. Goldhagen, *Hitler's Willing Executioners*, 362.

31. Ibid., 439, 455.

32. Ibid., 447.

33. See, for example, Robert R. Shandley, *Unwilling Germans? The Goldhagen Debate* (Minneapolis: University of Minnesota Press, 1998), Introduction.

34. Ibid. 582, n. 38.

35. Saul Friedlander, in Hartman, ed., *Bitburg*, 36.

36. "Daniel Jonah Goldhagen antwortet seinen Kritikern," *Die Zeit*, August 2, 1996 (available at http://www.zeit.de/1996/32/goldantw. txt.19960802.xml, accessed December 30, 2007); "Was dachten die Morder," *Der Spiegel*, August 12, 1996 (available at http://service.

spiegel.de/digas/find?DID=9079928, accessed January 4, 2008); the two pieces are translated as "The Failure of the Critics" and "What Were the Murderers Thinking?" in Robert R. Shandley, *Unwilling Germans? The Goldhagen Debate* (Minneapolis and London: University of Minnesota Press, 1998), esp. 129, 142–143, 159–160.

37. Daniel Jonah Goldhagen, *Hitlers willige Vollstrecher* (Berlin: Siedler Verlag, 1996), 12, translated in "Foreword to the German Edition," *Hitler's Willing Executioners: Ordinary Germans and the Holocaust* (New York: Vintage, 1997), 478, 482–483; and Goldhagen, "Motives, Causes, and Alibis: A Reply to My Critics," *The New Republic*, 215 (December 23, 1996), 37–45.

38. Shandley, *Unwilling Germans*, 5.

39. Wehler, "Like a Thorn in the Flesh," in Shandley, *Unwilling Germans*, 101.

40. Goldhagen, "Foreword to the German Edition," in *Hitler's Willing Executioners* (New York: Vintage, 1997), 480.

41. Shandley, *Unwilling Germans*, 17–18.

42. Jürgen Habermas, "Goldhagen and the Public Uses of History," in Shandley, *Unwilling Germans*, 264, 270.

43. Ibid., 272.

44. Evans, *Rereading German History* (London and New York: Routledge, 1997), 149–181. I make use here also of a transcript of a 2008 lecture titled, "The Goldhagen Affair Revisited," which is a revision of the earlier essay and was graciously provided by Dr. Evans.

45. Evans, *Rereading German History*, 164.

46. For a statement on this matter by Evans, as well as current sources, see Richard J. Evans, *The Third Reich at War, 1939–1945* (New York: Penguin Books, 2008), 177.

47. "Reflections on the Reception of Goldhagen in the United States," in Geoff Eley, ed., *The "Goldhagen Effect": History, Memory, Nazism—Facing the German Past* (Ann Arbor: University of Michigan Press, 2000), 159.

48. Ibid., 158.

49. Omer Bartov in Eley, ed., *The "Goldhagen Effect"*, 38–41.

50. Ibid., 40.

51. Caplan in Eley, ed., *The "Goldhagen Effect"*, 155, makes the point that

Goldhagen's views flew in the face of tendencies in historical research toward institutional and sociological explanations for the Holocaust.

Conclusion

1. See Peter Novick, *The Holocaust in American Life* (Boston: Houghton Mifflin, 1999).

Index

Ackerman, Hans: Speaker of Seagoville Family Camp Committee, 47

Ackman, K. Leslie (*Washington Post*), supports creation of USHMM, 125–126

Adorno, Theodore, 200

Allies, 9, 26, 28, 35, 93, 95, 112, 114, 150–151, 159, 162, 170, 211, 221, 227, 247–248

Aly, Gotz, 228–229

America First Committee: Isolationist Organization, 82, 85, 88, 265

American Federation of Labor: supports boycott of German goods, 69, 73

American Jewish Committee, 66–67, 71, 178, 264

American Jewish Congress, 66–67, 71–74

American League for Defense of Jewish Rights (ALDJR), 72

American Nazi Party, 4, 15–26, 59, 77, 100, 248; composition of, 15–16

American Protective League, 10

Anti-Defamation League: ethnic professionals, xx, 108, 124, 266

Anti-Germanism in US, xxiv, xxv, xxvi, 3, 13–15, 84, 90, 97–98, 100, 111, 133–134, 138, 179, 247, 249, 252; American media contribute to, 114–115; NBC Holocaust Miniseries, 115; and William Henry King, 12; created by USHMM, 133, 271; not created by USHMM, 134–136, 271. *See also* Kunwald, Ernst; Praeger, Robert P.

Anti-Jewish Actions, 70–71